Giacomo Leopardi

Twayne's World Authors Series
Italian Literature

Anthony Oldcorn, Editor
Brown University

TWAS 753

GIACOMO LEOPARDI
(1798-1837)
Drawing by G. P. Barricelli
Adapted from postcard
Photograph by Laura Barricelli

Giacomo Leopardi

By Gian Piero Barricelli

University of California, Riverside

Twayne Publishers • *Boston*

Giacomo Leopardi

Gian Piero Barricelli

Copyright © 1986 by G.K. Hall & Co.
All Rights Reserved
Published by Twayne Publishers
A Division of G.K. Hall & Co.
70 Lincoln Street
Boston, Massachusetts 02111

Copyediting supervised by Lewis DeSimone
Book production by Elizabeth Todesco
Book design by Barbara Anderson

Typeset in 11 pt. Garamond
by Modern Graphics, Inc., Weymouth, Massachusetts

Printed on permanent/durable acid-free paper
and bound in the United States of America

Library of Congress Cataloging in Publication Data

Barricelli, Jean-Pierre.
  Giacomo Leopardi.

  (Twayne's world authors series; TWAS 753.
Italian literature)
  Bibliography, p. 220
  Includes index.
  1. Leopardi, Giacomo, 1798–1837—Criticism and
interpretation. I. Title. II. Series: Twayne's world
authors series; TWAS 753. III. Series: Twayne's
world authors series. Italian literature.
PQ4710.B328   1986   851'.7   86–3140
ISBN 0–8057–6602–2

To my father
one of those cherished childhood memories
and to my mother
consummate leopardiana
now another cherished ricordanza

Contents

About the Author
Preface
Chronology

Chapter One
A Biographical Portrait: The *Epistolario*   1

Chapter Two
Philosophical Premises: The *Zibaldone*   32

Chapter Three
Poetic Myths: The *Operette morali*   70

Chapter Four
An Advanced Poetics   102

Chapter Five
The Poetry: The *Batracomiomachia* and the *Canti*   130

Chapter Six
Conclusion: In a Comparative Context   193

Notes and References   203
Selected Bibliography   220
Index   224

About the Author

Gian Piero Barricelli is professor of romance languages and comparative literature at the University of California at Riverside. He was born in Cleveland, Ohio, in 1924, and received a B.A., M.A., and Ph.D. from Harvard (1947, 1948, and 1953 respectively). He taught at Harvard and Brandeis before going to California in 1963, as well as at the University of Bergen and the School of Business Administration in Norway, and since has also taught at New York University. Among the honors he has received are Phi Beta Kappa, Harvard Humanities Award, two Fulbright awards, two University of California Humanities Institute awards, an Outstanding Educator of America designation, and his campus's Distinguished Teaching Award. He has been named to occupy for one year, at the College of William and Mary, the prestigious, endowed Chair of the William R. Kenan, Jr. Distinguished Professorship in the Humanities. He is also a professional musician, having taught music and composed various instrumental and vocal works; in addition, he conducted the Waltham Symphony Orchestra and the Cafarelli Opera Company of Cleveland for five seasons. Since 1963, he has served as music reviewer of the *Riverside Press/Enterprise*.

Professor Barricelli has published studies on Balzac, Leopardi, Plato, Diderot, Dante, Mann, T. S. Eliot, Calderón, Mazzini, Chekhov, Machiavelli, Turgenev, Chausson, Zweig, Pound, Boccaccio, Rulfo, Rojas, Liszt, Berlioz, Boïto, Busoni, painters from Botticelli and Blake to Nattini, Doré, Rauschenberg, and others, in addition to his own poetry and short stories, and has translated works of various authors like Virgil, Leopardi, Wergeland, and Machiavelli. He works primarily in the areas of romanticism and the Renaissance, and has made a specialty of the interrelations between literature and music and literature and law. He has recently coedited the MLA volume *Interrelations of Literature,* in which he coauthored an essay on law, and has published an essay-history of the Los Angeles Philharmonic. He is past editor of the *Italian Quarterly,* currently edits the American Comparative Literature Association's *Heliconian,* is associate editor for *Selecta,* the *Comparatist,* and *Bibliography: Literature and the Other Arts,* is chairman of the board of editors for *Modern*

Philology, and is forum editor for *Fantasy Studies.* Some of his oil paintings have been exhibited. At UCR he has been chairman of Comparative Literature and of the Department of Literatures and Languages.

Preface

Leopardi may not need another study in Italian, but in English—thinking primarily of the United States—he can stand an introductory volume that may be used as a reference and at the same time as a source of a few insights inspired by the countless commentaries he has elicited from numerous and fine scholars.

To an English-speaking readership, this volume purports to discuss the life and work of one of the leading poets in the Western tradition. Unfortunately, like his equally outstanding compatriot and novelist, Alessandro Manzoni, he has suffered, despite his prominence, from neglect in a literary community which, whatever its pride in comparatism and internationalism, still behaves as if the only literatures worth studying *in extenso* have been written in English, French, and German. The obvious error of this view is underscored dramatically when, for example, someone has reason to ask if from among numerous other authors one has read Leopardi, and receives a politely shy but negative, though not always apologetic, response even from professionals of literary history and criticism. Yet Leopardi is always a felt presence; he is complex, due to the intellectual and emotional richness of his motifs—a richness that has stimulated differing points of view with regard to his opus, primarily by Italian and often by British scholars. It is my hope, therefore, that in the United States the present study will help erase the provincial shyness (and where appropriate inject an apologetic wish) of some, as well as enhance the alerted desire and educated curiosity of others to whom the name of the "miracle of Recanati" is somewhat familiar.

It has not been my purpose to focus on scholars' disputes as to whether Leopardi was romantic or classic, imagist or symbolist, philosopher or moralist, erudite philologist or voice of the Risorgimento, materialist or idealist, patriot or recluse, pessimistic or elegiac poet. True greatness, such as his, transcends classifications. I have made my focus *the whole man*—meaning in this case the creative writer—which, after all, must represent the ultimate goal of any study of this sort. In so doing, I have brought together a large number of sources, in order to achieve an acceptably catholic point of view.

The plan of the work is methodologically simple. The intellectual and cultural biography in chapter 1 relies heavily, though not exclusively, on Leopardi's correspondence. After this, in chapter 2, comes a presentation of that vexing problem of his philosophy. The idea here was to abide by Leopardi's own statements, found largely in his notebooks and published thoughts, and not to intercalate notions which, though they may round out concepts conveniently for the sake of arriving at a calculated "system," also warp the author's thinking rhythm and meditative process. The chapter serves as an introduction to chapter 3, devoted to Leopardi's prose (which he thought of as an illustration of his philosophy) and providing, for the sake of reference, accessible summaries and commentaries. Similarly, the next section, chapter 4, deals with the more aesthetic matter of his poetics, and prepares chapter 5, dedicated to his poetry, this time with paraphrases (since poetry resists summary) and commentaries. Clearly, some poems, because of their special beauty and importance, had to be stressed over others. Finally, in chapter 6, I have attempted a concluding summary which places Leopardi—his uniqueness—in an international context.

All translations in this volume, whether from primary or secondary sources, are my own. I acknowledge with pleasure the financial assistance extended to me at various times by the University of California to complete this project. And I am deeply grateful to all those around me—family and friends—who have shown great patience as I worked on the manuscript, and especially to those who went beyond mere understanding and provided encouragement. To the Italian editor of this Twayne series, Anthony Oldcorn, whose suggestions were both copious and enlightened, goes my very special gratitude. If this study falters, as undoubtedly in places it does, it is not because of their lack of support. Or of lack of inspiration in the subject matter.

Gian Piero Barricelli

University of California, Riverside

Chronology

1798   Giacomo Leopardi born in Recanati on 29 June, of Count Monaldo Leopardi and Marquess Adelaide Antici.

1803   Monaldo's wife assumes control of the family finances, effectuating stringent economies.

1807   Giacomo begins studying under a tutor, Don Sebastiano Sanchini.

1809   First attempt at poetry: "La morte di Ettore."

1812   Writes his libertarian tragedy, "Pompeo in Egitto."

1813   Writes the "Storia dell'astronomia."

1815   Writes the *Saggio sopra gli errori popolari degli antichi* and completes his first translation of the *Batracomiomachia* as well as of Moschus.

1816   Supposedly the year in which he switched from philology to poetry, and in which his health problems start becoming manifest. Composes "L'appressamento della morte."

1817   Friendship with Pietro Giordani and beginning of the miscellaneous notebook *Zibaldone*. Falls in love with Gertrude Cassi Lazzari and writes "Il primo amore" and "Memorie del primo amore."

1818   Year of the *Discorso di un italiano intorno alla poesia romantica*, "All'Italia," and "Sopra il monumento di Dante." Leaves his home for the first time, going to Macerata with Giordani.

1819   Unsuccessful flight from Recanati. Deepens his study of philosophy, and writes "L'infinito" and "Alla luna."

1820   Pens "Ad Angelo Mai," "La sera del dì di festa," and has the idea for the *Operette morali*.

1821   Continued poetic activity, including "Bruto minore."

1822   More poetry, including "L'ultimo canto di Saffo."

1823   Disappointing sojourn in Rome; visits Tasso's tomb.

1824   Composes the *Operette morali; Canzoni del Conte Giacomo Leopardi* (Nobili edition) published in Bologna.

1825   Travels from Bologna to Milan, attracted by an offer from publisher Antonio Fortunato Stella, and back.

1826   In Bologna, falls in love with Countess Teresa Carniani-Malvezzi. Works on Petrarch's poetry, publishes *Versi* (Stamperia delle Muse edition) containing his "idylls," and returns to Recanati.

1827   Back in Bologna, thence to Florence. *Operette morali* published by Stella. Meets Ranieri in Vieusseux's circle, along with writers Gino Capponi and Alessandro Manzoni. Goes to Pisa.

1828   Writes "Il risorgimento" and "A Silvia." Returns to Recanati.

1829   More poetic activity: "Le ricordanze," "La quiete dopo la tempesta," "Il sabato del villaggio," possibly "Il passero solitario."

1830   Completes "Canto notturno di un pastore errante dell'Asia." Goes to Florence on the invitation of Pietro Colletta, where his friendship with Ranieri becomes firm. Falls passionately in love with Fanny Targioni-Tozzetti, who inspires poems like "Il pensiero dominante." Meets philologist Luigi De Sinner.

1831   Declines to be Recanati's deputy to the National Assembly in Bologna. *Canti* published (Piatti edition) in Florence. Goes with Ranieri to Rome.

1832   Back to Florence with Ranieri. Begins to receive a modest allowance from his family. Writes final page of the *Zibaldone*.

1833   Stops in Rome and proceeds with Ranieri to Naples. Possible year of "A se stesso."

1834   Writes "Aspasia," "Sopra un bassorilievo antico sepolcrale," and works on *Paralipomeni della Batracomiomachia;* second edition of the *Operette morali,* amplified, published in Florence (by Piatti).

1835   Composes the "Palinodia al marchese Gino Capponi"; a new and augmented edition of the *Canti* is issued by Saverio Starita.

1836   Bourbon authorities sequester the 1835 edition of the *Canti*. A third and augmented edition of the *Operette morali,* also sequestered, is issued by Starita. Establishes himself with

Ranieri in Villa Ferrigni, on Mt. Vesuvius, between Torre del Greco and Torre Annunziata, where he writes "Il tramonto della luna" and "La ginestra."

1837   Leopardi dies in Naples on 14 June, while cholera plagues the area. It is believed that Ranieri had him buried in San Vitale a Fuorigrotta.

> Therefore let the moon
> Shine on thee in thy solitary walk.

—Wordsworth, *Tintern Abbey*

> Meditating on that derelict stone afloat there in the abyss, you may feel most numinously a worm, abject and futile in the face of wholly incomprehensible immensities.

—A. Huxley, *Meditation on the Moon*

Chapter One
A Biographical Portrait: The *Epistolario*

His was an aristocratic humanism, but in more layman's terms he was to be known simply as "the poet of sorrow," and he began early in life to evidence a disposition for sadness. It is said that at four and one half years of age, Giacomo Leopardi shed more tears than any other member of his family at the death of his nine-day-old brother. Sensitive in the extreme, he was never able to reconcile loss with destiny—he sought but found no answer to this disparity—and out of the dialectic flowed the sophisticated verse. For even his prose was a form of poetry, and poetry, for him, operated as both an intellectual imperative and a psychological release. His biography is essentially the story of an inner life. It comes through in his works and notebooks, of course, but also very poignantly in his *Epistolario,* or *Letters.*

It was not difficult for his overprotective father, Count Monaldo, a mediocre writer who with modest justification saw himself as an intellectual, to detect special differences between his first son Giacomo, born 29 June 1798 in Recanati, and the other children, Carlo and Paolina, and later Luigi and Pier Francesco. Even before his precocious son had reached the age of ten, the count opened up to him the doors of the mansion's rich library, and for years thereafter the four dark, book-lined walls became the adolescent's haven and exile. The count was a peculiar man. In opposition to a long lineage of mayors and priors, soldiers (Knights of Malta), bishops, canons, and nuns in his family, he had leaned toward literature and had spent lavishly to assemble an imposing collection of books, esteeming highly whatever measure of distinction he had achieved by owning it. But the pleasures of the bibliophile had not translated into the rewards of the creator, for between the former and the latter there remained a considerable gap. Though well-intentioned and affectionate with his children, he was on the intellectual side beset, one might surmise, by a hidden sense of frustration which often gave his behavior and opinions an erratic quality. Stubbornness and selfishness were not unknown to him; profoundly religious, he yet cultivated secular literature and philosophy and procured a religious dispensation for his favorite Giacomo to read prohibited works; a close observer of the advances of science, he still held tightly to a number of superstitions; an admirer of his country's libertarian traditions, he nevertheless stood inveterately on reactionary principles, shunning the egalitarian ideologies filtering southward from France (troops of the French Republic had invaded the territory in 1796, and he had refused to go to the window to watch Napoleon ride by), adhering zealously as a citizen of the Papal States to Vatican policies, and externalizing this political attitude by wearing nothing but decorously austere, black garb with hanging sword (an important, if outmoded, trapping), while not renouncing servants, coachman, and coach even during times of financial stress. During this period, Giacomo, too, would wear the black, clerical gown.

In 1797, Count Monaldo had married the Marquess Adelaide Antici. Their diversity of character proved truly dramatic. In her male riding boots, she took to riding herd on the whole family, having convinced herself, not totally without justification, that her husband was an extravagant bungler of finances. The economic reverses in the wake of the alternating occupations of Recanati by Austrian and French troops lent an aura of prudence to her stern measures, to which she added her own brand of cold severity and bigoted piety. She could sulk as readily as she could scream. In retrospect, Giacomo could only remember her despotic economies and her puritanical Catholicism which, in good medieval fashion, preached the fear of God, the transience of mortal life, and the ultimate reality of heaven. Noticing that any semblance of motherly tenderness surfaced ephemerally if at all, Giacomo developed for her a gradual, festering feeling of hatred. But he remained forever the respectful, indeed most affectionate son who loved his family "more than [he loved] anyone else."[1] "The love I bear infinitely for my . . . parents will always keep me in this world as long as destiny will have me here."[2]

The two older children looked to Giacomo with feelings of mutual protection, and the latter, apart from being the most sensitive, also happened to be the most exuberant, arranging pastimes and directing games. Brandishing a twig as a sword, the young hero crushed many tyrants and safeguarded freedom any number of times.

Then he would retire to do his lessons in theology or mathematics, history or rhetoric, or foreign languages (Latin, Spanish, and French formally, as well as Greek, Hebrew, English, and German on his own, at different periods of his youth). A friend, Francesco Puccinotti, reported that Leopardi learned English and German while waiting for the ink to dry on the pages he had written (he never used a blotting sandbox). With frequent regularity, he would withdraw from play to the library and consume himself in all kinds of readings. It was not unusual for his eyes to tire bloodshot over the dimly lighted pages of classical or Christian texts and to close in a deep sleep as he drooped over his desk at late hours of the night. By the time he reached the age of fourteen, his teachers left him, claiming they had nothing further in which to instruct him. He seemed to be in a great hurry to read and learn—a frenzied hurry which kept him from many possible strolls along the sunny slopes of the countryside (he always remembered nostalgically those he had taken) or from more frequent frolic with his siblings. Instead, he translated ancient authors, like Horace (the *Odes*), and wrote commentaries on them; or he composed in Italian and Latin (plays, like the antityrannical tragedy "Pompeo in Egitto" ("Pompey in Egypt," 1812) or the pastoral tragedy *Telesilla* (1819); poetry, like "Le ricordanze" ("Remembrances," 1816) and "Il primo amore" ("The First Love") together with "Memorie del primo amore" ("Memories of the First Love," 1817); and essays, intended to lead to an autobiography of his inner life in the manner of Johann Wolfgang von Goethe, Vittorio Alfieri, or Ugo Foscolo; or he continued with his language of lifetime predilection, Attic Greek (the stories of how the eighteen-year-old prodigy deceived scholars in 1816 with the alleged discovery of a Greek manuscript in a torn codex, an "Inno a Nettuno" ["Hymm to Neptune"], and with two odes supposedly by Anacreon are well known). But not content with studying Homer, Virgil, Moschus (he translated elegantly the *Idylls* in 1815), Julius Africanus, Isocrates, and Theophrastus, he also revealed his critical and philological bent at sixteen, when he presented his father with a massive commentary ("Osservazioni") on neoplatonist Porphyry's life of Plotinus, a work that contributes to our understanding of the future poet's interpretation of nature and reality, both endless and ultimately unknowable, both pointing to the exiguity of man in the face of the infinite reality of being; and at seventeen, when he wrote a long *Saggio sopra gli errori popolari degli antichi* ("Essay on

the Popular Mistakes of the Ancients"), in which Vossler sees the
composite influence of the sarcastic Enlightenment, the religious
boy, and the budding philologist.[3] Even earlier, at fourteen, his
fascination with the infinite mystery of the starry heavens had made
him attempt a "Storia dell'astronomia" ("History of Astronomy")
which, with impressive Greek and Latin erudition, covers from the
beginning of the science to comet of 1811.

These were years during which the impassioned, teenage student
felt he had the world and fame in the palm of his hand. He later
admitted to a "furious dedication to study,"[4] an immoderate desire
and a mad and desperate effort that required the kind of physical
stamina his frail body did not possess. The cost of learning was
great. His eyesight began to fail, and later in life he endured sporadic
blindness; rachitis and other conditions of defective bone growth
gradually curved his spine and made him into a hunchback. No one
had noticed the progressing illness, or illnesses—for the list expanded as time wore on to include blood-coughing, asthma, kidney
problems, and dropsy. Count Monaldo seemed too enveloped in his
inconclusive world of letters to experience anything but a selfish
paternal pride in his son's splendid intellectual progress, and Countess Adelaide's only efficiency lay in handling bills and in nourishing
her pride by cultivating a facade of prosperity for her family and
for the benefit of the *Recanatesi*.

Recanati, as one critic describes it, stands "on a low hill some
fifteen miles from the Adriatic, . . . like a good many other provincial Italian hill towns. One long winding street stretches along
the crest of the hill; tall shuttered palaces of stone or faded brick
face each other in a stateliness that has lost its splendor. Through
the wide arches of the doorways one may catch a glimpse of an inner
court or a dessicated palm tree, a pillared balustrade or a sponge-
stone fountain. The main square has a tall watchtower, to look out
for pirates; the churches are numerous, and many of them old,
distinguished by a Romanesque portal or a Renaissance facade. In
winter, the narrow streets are dark and the north wind bites sharply
. . . , and even in summer the great rooms of the *palazzi*—carefully
shuttered against any damage by the sun—often preserve something
of [a] dank chill. . . . When the narrow side streets suddenly come
to an end, they frame a view of an astounding beauty: hillsides of
olive trees and vines falling sharply down toward the east to the

Adriatic, and, to the west, fold upon fold of blue mountain ranges stretching up to the mountains of the Abruzzi and the Maiella."[5]

Yet, even if "the golden streets and the orchards" were at his door, to Leopardi the town ws stultifying: he railed against it; his life there "was, is, and will perpetually be solitary,"[6] his health caused him constant problems, and, as he could lament not much later, in that setting "fate has condemned me to miss my youth, for I went from childhood to old age in a single jump."[7] No surprise, then, that at eighteen he felt old. Frequent depressions set in. An unpublished poem, "L'appressamento della morte" ("The Approach of Death," 1816), concludes with chilling finality: "May a slab cover me, and my memory perish." Death, of which he was traumatically aware because of his constant decline in health, loomed as a threat to preclude his acquaintance with fame. In the same poem, he wrote:

> And you too, Glory, farewell, who lowers yet
> My shadowed day which now does fall,
> And my life leaves no trace upon the world.
> For you I did sweat and burn in speechless thought,
> I would always seek but you in all this world,
> But here I had you not, nor shall I ever.

In addition, he underwent "conversions," perhaps in themselves intellectually healthy for the new and fresh directions they represented, but nonetheless jarring in the way in which they disrupted previously cherished and secure attitudes. The comfort that his father's Christian dogma had afforded him, and through which he had enjoyed whatever affection his parents were capable of displaying, crumbled in the face of rational doubts about theology and faith. The clerical garb which his parents had intended him to wear for a lifetime, disappeared; "I surely don't want to become a priest," he eventually declared in 1819.[8] In addition, he began to break away from a philological emphasis (he looked back in 1823 to when he "laughed . . . at philology")[9] and, by viewing more generously the accomplishment of modern literature, to cultivate more intimately the art of writing poetry. There are those critics who place inordinate emphasis on physiological factors to explain Leopardi's new orientation toward creative writing and readily quote any of his numerous references to his eye problem in his correspondence, such as: "For two months I haven't been studying or reading a thing because of my eyes . . . ,"[10] or "For six months a great weakness of my ocular nerves has deprived me of the use of my eyes and mind. . . ."[11] Supposedly, then, he cultivated an activity that spared his eye strain. But Leopardi often complained about his poor eyesight's interference with his "thinking, writing, and reading,"[12] and the fact will always remain that he was a born poet whom we would not have seen remain a perpetual philologist, even in good health. Disclaimers notwithstanding, he lived in a constant state of meditation, of poetic fashioning of the world around him, a condition that for him was, among other things, self-protective. For the greater the poetic and philosophical meditation, the greater the release, if only temporary, from the gloomy cruelty of the thought of death.

In 1816, Antonio Fortunato Stella, the editor of the often quoted review, *Lo spettatore italiano e straniero,* took an interest in Leopardi, offering him employment, publishing his works, among which was a translation of the first book of the *Odyssey,* and assisting in bringing him in touch with men of established stature like Vincenzo Monti, then considered Italy's major contemporary poet; Pietro Giordani, the skeptical ex-priest and most widely known intellectual of his day who became a lifelong friend and admirer of the poet; and Angelo Mai, the noted philologist and Orientalist whose discoveries of classical manuscripts inspired Leopardi's poem to him in 1820. Although from his association with the atheistic and ardent democratic liberal Giordani there grew several patriotic poems ("All'Italia" ["To Italy"] and "Sopra il monumento di Dante" ["On the Monument to Dante"], both 1818), the Milanese's influence on Leopardi, whom he described in his *Iscrizioni* as a future "honor of Italy as [he was] already a miracle of Recanati," is to be measured less in matters of philosophy or politics than in matters of humanistic studies. More important, Leopardi really confided in Giordani, as he had to some extent in his brother Carlo, and apprised him of the "obstinate, black, horrible, barbarous melancholy"[13] that devoured him, of his bitterness and disillusions, of his solitary life in the hated Recanati where his aspirations found nothing in common with his family's way of thinking and where his physical deformity and pursuit of literature became subjects of derision by the townsfolk. And Giordani, to whom he dedicated his translation of the second book of the *Aeneid,* had all the impulsiveness and sincerity of affection for the precocious youth that Leopardi's parents lacked; he became what Leopardi later called "the pillar against which my tired life leans."[14] He helped his friend in many ways; his effect was salutary, counterpoising, and sustaining. After a five-day visit to Recanati, Giordani managed to get Count Monaldo to agree to letting Giacomo accompany him to Macerata, the first time the young man left his home town without a member of the family. Through the encouragement, therefore, and continuously superlative (typical of Giordani) praise "bestowed on him by the foremost writer of Italy," as Leopardi called him—that "measure and form of my life"[15]—the poet's ever-present desire for literary greatness was bolstered and the friendship grew deep. This was the human Leopardi reacting, the poet in need of love and attention and in search of friends he could not find in his native town. Of course, there was always the other side of him, the metaphysical contemplator for whom friendship and fame, along with all other things human, appeared as illusions abetting the only reality, the "infinite vanity of all things" ("A se stresso" ["To Himself"], 1833).

Love is too weighty a word to describe the ephemeral sensation which had spurred Leopardi to compose "Il primo amore," a poem of personal disenchantment occasioned by the visit of a distant cousin, Gertrude Cassi, a lovely young lady of twenty-six who was married to a much older gentleman. Through her gracious smile and cheerful disposition, the silent chambers at Recanati acquired an unknown radiance, so that her stay of dreamlike brevity came to resemble an inner vision, and she an undefinable symbol of beauty blending in a sole reality what must have appeared to the poet as the finest aspects of nature and art. Still in the days when he was outfitted as a cleric and always moving in the shadow of his mother's stern humor which dampened conversation and expressions of joy, Leopardi probably never allowed Gertrude to suspect the impression she had made on him. Yet the experience may be considered, if not an enfranchisement, certainly an enrichment from which there emerged a consciousness of spiritual beauty—no less an illusion than all the rest, but a pleasant illusion of sweetness nonetheless. Later, when a peasant girl smiled at him from a field, or passed by on her way home to groom herself for a festive day, disillusionment with life's fleeting years continued to ring sharply in his verses, but the artistic release he obtained in trying to immortalize the ideal thought of those moments is not to be discounted. The poem dedicated to the coachman's daughter, "A Silvia" ("To Sylvia"—actually Teresa Fattorini), whose song he often heard from his solitary room and whose premature death reminded him of his own unlived youth and approaching end, further illustrates the sense of release.

For even the passionate loves he experienced later—always for married women and always resulting in disappointment—he transformed into poetic material.[16] Echoes of his feelings for Teresa Carniani-Malvezzi de' Medici of Bologna and particularly for Fanny Targioni-Tozzetti of Florence may be heard in "Il pensiero dominante" ("The Sovereign Thought," 1832), "Consalvo" (1833), and "Aspasia" (1834). Countess Carniani-Malvezzi was a cultured woman, a poet herself, with whom he established a comfortable intellectual rapport until his own emotions, growing warmer, forced a break (1826). Though middle-aged, she had, however, "made up for the youth he had not experienced," giving Leopardi "a kind of delirium and fever" at the outset, "like a love without restlessness," and "disabused [him] of disabusing," convincing him "that there really are pleasures in the world," and that he was "still capable of stable illusions."[17] Fanny Tozzetti, on the other hand, caused him genuine bitterness (1830–33). The capricious wife of a Florentine professor, she found herself flattered by the attentions of a well-known literary figure, and with dishonest encouragement brought about his inevitable disenchantment, the "ultimate deception," as he labeled it in "A se stesso." Leopardi needed love, indeed women: "I need love, love, love, fire, enthusiasm, life . . . ," he wrote to his brother Carlo;[18] this need could even outstrip that of fame: "I need not esteem, nor glory, nor similar things—but I need love,"[19] even though his lot from childhood had been "to desire and not be able to desire."[20] But his view of himself as a cripple, his fear of being scorned ("derided, spat at, and kicked,"[21] as he put it), and his belief that the anticlimax of realization would nullify the pleasures of anticipation combined to inhibit his pursuit of physical desire. "I would have a better opinion of myself if I thought myself capable of being loved."[22] There is no evidence that he ever experienced sexual enjoyment; but there is every evidence that his poetic tendency to idealize the feminine provided a surrogate. In a note he appended to his poem "Alla sua donna" ("To His Lady"), we read: "The author's woman, that is, beloved, is one of those apparitions of celestial and ineffable beauty and virtue that our fantasy often needs. . . . She is *the woman we do not find*. The author does not know if his lady (and calling her this he shows that he loves only her) is yet born or will ever be born; he knows she does not live on earth and that we are never her contemporaries; he seeks her among Plato's ideas, on the moon, on the planets of the solar and of the stellar systems."

As one may surmise, Leopardi's notion of love partakes of both romantic and classical inclinations that reflect broader and transcendent, however personal, dispositions. One reason may be obvious: the intellectual climate in Europe during his formative years. The philosophical Enlightenment and literary classicism were on the decline. As his notebook, called the *Zibaldone*, attests time and again in its 4,526 extraordinary pages, human experiences of any kind never remained superficial matters of mere record for him but were filtered through layers of scholarly meditation. The twenty-six entries on love (not counting specific types of love, like love of country, of fellow man, of self, etc.) suggest in the aggregate what analogous entries on other subjects (art, beauty, decadence, democracy, war, evil, nature, feeling, reason, and so on) also suggest: the combined influences of shifting historical orientations, all of which he transcended by achieving a highly personal synthesis. There are strong strains of eighteenth-century materialism: universal and individual reality as a cause and an end in itself, as well as an empiricist and sensationalist concept of custom (everything in life—man, nature, even memory—being a function of habit). Related to this are also strong eudemonistic arguments with reference to morality and considerations of the duality of nature and reason. But early in life he also developed a more romantic view of life; under the influence of Jean-Jacques Rousseau, the duality became a juxtaposition and eventually the notion of illusion surfaced to dominate. The noble savage untainted by civilization, man's irreducible individualism and the exaltation of feeling, and the spiritual, indeed gnostic, and to this extent classical, appreciation of history and the love of that intangible unity called country: these were a few of the notions that weighed on the opposite side of the ledger.[23] Central to Leopardi's meditations on love or on any other topic was always the disparity between man and nature, between the historical individual and the infinite or at least the indefinite, the basis of the tragic human condition or *Weltschmerz*, which in itself tended to give meaning to the new religions of love and of country. For Italian romanticism, like Norwegian romanticism as reflected by the poet

Henrik Wergeland, acquired a spirited political orientation, given the unrelenting presence of foreign troops on the peninsula which had aroused the indignation of many a writer, from Dante Alighieri, Francesco Petrarca (hereafter, Petrarch), and Niccolò Machiavelli, to Alfieri and Foscolo.

After reading their son's nationalistic poems in 1818, the same year as his *Discorso di un italiano intorno alla poesia romantica (Address by an Italian on Romantic Poetry)* in the impassioned political ending of which he extolled the dignity of Italian letters and traditions in comparison with those of foreigners ("we still drink this air and tread this soil and enjoy this light that a host of immortals enjoyed . . ."), Countess Adelaide and Count Monaldo, who detested the idea of an Italian "nation," came to regard Giordani as a perverter who was mainly responsible for Giacomo's now detectable opposition to the rules of the family and to its political and religious inclinations. The truth of the matter, however, was that Giordani's sway was primarily literary, and that, if "perverters" were to be identified, the parents should have investigated Dante and Petrarch, Alfieri and Foscolo, Plato, the Neoplatonists, Epictetus, Francis Bacon, the Baron de Montesquieu, Voltaire, Rousseau, Goethe, Giacomo's favorite Mme de Staël, and innumerable others attentively studied by Leopardi inside or outside his father's library. Besides, Giordani, Gertrude, and the publisher Stella represented three dimensions of the world beyond that narrow and stifling "hermitage, or better, prison"[24] of Recanati: friendship, love, and work, ennoblers of life whatever their ultimately illusory disadvantages.

By 1819, Leopardi longed to leave his native town. To Giordani he wrote: "Will I ever do anything great? even now as I go knocking my head against this cage like a bear? In this town of monks . . . and in this damnable house, where they would pay a fortune to see me become a monk, while for all intents and purposes, willy-nilly, I am made to live like one—and being twenty-one years old and with the type of heart I happen to have—rest assured that I'll explode in short order, unless I escape from here and become a beggar, as is bound to occur."[25] He thought of Milan, far from the Papal States. His parents forbade this, not surprisingly oblivious to the fact that the spiritual punishment they were inflicting on him was far graver than the physical illnesses of defective eyesight and spinal deformity. More than ever before, he felt estranged and alone. His prodigious intellectual evolution had left his family and his town far behind, and yet, he would ask himself, to what avail, if he would soon be breathing his last as an exile in "the most uncultured and deadest city in all The Marches"?[26] For a flashing moment he thought of suicide by drowning, an act of "final desperation,"[27] but he smiled at himself immediately with irony, knowing how his instinct would have spared him and returned him to the horrible "live burial" of Recanati. He recalled poetically the story of Brutus and the legend of Sappho, then returned to thoughts of leaving "the sepulcher of the living"[28] (as he would still remember his city in 1829), this time by escape. He arranged for a passport, but by coincidence his parents were apprised of the attempt and he got nowhere. In fact, the whole situation worsened: thereafter he was watched closely, was spoken to with diffidence, and his letters were opened. The exile had become a prisoner.

The poet-philosopher preferred meditation, however, to wallowing inordinately in personal lamentation, and he used to spend many a long hour atop a hill known as Mount Tabor. As usual, he reshaped his problem of desolation over his loneliness with his imagination wrestling in the throes of a broader consideration: dismay over his microcosmic insignificance compared with nature's vast powers and the long flow of history, and out of such thoughts between 1819 and 1820 grew his first meditative lyric, "L'infinito" ("The Infinite"), which pits boundless space and endless time against his tiny person and inadequate reason. His so-called conversion to philosophy took place in 1819, and it is not surprising that, with his attention focused on cosmic concerns, he put aside, at least temporarily, his earlier nationalistic fervor. The efforts of that secret political society, the Carbonari, extolled and joined by Stendhal, to establish an independent republic were viewed as vain by Leopardi in 1820. The supposed glorious destinies of nations merely seemed added deceptions; ancient Rome had proved that.

But the verdicts of reason could not deny the creative instinct that needed to feed on artistic illusion which, if marked by fecundity and nobility, would always remain a necessary stimulant for life and for action. The ode "Ad Angelo Mai" ("To Angelo Mai") praised so patriotically the philologist's discovery of many fragments of Cicero's *De Republica* that the Austrian police chief of Venice forbade its publication. And somewhat incongruously at a time when he began contemplating the idea of the *Operette morali*, Leopardi found himself hailed by Italian patriots who dreamed of a new Italy;

however detached from political immediacies his pessimistic philosophy tended to place him, he was being referred to as the rightful
descendent of Vittorio Alfieri and Ugo Foscolo, poets who had paved
the way toward their nation's future.

Springtime provided the poet with a number of inspiring illusions: nature, the granter of dreams, of cloudless skies, moonlight,
calm breezes and distant silences, of mountains, woods, and plains,
all that had captivated the ancient Greek imaginaiton, like a ther-
apeutic prescription designed to relieve the mind of the ineluctability
of our misery. "I am breathing the warmth of beautiful spring," he
wrote to Giordani in 1820, "like the only medicinal hope left for
the exhaustion of my soul. A few nights ago, before going to bed,
I opened the window in my room, and when I saw a pure sky and
a beautiful ray of moonlight, and listened to the tepid breeze and
some dogs barking in the distance, certain ancient images were
awakened in me, and I felt a stir in my heart, whereupon I began
screaming like a madman, asking mercy of nature, whose voice I
felt I was hearing after such a long time. . . . How can life be
tolerated without illusions and live emotions, and without imagination and enthusiasm . . . ?"[29] The atmosphere of the previous
year's "Alla luna" ("To the Moon") and of the coming "La sera del
dì di festa" ("The Evening After the Holiday," 1820) and "La vita
solitaria" ("The Solitary Life," 1821) prevailed for a while—but
only for a while. As usual, sober verities interrupted the promising
sequences of idylls, and it was not long before he saw himself again,
as he had in April of 1820, as "the most desperate man on the face
of this earth."[30] Now he would abhor himself if he had the strength,
but hatred is a passion and he could not experience passion any
more. He realized that he was prone to suppressing rationally every
illusion of feeling, and that in this sense his unhappiness was of his
own doing, but how could the ultimate absurdity of all existence,
what he had called "the misery of men and the nothingness of
things," yield any other conclusion? His "comfort" comes when he
"has the strength to cry."[31] Happiness is a dream, pleasure is not
a thing but a mere name, and virtue and moral greatness are lost
to him who lives in the world. Almost daily, Leopardi experienced,
if anyone in history did, the simultaneity of contradiction, the
contradiction between reason and illusion, between desire and fu-
tility, accomplishment and illness, life and death, poignantly sym-

bolized by what he called belonging to a noble family and living in an ignoble town.[32]

In 1821, various friends, Giordani among them, attempted to secure teaching positions for Leopardi. One of his aunts, the Marquess Ferdinanda Melchiorri, who had tried many times to persuade his parents to send him to her in Rome, almost succeeded in obtaining for him the recently vacated position of Latin scriptor at the Vatican Library. The poet himself solicited aid through his own contacts, but, partly because of his dogged rejection of the priesthood and partly because of his popularity as a dispenser of patriotism (for which the church had no use and which rendered him suspect), an offer never reached him. The selection committee might have argued that his reason tended to deny his feelings, which needed to believe, and by extension his faith, and might thus have decided, as Leopardi himself was to admit to his father, that he was by temperament "much more a disparager than an admirer";[33] but any question about his irreverence and possible atheism (some did question this) would not have corresponded with the truth. "I have never been irreligious . . . in fact or in principles."[34] For as his allusions to Rousseau and the French philosopher Félicité de Lamennais in the *Zibaldone* suggest, together with the forty-odd entries on religion and God the notebook contains, Leopardi's basic thoughts have a "religious" cast: the sense of man's smallness and loneliness on earth, the scorn for worldly goals and utilitarian purposes, the depreciation of human reason's vain pride, the cognizance of death's presence in every living thing, and the submission of his own being to a superior reality. "Man lives only through religion and illusion. This proposition is exact and irrefutable";[35] "Only Religion (more often than not favored and proved by reason) . . . can intervene to bring together somehow these two incompatible and irreconcilable elements of the human system, reason and nature, existence and nothingness, life and death";[36] "Nature is the same as God. As much as I attribute to nature, so much do I to God; as much as I detract from reason, so much do I from any creature. . . . Since I deem nature's work perfect, I deem perfect that of God; I condemn man's presumption to perfect of himself the work of the creator; I assert that any alteration made in the work as it has issued from God's hands can be nothing but corruption."[37] This type of religion aims little at giving comfort, and its God impresses through greatness rather than mercy; He is Creator more than Redeemer. Quite understandably, Cardinal Consalvi, the Vatican secretary of state who, had he wished, could have invited Leopardi to occupy the Latin post, felt he needed someone who espoused more "Christian" views.

The nationalistic vein (what there was of it) still pulsed and led to more poetry. In composing, Leopardi liked to evolve from a specific, private experience into a universal, synthetic vision. "Nelle nozze della sorella Paolina" ("For my Sister Paolina's Marriage") came toward the end of 1821, Paolina serving merely as a point of departure to exhort Italian women to inspire their men to perform the acts of sacrifice and heroism necessary for the salvation of the prostrate country. In the same month (November), "A un vincitore nel pallone" ("To a Victor in a Football Game"), a pseudo-Pindaric ode in praise of Carlo Didimi, a champion from Treja, revealed symbolically the kind of valor necessary for Italy's, indeed for Europe's, hopes of those years. And the following month, more poignantly though perhaps less historically correct, "Bruto minore" ("The Younger Brutus") described the vanquished general of Philippi as a vindicator of liberty and justice, and considered the power of nature over illusion and the vain struggle of man against destiny. Ideals perish unrealized with the same certainty that makes unattainment and misery inscrutable laws of the human condition.

More brightly poised against these poems (setting aside the passing bittersweet melancholy of rememberance of "Il sogno" ["The Dream"]) stands "Alla primavera, o delle favole antiche" ("To Spring, or About Ancient Fables," January, 1822), in which nature appears cruel but beautiful, inviting us through her gentleness to forget the more dire realities—offers, one might say, an alternative to Brutus' sword. But the suicide theme was too sharp to be brushed aside easily, and in May, "L'ultimo canto di Saffo" ("Sappho's Last Song") disclosed Leopardi once again overcome by the knowledge of nature's cruelty, especially to man who is condemned by fate to infelicity. Then, a few months later, came "L'inno ai patriarchi" ("Hymn to the Patriarchs"), extolling the serene pleasures of those who live in simplicity and are spared the relentless haunting of reason, which cannot soothe metaphysical travail with faith.

On 17 November 1822, what had seemed impossible happened: the count and countess gave their son permission to leave Recanati and visit Rome, thanks to the insistence of his good uncle Carlo Antici. The city of his studies and of his dreams, where he would delight in congenial conversations and where his literary aspirations would find a proper milieu and recognition—these visions glittered before him as he departed. It took but a few days for his melancholy disposition to make him lifelessly disillusioned again. "I don't even feel any pleasure at the very beautiful things I see, for I know that they are marvels, but I don't feel it, and I assure you that their multitude and greatness left me bored [the word is *noia,* the French *ennui*] after the very first day."[38] The classical Rome of Caesar and Brutus had become the pontifical city of Pius VII, subservient to the Holy Alliance (however unexceptionable its principles), and academically still unemancipated from the corruption and veneered pomp of the eighteenth-century Arcadia, before all of which the ancient monuments were no more effective than a theatrical backdrop. "There is boredom depicted on every face in Roman society."[39] At least, this was the part of Rome represented at the aristocratic salons to which the Antici family introduced him. Barring rare exceptions, such as a stimulating evening at the home of the Dutch ambassador to Tuscany, F. G. Reinhold, through whom he began to appreciate foreign intellects ("some learned foreigners—something quite different from the Romans"), he came face to face all too frequently with fatuous pedants, engaged in vapid conversation, and was even made to feel awkward because of his deformity. In addition, his family plagued him with requests which he tried genuinely to fulfill, though temperamentally unsuited to the task: Carlo wanted employment in Rome, Count Monaldo urged him to find Paolina a husband since the earlier projected marriage had never taken place, and Paolina herself pleaded the same cause in order to leave the Recanati homestead.

Leopardi, who could hardly pursue his own interests in the capital, unversed as he was in the diplomacy of courtesies and intrigues, was not a success. "Accustomed for such a long time to solitude and silence, my spirit is fully and most obstinately zero in the society of men."[40] However, he did manage to publish various philological tracts, was asked to translate all of Plato (fortunately he never signed the contract!), and almost secured a governmental post through the interest shown in him by the Prussian minister, Baron G. B. Niebuhr. But this did not materialize either, because Cardinal Consalvi, though transferred to another office by the new Pope Leo XII, was again involved and retained a lukewarm opinion of the poet. Niebuhr, however, himself a cultured man, became very fond of Leopardi, exclaiming that he had finally found an Italian worthy of ancient Rome, and offering to publish in Germany Leopardi's philological findings in the Vatican. This was some consolation to him, but not enough to erase the *noia* of the papal capital.

By the end of April, Leopardi was on his way back to "his burial grounds of Recanati"; "I left Rome . . . having enjoyed little or nothing there, because of all the arts that of enjoyment is the most concealed from me, so I wasn't sorry to return to the sepulcher, because I've never known how to live."[41] Academically, his Roman sojourn had left him with the knowledge that philology in the German manner, prevalent in the city, was an arid, albeit scientific, play of mechanical abilities, engaged in by the unimaginative people he had met in the salons; having learned the techniques of this inferior style of scholarship, he could barely contain a smile when praised for his mastery of them. He considered more highly his own philology, in the live, vibrant tradition of the philosophical interpretation of language. Psychologically, the sojourn had left him with only a questionable gain: "Rome made me perfect my insensitiveness toward myself: it made me review my whole life . . . ,"[42] and the paradoxically exhilarating experience of visiting the modest tomb of Torquato Tasso, like himself a great and unhappy poet:

Friday, February 15, 1823, I went to visit the sepulcher of Tasso, and I wept there. This is the first and sole *pleasure* I felt in Rome. The road to get there is long . . . [Tasso's tomb was in the monastery of Sant'Onofrio on the Janiculum] but wouldn't one come even from America to savor the pleasure of tears for only two minutes? . . . You must understand the crowd of emotions that stir in you when you consider the contrast between Tasso's greatness and the humbleness of his sepulcher . . . , the contrast experienced by the eye accustomed to the infinite magnificence and vastness of the Roman monuments, when it compares them with the smallness and bareness of this tomb. You feel both sad and frenzied consolation when you think that this poverty is still able to interest and animate posterity, whereas the very splendid mausoleums tht Rome shelters can be observed with perfect indifference toward the person they were meant for, whose name we don't even ask, or if we ask it we do so to identify the monument.[43]

For a while, the claustral isolation of Recanati came as a welcome relief from the disordered life in the Antici palace. But, again, only

for a while. The familiar contrast between illusion and reality reoc-
curred, perhaps abetted in part by his wavering despondency occasioned by renewed thoughts about women ("I often came close to
killing myself because of a love infatuation; . . . it isn't worth
loving women and suffering because of them,"[44] though "I do not
fault whoever is still capable . . . of really loving—in fact, I envy
him and congratulate him, because love, though a mere illusion
and a bearer of pain, yet dispenses a larger number of pleasures,
and if it causes much harm, this makes up for the very many delights
it provides").[45] To a Belgian friend he had met in Rome, A. Jacopssen, he confided philosophically, while contemplating yet another poem about women: "What is happiness, then, my dear friend?
and if happiness does not exist, what is life, then? I know nothing
of all this. . . . Indeed, it is solely up to the imagination to furnish
man the only kind of positive happiness of which he is capable.
True wisdom consists in searching for happiness in the ideal. . . .
I regret the times when I was allowed to look for it, and I notice
with a kind of dismay that my imagination is becoming sterile, and
refuses me the succor which it used to grant me."[46] The poem
germinating in his mind, regardless of his fear, was possibly "Alla
sua donna," actually written in September (1823). The idea of
perfection and absolute beauty defined by Plato and courted by
Petrarch encouraged Leopardi's wonderful illusion, less in his predecessors' terms of a reality than in terms of an unattainable concept
toward which all our artistic and natural energies aspire.

   "[Philosophy] . . . was not taught to me by my books or by my
studies or by anything else except experience."[47] It is as much the
experience of life that Leopardi alluded to as it is of thought, of
private meditations, such as those he engaged in atop Mount Tabor
when he could direct his mind to his favorite topic, "the sadness
and vanity of knowledge,"[48] and thereby "laugh at men and at [his]
own miseries."[49] The *Operette morali,* to which he dedicated most of
1824, stem from a variety of meditations, exploring in carefully
controlled, usually dialogued prose, ever greater depths of thought
and often dressing his ideas in biting irony. Like Lucianic or Swiftian
counterparts to the poetry, they talk of man's fallacious illusions,
his inane belief in progress and civilization measured by sheer tech-
nological invention rather than by the soul's betterment, the vanity
of his wealth and glory and honor and liberty and patriotism, of
his proclaimed centricity in the universe contending with his un-

admitted puniness, of his felicities and pleasures, and—always a
point of convergence in the poet's philosophy—the bitter truth of
nature's thorough indifference to man's despair. Thus the *Operette*
renewed his self-confidence as a thinker and artist, proving to himself
that as a creative writer he was not drying up and that he could
still kindle dreams he had feared extinguished, in fact, that he could
still arouse in himself the sustained passion he needed to express
them.

The period that followed and lasted until the summer of 1827
was largely one of travel (his parents having resigned themselves to
his need to move about by this time), of intensified illness, especially
during the winter seasons, and of financial discomfort. The first
verse of "Al Conte Carlo Pepoli" ("To Count Carlo Pepoli"), a poem
written in honor of a recently acquired friend from Bologna, sets
the spiritual tone for the period: "This troubled and travailed sleep
we call life." But at least on the surface, all was not bleak in Florence,
even if one discounts the aborted relationship with Countess Mal-
vezzi. His old friends did not diminish their support: Giordani and
the Swiss founder of the review *L'Antologia,* Giampietro Vieusseux,
invited him to collaborate on that liberal periodical; the publisher
Stella offered him the supervision of several important editions of
Cicero and Petrarch—a pedantic pursuit about which he was not
overly enthusiastic ("You propose to give us all of Cicero in the
original . . . a vast and costly enterprise, for which critical ex-
amination of the texts is of the utmost importance. . . . I would
gladly undertake [it]. . . . But being so far away, and in a city
totally empty of modern publications, especially in matters philological . . . ," etc.);[50] Niebuhr's successor, Karl Bunsen, inter-
vened with the pope in an attempt to procure employment to relieve
his economic distress: the Chair of Greek and Latin Eloquence at
the University of Rome. All in vain: Leopardi was not prepared to
don the "mantelletta,"[51] his supposed political leanings invited the
vigilance of the Austrian police and the pontifical censors, and an
acquaintance (Pietro Brighenti), who as an unsuccessful publisher
needed money, did not serve him well when he turned informer for
the police on his friends' political opinions and activities. He might
have fared better had he gone to Rome in person, as Bunsen had
strongly urged. But Leopardi, who frequently used his poor health
as an excuse not to do things he might have undertaken had he had
a little more aggressiveness, complained of a recent "intestinal ma-

lady."[52] He was genuinely disappointed, though, at being turned down: "how little, in fact not at all, we can put our trust in this Gothic government, whose most solemn promises are worth less than those of a drunken lover."[53] An ecclesiastical benefice available to a member of the Leopardi family tempted the hard-pressed poet for a while, but his conscience interfered. Marked by contrasts, his life developed a further one: the fame being achieved by his published works, evident by the way in which people practically stood in line to catch a glimpse of him ("that *hunchback Leopardi* counts for something in the world,"[54] he was to say jokingly), and the continued difficulties of all sorts he was experiencing.

Except for Bologna, where Leopardi actually came upon the literary circle he had long craved, he found little to attract him in other centers like Milan, Ravenna, and Florence. Part of him continued to miss Recanati with his family there, despite everything, and above all, its solitude, but the other part "could stay very well [in Bologna]."[55] "I live here liked, honored, and esteemed, much more than I deserve."[56] As for Milan, "There isn't a single social activity here except horseback riding and coffee; by comparison, Rome and Bologna are like two Parises . . . ," and—graver still for him— "there is no city in the world less studious of antiquity or of classical languages";[57] Ravenna, which he visited off and on during his prolonged stay in Bologna, receives scarce mention in his correspondence; and Florence, where he went in 1827 and was treated "with great kindness,"[58] soon became a "melancholy" city in which "these alleys, called streets, choke me; this universal filth infects me; [and] these most inane, most ignorant and arrogant women irritate me."[59] Besides, the Florentine Liberals, with their belief in improving the human condition through legislative reform and education and in valuing literature more as a means toward political and social progress than as an end in itself, appeared ingenuous to him.[60] If there was one city besides Bologna, which interested him only intellectually, about which he could rave, it was Pisa, that "romantic" mixture of "a large city and a small city,"[61] with an exquisite climate and a beautiful language, where he could "dream with open eyes,"[62] whose embankment along the Arno River he declared "such a beautiful, broad, magnificent, gay, and smiling spectacle that it makes you fall in love with it . . . I really don't know if in all of Europe there are views like this."[63] A visit there in 1827–28 to avoid the cold of the interior renewed his creative energies which had again come to a standstill since March of the previous year. Even if the new mood was cut short because of the death of his younger brother Luigi, Pisa inspired the serenity of "Il risorgimento" ("The Awakening"), a poem bespeaking a renewed desire for inner contemplation, for sad and happy memories, for the stirrings of the heart, for hopes and "bitter truths." The mood continued and was epitomized in "A Silvia" later that month (April 1828).

Still, Florence too offered him advantages. If Leopardi's rapidly deteriorating eyesight only allowed him to see the city's marbles and flowers in gloomy terms, the city brought him in touch with distinguished literati and historians: Niccolò Tommaseo, Giambattista Niccolini, Stendhal, Alessandro Manzoni, and Pietro Colletta, not to mention once more Giordani and Vieusseux. They were "acquaintances more than friends,"[64] perhaps, but nonetheless significant, except for Tommaseo, whom he eventually called "an Italian, or rather, Dalmatian ass," that "mad beast . . . [who became his] personal enemy" in publishing matters.[65] It was here that he wrote one of his best prose works, which he added to the growing *Operette morali*, the "Dialogo di Plotino e di Porfirio" ("Dialogue between Plotinus and Porphyry"). It is also one of the most important, because it disclosed a new phase of his thought, one that took shape slowly as it questioned more and more Brutus's solution of suicide and averred that life is here to be lived, and lived with a solemn sense of responsibility which stems from a feeling of love and compassion for our fellow man and which brooks no excuse to abandon our brethren in the throes of the human struggle against the forces of nature. Leopardi convinced himself that the duty of confraternity fosters in each of us a superior inner life, and if it is an illusion it is nonetheless sacred because it seeds our existences with love and beauty and goodness to the detriment of private egoisms: "Let us live, my Porphyry, and comfort each other mutually." Action obviates sulking. Leopardi carries on a dramatic dialogue with himself in the Petrarchan tradition of the *Secretum*, but he fights doubt at every turn, and he does so in a period when his severe physical suffering should have aggravated the despondency stemming from his agony and spleen—from his existential *noia*. For this reason, it should be stressed, in opposition to those critics who wed the poet's world view to his physical condition, that while the physiological inevitably taints the spiritual, misery of the flesh did not color fundamentally, much less direct, his philosophy of life. Angrily, he commented on a review of the *Operette morali* in the German journal *Hesperus:* "Whatever my troubles, which they have thought proper to display and perhaps to exaggerate somewhat . . . , I have had the courage not to try to diminish their weight either by frivolous hopes of a supposed future and unknown happiness, or by cowardly resignation. . . . Before dying, I must protest against this suggestion of weakness and vulgarity, and request my readers to concentrate on attacking my observations and arguments rather than on accusing my infirmities."[66]

Leopardi returned to Recanati toward the end of November of 1828 in the company of the philosopher-theologian Vincenzo Gioberti. The encounter of these two prominent figures could only have left impressive memories. Leopardi regarded Gioberti as a person "of rare genius and learning,"[67] though at the time his friend was only in his late twenties and had not yet published his absolutistic views on the Good and the Beautiful, the moral mission of the Italian people, and his anti-Jesuitic barbs. But these subjects informed their conversations during the few days of his visit. After Gioberti's departure, the poet found himself in the middle of a family squabble over Carlo's marriage to a cousin on his mother's side, Paolina Mazzagalli, a marriage the count and his perpetually harsh wife had tried at all costs to prevent. Although he always longed nostalgically to return to the home and solitude—and also the warmer weather—of Recanati (his later correspondence is full of references to how the cold elsewhere in Italy anguishes and "kills"[68] him), once he got there he soon saw the town as "infamous" and "hated" and full of "savage people."[69] The love-hate contrast never abated. This particular family controversy may not have taken him by surprise, but it did renew needlessly his domestic discomfort. And then, with Carlo away, the mansion appeared all the more spectral.

For publisher Stella, Leopardi had been working on an anthology or "Crestomazia" of Italian literature, an "immense work" in two volumes (prose and poetry) which required "a multiplicity of readings," and whose more than eighty authors drawn from all centuries would be "most useful inside and outside of Italy" and "worthy of Italy."[70] Much of what he remembered from his earlier years in his father's library found its way into the prose volume at least (he was not satisfied with how the poetry one was turning out); he stressed stylistic qualities above all in his choices (he admired the scientific prose of Galileo Galilei), and did the best he could with the ultimately meager resources of Recanati. He vowed not to accept any more tedious editorial jobs. And he never finished an "Enciclopedia delle cognizioni utili e delle cose che non si sanno" ("Encyclopedia of Useful Knowledge and of Things Not Known"), promised to Stella.[71] Had it not been for the intemperate northern winters, he would have accepted Bunsen's offer of a chair at the University of Bonn or Berlin. Unable to venture beyond the Alps, he continued to look about for a teaching position in Italy, approaching trusted friends in Parma who offered him an inadequately salaried chair in natural history in that city's university; he declined it in the hope that Colletta would find him something better in Florence or Leghorn. When this, too, failed, Colletta begged him in 1829 to accept hospitality in his own home, an act of generosity that embarrassed Leopardi into refusal. It was during this period of almost daily exasperated sensibility—"I can do nothing, I am nothing,"[72] he said—that he composed some of his finest verses: "Le ricordanze" ("Remembrances"), a reliving of his earlier years of vanished hopes in which the mythical girl Nerina[73] appears, symbolizing a disintegration of youth under destiny's inexorable force; "La quiete dopo la tempesta" ("Quiet after the Storm"), an account of how man's sole happiness is a negative derivative of nonsuffering; "Il sabato del villaggio" ("Saturday in the Village"), a reminder of how the day before Sunday, like youth, is always lovlier in its promise than in its fulfillment; and probably "Il passero solitario" ("The Solitary Thrush"), conceived years before and dealing with the natural passing of time for the song-thrush and its painful passing for the poet. But as he penned these idylls, he engaged simultaneously in more heavily philosophical conjectures, not simply explaining man's duty to his fellowmen but also facing squarely the nature of the goal of human life and of universal existence. The problem, of course, presupposed no satisfying response. But a striking poem, written at the outset of 1830, contains Leopardi's reaction: "Canto notturno di un pastore errante dell'Asia" ("Night Song of a Wandering Asian Shepherd"). The poem uses as its point of departure a Russian traveler's simple account of the customs of certain shepherds and rises to broad philosophical heights concerned with the domination of life by suffering and ennui and the inevitable plunge into the abyss of nothingness.

Another reversal for Leopardi: Italy's leading academy, L'Accademia della Crusca, awarded its quinquennial prize of 5,000 scudi to the distinguished historian Carlo Botta instead of voting to have it shared with the author of the *Operette morali,* who, as widespread contemporary opinion held, was equally deserving. Leopardi had entered the contest, though fearing that the Academy favored Manzoni for his historical novel *I promessi sposi (The Betrothed).* But Manzoni had not entered, and Leopardi wrote to Vieusseux, on whose circle (which included Niccolini) he thought he could count: "I beg you to recommend my affair to all those friends who you think might help me. If I have hope in anyone, I have it only in you and in them."[74] But the voluminous *Storia dell'Italia, in continuazione a quelle del Guicciardini (History of Italy, Continuing the Histories of Guicciardini)* gave Botta the nod—and the money, which Botta needed desperately, even more than Leopardi, who had in any case said that he could never "peddle his mendicity."[75] Nevertheless, under these new circumstances, it was not difficult to persuade him to accept a monthly subsidy of eighteen francesconi raised by a small group of friends and admirers headed by Colletta in 1830 to enable him to live in Florence (he was once again determined to leave "the horrible night"[76] of Recanati) and prepare his poems for publication.[77]

The *Canti,* a title suggesting various poetic forms—songs, idylls, hymns, and elegies—were first published by the Florentine editor Guglielmo Piatti in 1831 with the grimly proud words "from Recanati" appearing under his name, and with a grateful introduction, "Agli amici suoi di Toscana," to all his sponsors, many of whom were unknown to Leopardi: "I have lost everything; I am a trunk which feels and suffers. Except that at this time I have acquired you; and your company, which replaces my studies and my every delight and hope, and would almost compensate for my ills if, because of this very infirmity, it were possible for me to enjoy it as much as I should like, and if I were not aware that my fate will soon deprive me of this too. . . ." To be sure, Leopardi wanted to repay his debt, even if it meant having to return to Recanati. Like the exiled Dante, who suffered from having "to climb another's stairs," as he put it, to sue for patronage, the poet was tired of living continually off someone else's kindness. In October, he met the Swiss philologist Luigi De Sinner, to whom he sold his scholarly manuscripts, and this helped somewhat.

Rather surprisingly, the town of Recanati paid tribute to its illustrious son by electing him deputy to the meeting of the National Assembly expected to convene in Bologna. He declined. Because of the political turn of events, the meeting never took place—something to which Leopardi was totally indifferent. He had become involved with Fanny Targioni-Tozzetti, who provided the irritating experience of "Il pensiero dominante" and of "Aspasia," and who made his desire for love disintegrate into bitterness. In the light of his personal debacle, political exigencies seemed secondary. Manzoni tended to remain concerned yet aloof from them; Leopardi, if anything, cast their immediacies aside and retained some feeling only for the broader aspects of national idealism. And this, despite the fact that at this point the Austrian troops were crushing the patriotic revolution which had erupted in Modena and reached the provinces of the Marca Anconitana. "You must know that I abhor politics, because . . . I see that people are unhappy under any form of government; the fault is nature's that made man for unhappiness— and I laugh at the happiness of the *masses* because my little brain can't conceive of a happy *mass,* made up of unhappy individuals."[78]

When in Florence at Colletta's invitation, Leopardi had renewed contact—now friendship—with Antonio Ranieri, a Neapolitan exiled from his native city on account of his liberal opinions. He had first met him in 1827. There now began the "brotherhood" which was to last until the end of his life and which still remains mystifying, given the fact that Ranieri was neither the most cultured nor the most refined of his acquaintances.[79] But culture and refinement notwithstanding, Ranieri was intelligent and elegant, and above all he had a gift for conversation. He assisted Leopardi fraternally, and persuaded him to leave with him for Rome. But the papal capital was "like a very bitter exile";[80] later they both returned to Florence. It seems that Leopardi bore most of the expenses of their life together. During the winter months between 1831 and 1832, the Accademia della Crusca honored the poet by making him a corresponding member. In the words of the Academy's secretary, Giambattista Zannoni: "The beautiful style in which you write Italian prose and verse, the lofty merit of your ideas . . . , as well as your great expertise in literature and the learned languages of Greece and Rome, have moved the members of the Academy to make you one of their college, in which action they see a memorable honor redound to themselves." And Leopardi's humble response: "I recognize no merit [for this honor] in myself, . . . unless one could call merit the immense and inexpressible love I bear this dear and blissful and blessed Tuscany, home of all elegance and good custom and eternal seat of civilization, for which I ardently desire permission to call my second homeland. . . ."[81] But a quick delusion followed: he and Ranieri were not allowed to publish a projected weekly, *Lo spettatore fiorentino,* already contracted with publisher Giovanni Freppa. He sank once again into a depression. Besides, the poor state of his finances (now often aggravated by the presence of his Neapolitan friend) did not permit him much leisure to bask in the important Crusca recognition and for the first time in his life he turned to his father for help—which meant to the family administrator, Countess Adelaide. He was accorded the modest sum of ten to twelve scudi a month for most of his remaining years, and this sufficed to relieve him from complete dependency on Ranieri.

The year 1831 had seen the appearance of an anonymous publication, *Dialoghetti sulle materie correnti nell'anno 1831,* whose reactionary tone should have betrayed the authorship of his father Monaldo, but a number of readers immediately thought of the author of the *Operette morali.*[82] In Rome, Lucca, Milan, Tuscany, even in France, they all talked about Giacomo Leopardi as a convert, like Vincenzo Monti, to more conservative thinking. Irritated, Leopardi published declarations of nonauthorship as widely as he could, since he considered the book "infamous, most infamous, most villainous"[83] for its antiliberal, antimodern utterances. When calm was restored, he continued to work on various projects, and to dictate his thoughts for the by now extensive *Zibaldone.* The last entry came on 4 December 1832.

A lingering yearning for love underlies some of the poetry written at this time in Florence, especially "Amore e morte" ("Love and Death"; "Consalvo," too, dates from this period). Not uncharacteristically, he willingly allowed his dreams to penetrate the creative process, as if out of a desire to fortify himself by a residual will to love, though aware that his creativity was stimulated by nothing more than the fleeting hope of a momentary illusion. What he had declared in 1820 still obtained: "I consider love the most beautiful thing on earth, and I feed myself on vain images."[84] On the other hand, several dialogues written for the *Operette* at this time (the "Dialogo di un venditore di almanacchi e di un passeggere" ["Dialogue between an Almanach Vendor and a Passer-by"], and the

"Dialogo di Tristano e di un amico" ["Dialogue between Tristan
and a Friend"], for example) stand among his most bitter and ironic.
The same mood prevails in "A se stesso," written in 1833, with its
profound, however unacrimonious, despair which refocuses his view
of reality, the sweet dreams of love, and women particularly, that
breed he had once seen as goaded by "ambition, interest, perfidy,
[and] insensitivity."[85] He had not changed his mind. All this left
him with a feeling not only of vapidness, but also of self-deception,
shame, and scorn. Nature with its inscrutable laws does not grant
man even the most modest privileges to abate the penalty of being
born. From the private to the universal malady: the step was taken
repeatedly and easily by Leopardi, not because the private fashioned
the universal but because the private was but a microcosm of the
macrocosmic universe. Perhaps his most pessimistic thoughts oc-
curred in 1833, the year he jotted down the following words addressed to Ariman ("Ad Arimane"), the evil spirit of Iranian
mythology: "During my lifetime, I was . . . the apostle of your
religion. Now recompense me. I ask you not for what the world
calls goods; I ask you for what is considered the worst of evils:
death. . . . I cannot, I cannot bear life any longer."[86] Leopardi
followed this utterance immediately with a proud and tearless silence.

Aware of his friend's depressed state, to say nothing of his weak-
ened physical condition, Ranieri, recently pardoned by the new king
of Naples, Ferdinand II, obtained from this monarch the privilege
for Leopardi and for himself to live unmolested wherever in the
kingdom they chose. The two friends left Florence, stopped briefly
in Rome, and arrived in the southern capital in October of 1833.
Leopardi wrote to his father: "As for my health, which was never
worse than now, the doctors have advised the air of Naples as the
best remedy. . . ."[87] The following year, Ranieri introduced him
to August von Platen. It took a while for the dejected poet, who
rarely left his twilit room and by this time shied away instinctively
from facile friendships, to recognize in the German lyric poet a
kindred spirit. Von Platen left this description of Leopardi at thirty-
five: "At first sight, Leopardi seems absolutely horrible, if one has
come to imagine him through his poetry. Leopardi is short and
hunchback, his face pale and suffering, and he aggravates his bad
condition with his way of life, because he makes day out of night
and vice versa. Not being able to move or apply himself, because

of the condition of his nerves, he leads one of the most most miserable lives you can imagine. However, when you get to know him more closely, all that is disagreeable externally disappears, and the fineness of his classical education and the cordiality of his manner dispose you toward him."[88] Though von Platen visited him frequently, the contact was brief, since the German was to die one year later (1834) in Sicily. Ever more alone in the writhing depths of his private world, Leopardi could once more only gaze at himself scornfully, mindful of Ariman's liberation in death. Human effort is folly, and the glib optimism which directs our belief in progress is a ludicrously grim joke when suffering is the perennial sentence we receive from the ironic tribunal of existence.

"Aspasia" appeared in 1834, a moment of self-contemplation and a recollection of his previous humiliating passion for a Florentine lady. Contrary to his earlier hopes (although he was always aware of the deception), illusions such as Beauty, Nature, and Virtue held forth no promise. In the same vein, he wrote "Sopra un bassorilievo antico sepolcrale" ("On an Ancient Sepulchral Bas-Relief") and "Sopra il ritratto d'una bella donna, scolpito nel monumento sepolcrale della medesima" ("On the Portrait of a Beautiful Woman, Sculpted on Her Tomb"). And with the crumbling of the ideal of Beauty went a profoundly skeptical reaction to the century's confidence that the invention of machinery and the development of a new science and political economy were destined to catapult man into an unprecedented Eden of social existence and wealth. The subtle irony of "Palinodia al marchese Gino Capponi" ("Retraction for Marquis Gino Capponi," 1835) aims at unmasking the vanity of utilitarian Golden Age forecasters. The gratifying publication of new and augmented editions of the *Operette morali* by Piatti in 1834 and of the *Canti* by Saverio Starita in 1835 did not brighten his mood. Most of the time he spent composing a prose piece of bizarre patriotic fantasy, the satirical *I Paralipomeni della Batracomiomachia (The War of the Mice and the Crabs,* completed in 1837), which reiterated his ridicule of the revolutionary efforts. It was clear that he did not get along too well with Neapolitan intellectuals and their proselytizing Catholicism; he called their land "semi-barbaric and semi-African," and the people "Lazzaroni and Pulcinelli—nobles and plebeians, all thieves and damned barons, most worthy of the Spanish [oppressors] and the gallows."[89] In addition, the Bourbon authorities issued an order to sequester the recent edition of the *Canti* as well as another

edition of the *Operette* (1836, by Starita), and Starita seems to have
tried to clear himself in niggardly fashion at Leopardi's expense.
Paris suddenly looked very inviting under these circumstances, and
the poet of Italic songs mentioned several times his resolve to transfer, regardless of his health, to the French capital, where De Sinner
had moved, "To end my days."[90] In the *Paralipomeni,* therefore, the
rats, crabs, and frogs represent the Neapolitans, the adherents of
the papacy, and the Austrians—with the Spanish thrown in for
good measure.

Still, it cannot be denied that the cultural activity of Naples
during those years brought Leopardi out of his social lethargy. Then,
toward the end of 1836, an epidemic of cholera aroused in him a
strong will to live, if only to see Recanati once more, the town and
the people he associated in his imagination more with his bygone
happiness (his nostalgic "lost youth") and serenity than with his
claustration and suffering. Something always told him, almost be-
lying his philosophy, that when he was most dismayed at "The
surrounding nothingness"[91] and wrote things "not worth an iota"
(un fico),[92] his "travail derived more from the feeling of [his] particular unhappiness than from the certainty of universal and necessary
unhappiness."[93] Yet the unhappiness remained "necessary." And as
if to corroborate this, Leopardi's health worsened. Doctors advised
him to stay at the villa of Giuseppe Ferrigni on the slopes of Mount
Vesuvius, between Torre del Greco and Torre Annunziata. The view
of the buried cities and barren plains, and the contrast between
nature's mysterious laws and infinite powers on the one hand, and
man's antlike, travailed condition stupidly comforted by notions of
progress on the other, combined to make "La ginestra" ("The Broom
Plant") a magnificent epilogue to the poet's whole spiritual life.
More than in any other poem, perhaps intensified by the proximity
of death, Leopardi's sense of fraternity and humanity reached une-
qualed heights of urgency, of sublimity, and of compassionate love.
He reminds us of Plotinus's "Let us not refuse to share the ills which
destiny has allotted to our species." In some respects a testament,
"La ginestra" finally manages to synthesize and reconcile the seemingly mutually exclusive movements of reason and illusion in a noble
plea for love and action.

Enrichetta Carafa, one of Ranieri's nieces, left a brief account of
one of Leopardi's favorite strolls by Vesuvius: "By strange coincidence, a young peasant girl lived not far from the villa, named

Silvia—a very rare name in those parts, and perhaps she was the only one there then with that name. During his country strolls in Antonio Ranieri's company, Leopardi often reached the rustic dwelling of Silvia and used to stop there to chat with her about country matters and domestic things, making himself simple like that simple creature."[94] Always the classicist at heart, and even so more bucolic-than epic-minded, Leopardi was always more attracted instinctively to innocence and the simple pleasures. The "simple" imagery in his poetry betrays this propensity which stems from equating simplicity with true nobility, or, in more Rousseauan terms, niggardliness wtih civilization. "The more I learn of the wickedness and lowness of men, the more I become animated and fervent toward noble and good hearts. . . ."[95] Compared with this "fervor," the intellectual stimulations of the city, of Bologna and Florence, were less inspiring, and this helps to explain his recurrent desire for the "solitude" (the equation's third term) of Recanati. Toward the end of his life as toward the beginning of it, he could aver that by temperament he was a "perpetual solitary," or, "as they say in English, [someone] more *absent* than a blind or deaf man would be. . . . In my eyes, men are what they are in nature, that is, a most minute part of the universe; my relationship with them, and theirs among themselves, do not interest me in the least, and this being true, I observe them but very superficially. But be assured that in matters of social philosophy, I am in all respects a real ignoramus. So I am used to observe myself constantly, that is, the man in himself, and similarly his relationship with the rest of nature, from which, regardless of my solitude, I cannot free myself."[96] Civilized man in the generic sense was one thing; but the simple person, like Silvia, was quite another—not the type he would observe superficially but indeed the type for whom he would exhort mankind to a spirit of defense against the calamities and cruelties of nature. Silvia, the *ginestra:* was there a difference?

On the more immediate economic side, the poet, whose impecuniosity had now become distasteful to him, sent a plea for money to his parents. Almost certainly, Count Monaldo would have been moved to succor his famous son, but Countess Adelaide, as impervious to pity as ever, forbade him as well as her brother Carlo Antici to lend a helping hand. By this time, dropsy had set in, and Leopardi's health plunged to an unprecedented level of weakness. He could only dictate; Ranieri and Ranieri's sister Paolina took turns reading aloud to him, sometimes all night long. In 1837, he was back in Naples with the Ranieris who stood by him hopelessly in alarmed apprehension. The previous December, Leopardi had written to his father: "My mother will understand that my asking for a special allowance could not and did not happen until my need reached the item *bread;* when she finally comes to realize that none of you in his lifetime ever found himself—nor will he, thank God— in terrible natural distress, as I *very often* found myself through *no* fault of my own; when she sees in what clothes I stand before her, and when she further realizes that the rejection of one of my promissory notes means a protest to the authorities, and a protest on one of my notes—since I am unable to pay the equivalent sum—means my immediate arrest; then perhaps she will feel some regret for her hostile prohibition. . . ."[97] But she did not, and preferred to find refuge in her arid brand of religious faith. Still and consistently, the poet harbored no bitterness in his heart. In May of 1837, he thanked his parents for the usual tiny monthly sum he had received and for their past thoughtfulness; to his father, he wrote: "I thank you and mother for the gift of the ten scudi, I kiss the hands of both of you, I hug my siblings and beg you all to recommend me to God, so that, once I shall have seen you all again, a good and timely death will put an end to my physical ills which can be cured in no other way."[98] This is the last sentence in his correspondence, and echoes the same pain of years before: "Condemned through lack of means to this horrible and detested abode [of Recanati], and already dead to all pleasure and hope, I only live to suffer and I only invoke the repose of the tomb."[99]

Ranieri convinced Leopardi to return to the more salubrious climate of the Ferrigni villa. It was 14 June. While preparations were almost completed, the poet dictated the final verses of his last poem, "Il tramonto della luna" ("The Setting of the Moon") in which the lifelong drama of reason and illusion surfaced in the form of kindly memories, pulsating with a vague, unfulfilled longing for peace and rest. To make the trip comfortable, Ranieri and his sister got him to change his hours back to normal, if only for that day, but grew concerned at meal time when their friend could not take his usual soup (he disliked ass's milk but he had done well with an ice cream— but ices were something of which he was excessively avid) and, complaining of not feeling well, asked himself for the physician, Dr. Mannella. The doctor knew of Leopardi's asthma, among other ailments (leg swelling, insomnia, colitis, and chronic bronchitis), but this time matters were worse. He advised Ranieri to send for a priest. Paolina Ranieri supported his head and dried the perspiration from his forehead, then the poet looked straight at Antonio saying that he could no longer see him. Shortly afterward, Leopardi died. [100]

He was buried in the little church of San Vitale in Fuorigrotta, [101] and Giordani provided the epitaph:

> TO COUNT GIACOMO LEOPARDI OF RECANATI
> PHILOLOGIST ADMIRED OUTSIDE ITALY
> CONSUMMATE WRITER OF PHILOSOPHY AND POETRY
> TO BE COMPARED ONLY WITH THE GREEKS
> WHOSE LIFE ENDED AT THIRTY-NINE
> MADE MISERABLE THROUGH CONTINUOUS ILLNESSES
> ERECTED BY ANTONIO RANIERI
> COMPANION FOR SEVEN YEARS UNTIL THE FINAL HOUR
> TO HIS BELOVED FRIEND.
> MDCCCXXXVII

Ranieri also saw to it that a death mask was made, but his own words describe the poet just as well: "He was of middle stature, bent and slim, his color between white and pale, his head large, his forehead square and large, his eyes pale blue and languid, his nose sharp and fine, his features very delicate, his speech modest and somewhat faint, his smile ineffable, almost celestial."[102]

Leopardi's was a life of sorrow, of serene honesty and gentleness, and of dignity of spirit; it was also a life which questioned and sought much and which rejected more, for he never claimed to have uncovered viable answers. Like the waves of the sea, his moods constantly rose and fell; his heart could not abandon what his intellect could. In the words of one critic, [103] he explained nothing, but he said everything.

Chapter Two
Philosophical Premises: The *Zibaldone*

That Leopardi merits the title of philosopher has been variously debated but ultimately recognized over the years: directly, if we take notice, among other sources, of his inclusion in the *Encyclopedia of Philosophy;* and indirectly, if we remember, as examples, the references to him in Miguel de Unamuno's *Del sentimiento trágico de la vida (On the Tragic Sentiment of Life)* or the allusions to him in Arthur Schopenhauer's *Die Welt als Wille und Vorstellung*[1] *(The World as Will and Idea)*. Leopardi certainly thought of himself as a philosopher when he referred frequently to his "system," and specifically when he wrote the *Operette morali,* which he considered a full exposition of this system. To be sure, he asserted that his constituted a philsophy or an ultraphilosophy derived from experience rather than from books, but the expressed experience still forms a body of thought shapable by coalescing the *Operette* with the *Pensieri* and many pages of the *Zibaldone* in some kind of "systematic correlation."[2]

As early as 1843, Gioberti spoke of the "profound melancholy" which "animates" Leopardi's world view, of "a tranquil and logical despair, which appears . . . not like a disease of the heart but like a necessity of the spirit and a summary of a whole system."[3] Yet some prefer to think of him as a moralist rather than as a philosopher in the stricter sense. Francesco De Sanctis noted that Leopardi's whole philosophy revolves around the problem of the existence of evil in practical rather than in speculative terms, "implying by itself the goal and significance of life itself," since he was alien to abstract, metaphysical speculation.[4] And, more recently, C. Luporini, who cannot place him in the historical lineage of "problematic and critical connections" of philosophical thought, sees him as a "great moral philosopher."[5] Between De Sanctis and Luporini, Benedetto Croce's opinion stands more stark and severe; Leopardi's thought, for him, as "a doctrine of evil, of suffering, of the vanity of nothingness," has no philosophical value.[6] The Neapolitan philosopher saw this doctrine as a pseudophilosophy and state of mind, as intrinsically nothing but an expression of the poet's own regret and bitterness.

Philosophers often play with words and always welcome systematic speculation. Leopardi was more genuine. What is philosophy except an investigation of causes and laws underlying reality? If Leopardi sought these, he sought them not in the manner of a mathematician working out a formula to solve a problem, but with a questioning sense of human immanence as well as personal involvement, first on the social and finally on the cosmic level. He sought to know how to act in a purposeless universe. Indeed, his philosophy is deeply negative, "a pessimistic catechism"[7]—though it is constantly denied by his vitality as a poet and his consciousness as an artist—and it is arrived at after an endless scrutiny of the world as it conditioned man from the dawn of civilization. His claim to rely on experience rather than on books notwithstanding, Plato and Blaise Pascal, Gottfried Wilhelm Leibniz and Lucretius, Aristotle and Machiavelli, John Locke and René Descartes, Sophocles and Horace, Baron d'Holbach and Johann Gottfried Herder, Seneca and Giovanni Battista Vico, Thomas Aquinas and Martin Luther, *Job* and *Ecclesiastes,* among others, are all absorbed into his philosophy. If regret and bitterness entered his weltanschauung, they did so because the poet lamented the human condition. Therefore, as he admitted, he "embraced naturally the Stoic philosophy,"[8] not for its indifference to pain but for its posture of endurance. This posture becomes significant because, stemming as it does from an adverse (yet so often poetic) view of Nature (reality)—the keystone concept in his entire "system"—it places Leopardi centrally among post-Renaissance proto-existentialist thinkers from Pascal to Sören Kierkegaard in such a way as to make us realize how exaggerated is the prominence in the existential textbook of writers like Jean-Paul Sartre and Albert Camus, who in the long run gave this particular world view little more than an insulated lexicon and a piquant revision of some concepts like choice, responsibility, and revolt. Indeed, given his "courage," "complexity," and "depth" as a thinker, "we recognize [in Leopardi] the anticipator and teacher 'of that philosophy of our time, Existentialism . . . , the anguished realization that our existence is a problem, the tormented search for truth that will never end.' "[9]

Friedrich Schlegel liked to blend "the poetizing philosopher and the philosophizing poet" into "prophets" in the continuing critique of pure reason,[10] and this should remind us very much of Leopardi. As in the *Canti* we see the philosophizing poet, so in the *Operette morali* we see the poetizing philosopher. In the background of the *Operette morali* lie his notebook, the *Zibaldone di pensieri,* and a collection of thoughts reminiscent of the seventeenth-century French moralist François de la Rochefoucauld, the *Pensieri* (largely derived from the *Zibaldone*).

The 4,526 pages of the hodgepodge notebook-diary or *Zibaldone* present an encyclopedic medley of thoughts and analyses, observations and recollections, all set down in Leopardi's incredibly small handwriting, and dating from July 1817 to December 1832. Just by consulting an index, we gain a staggering impression of the myriad of intellectual problems and sources that shaped his mind, even if we might hesitate to call them influences because of how he transcended not only most of what he read but also most of his own concerns. Thematic threads weave throughout it, sometimes functioning as recalls, but generally a shift of focus alters the theme's tone; indeed, the tonalities often appear contradictory and force us to modulate our attention to allow for the contrast. But the themes themselves remain the same; after all, the entries in the notebooks cover the brief span of fifteen years—not much time for radical changes of opinion. To the extent that the fragment and the short essay can say more by implication than the full-blown treatise, the *Zibaldone* represents the whole that is greater than the sum of its parts. And it is a whole that is too vast to embrace. No single point of view suffices to envelop the intellectual vision. Leopardi could never have arranged all that it contains in a series of systematized publications. "The experience of the *Zibaldone* is not the experience of a work; it is the experience of the *impossibility* of the work."[11] From linguistic notes to archaeological and scientific notes, comments on religion, history, and art, literary opinions, lines of verse, memories of childhood, hopes, regrets, to snatches of popular songs, anecdotes, sayings, confessions, ironies, lamentations, observations, and, of course, discussions of philosophical concepts—the *Zibaldone* (not unlike Samuel Taylor Coleridge's *Biographia Literaria*) "is Leopardi himself—sitting alone in his library at Recanati and writing until his eyesight failed, with his lexicons and encyclopedias beside him—a tribute to scholarship, taste, and addiction to truth, and also (for no man who could share his thoughts with his fellows would keep such a diary as this one) a tragic record of human solitude."[12]

Just under two thirds of the *Pensieri's* 111 entries stem from the *Zibaldone,* which gave them "their first life,"[13] so that this work too, assembled during his Neapolitan sojourn and published post-humously by Ranieri as part of Leopardi's collected works in 1845, bears the same broadly philosophical imprint. Best described by Leopardi himself, they represent "reflections on the character and behavior of men in society,"[14] many of them dating back to the early 1820s. For this reason, as well as for the fact that they constitute an unfinished opus, never really properly polished by the author, the *Pensieri* in tone and subject matter reflect attitudes of his youth and present "a Leopardi become rigid, so to speak, in his convictions, and at the same time devoid of that serenity which a conviction held for some time ought to give."[15] Contrary to the intellectual variety and attendant excitement of the *Zibaldone,* they focus on Leopardi as moral philosopher—as bitter moral philosopher, so much so that the author's introduction contains an apology: "For a long time I refused to believe true the things I shall say below, because, apart from my nature being too far removed from them and one's mind always tending to judge others according to one's self, my inclination has never been to hate men but to love them. But in the long run, experience almost violently convinced me of their truth."

The importance of both the *Zibaldone* and the *Pensieri,* however, lies not in the significance of any one thought, but of one thought compared with another, in the cerebral process involved, since Leopardi ultimately denied reason any stature but deemed vital the striving and the quest. It lies also in the secret diary aspect of the collections—the secret diary of one of the world's foremost poets. How fascinating it would be to possess the same for Shakespeare, Virgil, or Goethe, to know what thoughts crossed their minds daily in all candor, without their being wrapped in the veil of editorial retouchings or tactful recastings for publication! Here we see the basic culture and moral philosophy of the Enlightenment stripped of its optimistic leanings and courting nihilism. Leopardi's speculations do not lead to theoretical conclusions but to endless questioning, toward a series of meditations that demolish ideologies and hopes, rational structures and illusions, progressive faiths and cherished beliefs, without for all that renouncing the dream of a change.[16]

Nature and Reason

Given the central position occupied by Nature in Leopardi's way of thinking, one is tempted to define philosophy, for him, as an ordered representation of it. Taking their clue from the unflattering "stepmother" image of nature in "La ginestra," critics have commonly emphasized the pessimistic optics, claiming that Leopardi saw man's insignificance, his suffering and unfulfillment, as natural conditions perpetrated by this cruel stepparent whose utter indifference to man's condition conveys hostility and whose abstractness spells inscrutability. One is reminded of Franz Moor in Friedrich von Schiller's *Die Raüber:* "I have every right to be resentful of nature!" She is the parent whose beauty attracts and whose enmity repels—hence another deception. This is all quite true, especially when by philosophy we understand an imaginative construct, as we would for William Wordsworth. But since, for both poets, imagination stands for more than reasoning or feeling (Wordsworth's "feeling intellect" and "discerning intellect") and is capable of seizing the whole of life in a single manifestation, and since Leopardi pushed his inquiry ever farther, by philosophy in his case we may—always within certain "poetic" strictures—also understand reasoned speculation.[17] For there is another dimension to his view of nature which rounds out the perception, making it less one-sided than the clues of the "broom-plant" would indicate. One passage toward the end of the *Zibaldone* is particularly significant because it reveals, in 1827, not a change from his basic and balanced perceptions of the early 1820s, but a more mature disposition toward the phenomenon of nature, one rich with a-religious and materialistic implications:

Certainly, many things of nature go along well, that is, in such a way as to conserve them, make them last . . . , but more often than not they go badly, they are badly arranged—things moral as well as physical—to the extreme inconvenience of living creatures. . . . These are regular, natural evils. However, we cannot argue from this that the fabric of the universe is the work of an unintelligent cause, though we think we can argue with certainty from those things that go well that the universe was created by an intelligence. We say that the evils are mysteries, that they seem evil to us but actually are not, though it does not dawn upon us that even the good things are mysteries, and that they seem good but actually are not. (Z, 4248)

Nature loses some of its oppressiveness in the drama enacted in the *Zibaldone* between itself and reason. "Only nature is mother of greatness and of disorder; reason is quite the opposite" (Z, 252);[18] "Nature can supplement and does supplement reason an infinite number of times, but never vice versa, even when reason seems to produce great deeds (something quite rare), for even then the impelling and moving force is not that of reason but that of nature; on the other hand, remove the strength administered by nature and reason will always be inoperative and impotent" (Z, 333); "Reason is the enemy of nature, but not primitive reason . . . [which] nature herself placed in man, for in nature there are no contradictions; the enemy of nature is the unnatural use of reason . . . [by] corrupt man . . . not primitive man" (Z, 375). These thoughts lead logically to the assertion in favor of the "superiority of nature over reason, of habit (which is second nature) over reflection" (Z, 3518). The assertion is significant not just because it mitigates the harshness of the common critical perspective but also because it orients us toward Leopardi's ever-present appreciation of nature, usually of nature in her simple presences and manifestations. The disorder of cataclysms is horrible, but nature remains great because inherently beautiful, therefore impressive. Clearly he means nature in the broadest sense, "live nature, its ways, causes and effects, its manners and processes, its goal or goals, intentions, the destiny of the life of nature and of things, the true destination of their being, indeed the spirit of nature . . . both *material . . . and moral . . .*" (Z, 3241). There lies in its bosom a poetic element which reason cannot claim. "Nature, by which I mean the universality of things, is composed, conformed, and ordered in accordance with a poetic effect, . . . to produce a poetic effect, . . . [whereas] there is nothing poetic . . . in exact, geometric reason, . . . in the metaphysician who, . . . in his speculations uses . . . nothing but cold reason. Pure and simple reason and mathematics never were able and never will be able to discover anything poetic" (Z, 3241–42); indeed, "whoever ignores the poetic side of nature ignores a very large part of nature; in fact, he absolutely does not know nature because he does not know her mode of being" (Z, 1835).

As a poet, and with a frame of mind that wanted to value illusion and the imagination, Leopardi never varied his attitude toward reason. Reason, as Rousseau had claimed, never did anything great and, being purely humanly based, has never progressed in the human species (cf. *Z, 4492*). The whole idea of erecting altars to the Goddess Reason (cf. *Z, 357*) demonstrates the utter ingenuousness of the French revolutionaries (cf. *Z, 160–61*). Reason has "stiffened and sterilized" our lifes (*Z, 21*), pushing man into indifference (*Z, 363*) if not into actual impotence (*Z, 2942*). Pierre Bayle had chastised it (*Z, 1555–56*), and none other than the supreme rationalist Aristotle himself had cautioned against its inordinate use (cf. *Z, 2683*). Not many years after Leopardi wrote these lines, another writer, the novelist Honoré de Balzac, was to warn repeatedly and more overtly than his colleagues about the paralyzing effects of excessive analysis in works like *A la recherche de l'Absolu (In Search of the Absolute)* and *Le Chef-d'oeuvre inconnu (The Unknown Masterpiece)*. A half century before, Immanuel Kant had dealt rationalism, as well as empiricism, a severe blow, a state of affairs which the ensuing generation, invoking feeling and intuition, welcomed perhaps a bit too enthusiastically. Leopardi may have been echoing a romantic attitude bent upon reprimanding the classical age for its excesses and misplaced confidence, but as usual he went speculatively beyond what was in the air and expanded the critique of reason immeasurably to include the whole concept of nature on all levels. Tersely put, reason depoetizes.

Leopardi could not abandon the notion of the poetic. Reason may dismantle and reconstruct nature mechanically, but this hardly gives reason an understanding of what it is dealing with, nor does it acquire any autonomy thereby, any exclusive and valuable existence in itself. In fact, as an "artificer of mythology," reason becomes, like everything else, an illusion—though the mythology is "very ugly and bitter" (*Z, 1841–42*), if only because it builds man's hope that through philososphy, whose tool is reason, the human lot will improve. Philosophy, like reason, must relate to poetry:

It is wholly indispensable for a [true philosopher] to be a consumate and perfect poet, but not to reason as a poet; rather, as a very cold reasoner and calculator to examine that which *only* the very impassioned *poet* can know. A philosopher is not perfect if he is only a philosopher, and if he uses his life and himself only to perfect his philosophy, his reason, in the pure search for truth, which is nonetheless the single and pure goal of the perfect philosopher. Reason needs the imagination and the illusions it destroys. . . . (*Z, 1839*)[19]

In this sense, Leopardi has high regard for those philosophers with great qualities of imagination and heart (cf. *Z, 3245*), among whom he included Plato, Descartes, Pascal, Rousseau, and Mme de Staël. Perhaps a one-sentence entry in the *Pensieri* summarizes it: "[There is] no greater sign of not being much of a philosopher or a wise man than to want all of life to be wise and philosophic" (*P, 27*).[20] This was the barb Leopardi stuck in the side of the French Enlightenment's glorification of the pure rational process.

In his study on Leopardi's concept of nature, Bruno Biral[21] suggests how the poet stresses the primacy of man and feeling, whatever the antimetaphysical consequences of this attitude. Originally, Leopardi had leaned in another direciton. Baron de Montesquieu had enabled him to reject the world of Platonic ideas and of absolute values; Copernicus had shown him how to destroy old anthropocentric metaphysical structures; and the eighteenth-century Idéologues had demonstrated to him that the limits of our ideas are the limits of matter. But if for him reason lacks reliability, the picture is not as neat and the metaphysics of nature cracks. Nature does not move in a preordained plan; she creates man and then, as the poet Alfred de Vigny would have said, abandons him, following her own mechanistic laws which demonstrate no concern for his fate and happiness. Perhaps, as has been suggested, it was less nature than the idea of nature that Leopardi admired.[22] Nature is beautiful and therefore inspirational: these are aesthetic qualities; she is indifferent and therefore harmful: these are moral qualities. Hence the "Dialogo della Natura e di un Islandese" ("Dialogue between Nature and an Icelander"), in which the Icelander still cannot escape Nature even in the heart of Africa and sees her there, enormous, grotesquely shaped, half-beautiful, half-terrible: "From far away he espied a huge bust, which he first took to be made out of rock, resembling the solitary colossi he had seen many years before on the Easter Islands. But once he got closer, he found that it was the enormous shape of a woman seated on the ground, her bust upright, her back and elbow leaning against a mountain, not simulated but alive, her face halfway between beautiful and terrible, her eyes and hair very black; she was staring at him. . . ."

This mechanical hulk, rhythmed to the "perpetual circle of production and destruction" (an absurdity to the Icelander), was not what Leopardi believed had to come under the heading of Necessity, or the Norm. He could not accept, as Ugo Foscolo could, the notion

that all that was had to be and could not be otherwise, and that if
it did not have to be, it would not be. Even if he espoused certain
aspects of the mechanistic vision, he had to make distinctions simultaneously between good and evil, and not be impervious to them
as Nature asserted to the Icelander. Therefore the pages of the
Zibaldone are filled with counterstatements: if, on the one hand, we
read that nature being life is also happiness or that the harmony of
nature aims at a being's happiness, we also read that for us the
universe is mainly bad and that nature is regularly and perpetually
a persecutor and a mortal foe of all individuals of any genus and
species (cf. *Z, 3814, 255, 4258, 4485–86*). Our stance, then, must
be one of diffidence before the machine. Mechanistic final causes
may not be totally discarded, but human values do exist, and man
must continue to judge by them. This does not mean that he can
escape the inexorable "stare," but this at least makes him realize
that nature, however lovely at times, is responsible for evil and
unhappiness by not providing adequate conditions for happiness.
Says Nature to the Icelander: "Did you perhaps imagine that the
world was made for you? You should know that in my creations,
orders, and operations—barring very few—I always had and continue to have in mind something quite different from man's happiness or unhappiness. . . . And, in fact, even if it so happened
that I extinguished your entire species, I would not notice it. . . ."
Thus is Leopardi's view of nature, as a mysterious principle of being
for man, akin to Eduard von Hartmann's later claim that nature is
"unconscious," acting like a neutral absolute.

As Biral suggests, Leopardi does not see nature as the Marvelous
Clock of eighteenth-century philosophers, but as one of two great
mutual antagonists, the other being man, and like Pascal he finds
his own reason frightening and anguishing with reference to man's
finality and nature's infinity. "In the 'Dialogo di Tristano e di un
amico' he declares that his philosophy is 'painful, but true.' True,
because reason demonstrates that nature operates by mechanical laws;
painful, because man, who has an unsuppressible desire to love and
to be loved in return, cannot accept the extraneousness of nature.
Knowledge of the truth is painful."[23] This concept makes the poet
one of the most tragic of romantic thinkers; his exasperated individualism places him in the lineage of proto-existential thought.
His "rebellion" (though Leopardi was always too serene to rebel)
assumes a Stoic posture and searches for a way to confirm the human

values he clings to—the philosopher *is* poet—and this he finds ultimately in the confraternity of society. A simple broom-plant, one of nature's unassuming beauties—that "poetic side of nature"—guided him to this view toward the end of his life.[24]

The notion of brotherhood was more poetically than religiously inspired. It was not, for Leopardi, an emanation of Christian philosophy. His concern with Christianity occupies only two years of the *Zibaldone:* 1821 and 1822. In his basic nonacceptance of it, he differs widely from Manzoni. Leopardi rejects the Christian shift of emphasis from life, as Pagan antiquity had stressed, to death. The key passage reads: "Life is naturally made for life and not for death. That is to say, it is made for activity and for all that is most vital in the functions of living creatures" (*Z*, 2415). This went contrary to the prevailing romantic attitude in Europe, expressed in German painting by Caspar David Friedrich and Philipp Otto Runge, in Russian by Aleksandr Ivanov, and in literature by René de Chateaubriand, Alphonse de Lamartine, and Silvio Pellico, to take a few random examples.[25] While Christianity was being at least sentimentally rehabilitated on the Continent, those writers were few who, like Leopardi and Vigny, preferred to profess Stoic rather than Christian beliefs. For Leopardi, nature and Christianity contrast:

Christianity is a mixture half favorable and half contrary to civilization, of civilization and barbarity—the effect of civilization and the enemy of its progress. . . . Christianity in its perfection . . . is incompatible not only with the progress of civilization, but with the subsistence of the world and human life. How is it possible for something to last that holds itself for nothing, . . . and that longs for its own dissolution? . . . Among all ancient and modern religions, Christianity is the only one, implicitly or explicitly, by its very essence, constitution, character, and spirit, that makes us consider evil what naturally is, was, and always will be good, and consider good what is always evil—beauty, youth, wealth, etc., even the happiness and prosperity we long for and all living beings will eternally and necessarily long for. . . . The world cannot subsist unless it has itself as an end. (*Z*, 2456)

Though in an intense philosophical moment in 1826—as intense as his depression in 1833 that resulted in "A se stesso"—he declared, almost like Lord Byron's Cain, that "Everything is evil" (*Z*, 4174), Leopardi could not proclaim the Christian "vale of tears," and, as one critic observes, on this question he does not alter his first focus.[26]

Along with its being unnatural, Leopardi also put Christianity aside because of its relation to reason. He did this in part because of his disagreement with Enlightenment rationalism. "Even if we want to consider the Christian religion as the fruit of human reason in the context of those times and places, it is undeniable that in turn it influenced very much reason itself, turning it to its depth, to the abstruse, to the metaphysical" (Z, 1065). As unnatural as reason is, not because it forms an essential part of the living being but because as it develops it becomes the principal obstacle to human happiness (Z, 1825), so is Christianity unnatural and wrong. Hence the religious question becomes part of the more fundamental debate between nature and reason.

However, as we have seen, nature herself holds an ambivalent position in the mind of the poet, who modulates in his notebooks from admiring to condemning statements. But the early Rousseauan position of 1823 in which nature is good and civilization bad will change by 1829 when Rousseau is put aside and man emerges as the victim—the basic thought (as distinguished from his poetic attitude vis-à-vis nature) that will induce him to defend himself against the charge of misanthropy and generate the idea of brotherhood in 1836:

My philosophy not only is not conducive to misanthropy, as it may seem to those who look at it superficially, and as many accuse it of being; but by its nature it tends to heal, to extinguish that ill-humor, and hatred—not systematic but yet real hatred—that so very many who are not philosophers—and who would not be called or thought of as misanthropists—bear. . . . My philosophy makes nature guilty of everything and by exculpating men entirely, turns the hatred (or, if no more, the lament) to a higher principle, to the true cause of the ills of living creatures. . . . (Z, 4428)

The second half of the *Zibaldone* contains a "Lucretian polemic"[27] against the system of the universe, again pitting Leopardi against his contemporaries who could only find words of praise for its incomparable order. We are traduced by appearances. The year 1829 brings a diatribe against the stepparent: "Nature, by necessity of the law of destruction and reproduction, and to preserve the present state of the universe, is essentially, regularly, and perpetually the persecutor and mortal enemy of all the individuals of every sort and species to whom she gives birth; and she begins to persecute them from the very time she produced them. This, being the necessary consequence of the present order of things, does not give a great idea of the intellect of whoever is or was the author of this order" (*Z*, 4485–86).

Leopardi's position between poetic and simple nature on the one hand and the cosmic nature of reproduction and destruction on the other constitutes a moving dialectic in the pages of the *Zibaldone*, though the emphasis shifts from the first half to the second. Mario Vinciguerra has brought a balanced perspective to it, saying that as part of nature man cannot step outside it and judge it. That part of the universe we know "has nothing to say in response to the queries or accusations of the rebels, because it itself is not an autonomous entity." So long as we are the children of a "natured nature" (*natura naturata*) and not of a "naturing nature" (*natura naturans*), we cannot make accusations. This inwardly the author knew. "And here we find ourselves in front of the great Leopardian drama."[28]

Beauty

Leopardi's focus on the problem of nature spins off into the related concerns of beauty, love, pleasure, and death, where the same pathos-logos obtains. Any analysis of the universal system of being, he declared, must necessarily deal in a major way, among other things, with the beautiful (cf. *Z*, 1833). But only "among other things." In the Copernican world, beauty is not a central concept as it had been in Plato's *Philebus;* not an inherent, nonrelational property, it is therefore not an absolute (*Z*, 1184). If it enhances our otherwise negative view of nature, beauty represents but a moment of our interpretation of nature—and a subjective moment at that, derived from the experience of the senses. No innate idea of beauty or instinctive capacity for taste and judgment exists; all comes to us exclusively through habit and comparison. No absolute standard shapes our view. "Only by seeing much does one without thinking form a judgment, a discernment, a fine sense to distinguish the beautiful from the ugly" (*Z*, 1186).[29] Beauty exists by "no eternal and necessary laws" (*Z*, 1412), and being relative, it cannot be considered the sole concept of aesthetic experience. In fact, it depends entirely on perception, on "circumstances extrinsic . . . to the sphere of beauty" itself (*Z*, 1184), and is consequently, like taste, something refined by experience (*Z*, 1187). An aesthetic experience is not an idea found in nature, and there exists no consensus on it: simple, uncorrupted souls like children disagree with those who live in primitive contexts on seas and farms, who disagree with educated and erudite persons, who in turn disagree with artists and poets, and so on, "even in essential matters, more or less, according to differences among nations, climates, opinions, habits, customs, styles of living, centuries . . ." (*Z*, 3206–8). Among other things, Leopardi was a genuine relativist.

In this as well as other considerations, essential for him was the notion of habit, or *assuefazione* (*Z*, 1945, 1186): "In brief, everything is habit" (*Z*, 1371). For if it can be argued that opinion forms a substantial component of one's awareness of beauty (*Z*, 1319–21), an even more fundamental component is the *effect* of beauty which shapes that awareness. And it is the effect that forms the habit, the individual's customary way of viewing beauty. The conditions of its apprehension always relate to a subjective response. To paraphrase Joseph Addison, taste is not to conform to beauty but beauty to taste.[30] It was clear to Leopardi, not immune to the romantic spirit of rebellion against traditional rules, that beauty possesses no self-contained properties but lies in the experience of the percipient— which means that it can only be appreciated under relative conditions. As the moral-sense theorist Francis Hutcheson had insisted a full century earlier, the word "beauty" is to be taken for the idea raised in us.[31] For this reason, as any number of eighteenth-century philosophers, largely British, had pointed out, its elements or aspects are not shared by all human beings—hence the problem important to Kant's *Critique of Judgment:* "How, if the aesthetic judgment arises from the subjective feeling and predicates nothing of the object, can it claim to be more than an autobiographical report and can, indeed, claim to be universally binding?"[32]

Leopardi had his response. He admired Kant as one of the great modern philosophers but did not consider that his metaphysical speculations had made any breakthrough ("even his disciples ignore . . . his discoveries, whatever they may be" [*Z*, 1857]). At least on the instinctive level, he must have known more than his words "whatever they may be" suggest, for as one critic comments, "it is surprising that Leopardi's [philosophical] thought has not been sufficiently probed and historically validated yet, Leopardi who—mind you—reached the same conclusions in critical philosophy as Kant, without having read him, reconciling empiricism and rationalism and denying metaphysics all foundations because the human conscience cannot go beyond phenomena. . . ."[33] Still, Kant dismantled metaphysics or pure reason in order to reestablish it on firmer grounds, while Leopardi devaluated it out of his characteristic skepticism. Leopardi had a more vigorous perception of reality than the Königsberg philosopher; ontologically, he recognized the phenomenal existence of an outer world as separate from that of the thinking subject, and he thus eschewed the idealistic manner of viewing being. There was no categorical imperative. Not that he was a thoroughgoing materialist in the Enlightenment sense, but in his traditional separation of matter and spirit and in his pronounced awareness of the physical nature of reality, he did tend in the materialistic direction. This view, too, proceeded undoubtedly from his skepticism, which did not endow matter with positive connotations. That part of matter that is associatable with spirit he preferred to identify simply as "nature." And this part of nature was related to the concept of beauty, the part bound to the thinking subject.

Given the relativity of one's apprehension of beauty, the poet distinguished between the abstract, metaphysical consideration, about which he had little to say (it is a "chimera" [cf. *Z,* 1256, 3207]), and human, tangible beauty that beckons our vision and lures our senses. Pure beauty, he recalls Montesquieu as saying, the kind that boasts perfect proportions, rarely kindles great passions anyway. Human beauty, on the other hand, which may not be apprehended immediately (*Z,* 1794–95), impresses our sensibility and moves the psyche with desire. However, like reason, alas, it is deceitful. Theophrastus was right: he called it a seduction and a lie (*Z,* 306), and in its anticipation Sappho and Petrarch had experienced a sense of fear which developed from the certainty of a nonrealization of desire (*Z,* 3443–46). Therefore, Leopardi's answer to Kant, while never stated *ad hominem,* remains implied: since the aesthetic judgment of beauty cannot be predicated on objective properties and so cannot be universally binding, and since the subjective apprehension deceives, beauty is—too—an illusion. E. von Hartmann also had declared that all is illusion.

Love, Pleasure, and Death

The same dichotomy Leopardi made between two ways of viewing beauty—the abstractly reasoned and, more personally, the immanently perceived—he made for the related question of love. As has been intimated, multiple perspectives characterized his questioning mind and enabled him to cultivate contrasts ("Everything is animated by contrast and languishes without it" [Z, 2156]) and engage in an almost Hegelian dialectic without, however, stressing the synthesis unduly. The synthetic function, he might have said, tends toward a deceptive idealism, while the primary opposition is realistic, human and natural. Improperly, some critics have made contrast, in his case, synonymous with contradiction. Leopardi's thought process is not contradictory; it is complementary. This does not mean that Leopardi is a writer and thinker existing biographically in a timeless realm, or, to use Umberto Bosco's phrase apropos of Petrarch, that he is a "poeta senza storia," a poet without a history. Yet, if his thought evolves, as surely it does between his early and later years (though never forgetting that from the first entry in the *Zibaldone* to the hour of his death covers just under two decades, not more, however intellectually intense these years were), the evolution is not characterized by an accumulation of knowledge which then results in a change of intellecutal direction—which then *could* be seen as contradiction—but rather by an intensification of knowledge which then results in a shift of emphasis. The problematic nature of his reasoning suggests a process: he reacts to the provocations of Kant, Strato of Lampsacus, the *philosophes,* Rousseau (if Leopardi put aside his sentimentalizing about nature's goodness he did not discard the poetic sensitivity the idea of nature arouses), Descartes, etc., but the process is not a true repositioning. The crux of the matter always is less the contradiction than what De Sanctis calls the constant interplay between enthusiasm and skepticism,[34] or the fusion of opposite perspectives. The true process lies in reconciling potentially contradictory attitudes. With reference to felicity, for instance, Leopardi wrote:

It seems quite contradictory in my system with regard to human happiness that I should praise action, activity, abundance of life so greatly, and thereby prefer the ancient way of life and condition to the modern one, and at the same time consider as the happiest or the least unhappy of all the ways of life that of the most stupid of men, of the least animated animals, that is, of those that are poorest in life, the inaction and sluggishness of savages. . . . But in truth, these two things go very well together, proceed from one and the same principle, and are necessary consequences of it no less the one than the other. (Z, 4185)

Even more to the point, his most concise statement on the matter was inspired by nature: "Nature has various qualities and principles that are at once harmonious and contrary; in fact, they harmonize and sustain themselves mutually by virtue of their contrariness. And not only does one of the contraries not destroy the theory of the other, it rather demonstrates it" (Z, 2045–46). Leopardi's cognitive trait is not contradiction but relativism.

In the matter of love (between individuals), he distinguishes instinctively between the concept and the private experience, to which he is unavoidably and immediately drawn. But he goes further in working out the phenomenon in conjunction with self-esteem (and its variant, self-love), desire, matter, infinity, pleasure, self-preservation, and, of course, illusion. All these concerns cast relative hues on each other, since they depend on how the mind perceives them in relation to each other. On the highest or ideal level, love "is the life and vivifying principle of nature [as hate is the "destructive and fatal principle"]. . . . Things are made to love one another mutually, and life is born from this" (Z, 59).[35] But realistically our capacity for this is far from infinite. The following excerpt from the *Zibaldone* states the problem:

Man's desire to love is infinite if only because he loves himself with limitless love. He therefore wants to find objects that he likes, to find the good (and by good I also mean the beautiful . . .); he wishes, then, to love. . . . And he wishes it boundlessly. . . . This desire is innate, inherent, inseparable not only from man's nature but from any other creature, because it is a necessary consequence of self-esteem [*amor proprio*], which is a necessary consequence of life. But it does not prove that man's ability to love is infinite, just as his infinite desire to know does not prove that his ability to know is infinite; it only proves that his self-esteem is limitless or infinite. . . . We can only know and love most imperfectly. [We would have to know and love something infinitely for our ability to be infinite.] Therefore, our knowledge and love, though directed toward an infinite being, are not infinite, nor could they ever be. Therefore, our ability to know and to love is essentially and effectively limited like our ability to act physically. . . . Therefore, our infinite desire to know (that is, to conceive) and to love can never be satisfied by reality . . . [to the extent that] it can really possess an infinite object . . . ; it can only be satisfied by illusion (or false conceptions, or false persuasions of knowledge and love, of possession and pleasure). . . ." (Z, 388–90)

The phenomenon of love leaves us in a state of greater vagueness, confusion, and indefiniteness than any other passion (Z, 1017); if one cultivates it, one risks being traduced by "all the *most extravagant* illusions of love" (Z, 1651). At any time, the seduction remains. It is nurtured particularly by the sense of the infinite, or the indefinite, the quality that makes hope more attractive than pleasure (assuming the latter can be experienced). The sensibilities that stir desire and hope are heightened, even if in the true lover these sensibilities, as we learn in "Aspasia," exist confusedly. "This infinite," however, being "inseparable from true love . . . with all its storms, is the source of the major joys man can experience" (Z, 1018).

Even so, our inability to realize desire fully is always such as to make us feel something missing, a betrayed hope, in love's great transports (Z, 142). Among all desires, that of love is the most painful, in its course and duration (Z, 3446)—a thought which leads Leopardi sometimes to the dark conjecture that only through pain can one arrive at the pleasant, indeed at its mere "shadow of happiness." The finest moments of love, he believed, belong to those times of "quiet and sweet melancholy," when one cries without knowing why, and when one comes close to resigning oneself calmly to some misfortune without knowing which. "In that calm, your less agitated soul is almost full, and almost tastes felicity" (Z, 142). In his *Temple de Gnide* (Section V), Montesquieu had suggested as much.

But, drawn down to the level of experience, Leopardi soon replaces philosophy with psychology, and the entries in the *Zibaldone* tend to become gloomier or simply more observational, within a few years' space (1818 to 1823, for example). On the sensual plane, love tends normally toward equals rather than toward opposites (which it may do, too, but only when it yields for special reasons to our interest in the extraordinary [Z, 2045]). Given its usual affinity for the infinite, it finds its energy in the imagination, which becomes specifically active when the element of mystery shrouds the desired object (Z, 3909–10). Sensual love, furthermore, can be transformed and spiritualized by external factors, by "opinion'" or social pressure, such as the knowledge that the other party is one's sibling (*Z, 3915–19*), thereby creating a taboo for sensual expression. The known often hinders. In the absence of the unknown, the fecundating powers of the imagination lose their sensual vigor. This line of argument makes it sound as if Leopardi felt keenly about carnal love between the sexes, but such an emphasis would prove misplaced. Like his Asian shepherd, he looked upward while asking secular questions of himself, of humanity, and of love; in his vocabulary the noun "love" applied just as often to concepts, like youth, art, mankind, solitude, even country, and on several occasions he insisted that when one loves a woman one actually loves the idea of beauty that woman represents. He did not emphasize the carnal play of the sexes *(volutà),* even if he liked to speculate idly with Mme de Lambert *(Réflexions nouvelles sur les femmes)* about three types of women within the ambit of love (*Z,* 677), or about their craving sense of rivalry with their lovers (*Z,* 1362, 4102), or about the titillating role of clothing in lustful attraction (*Z, 3304–6*). The physical quickly made way for the spiritual. It is the young and inexperienced beginner, he wrote, who in matters of love considers only the face (*Z,* 1882). Something less immediate and superficial is involved, something mystical, as the following paradoxical passage illustrates:

When the use of clothing was introduced, woman became almost mysterious to man (especially to the inexperienced youth), and man to woman. Their hidden forms left room for the imagination. . . . In the natural state, man's innate inclination toward woman . . . , nowhere needing to exercise the imagination, produced very simple, distinct, clear, and material thoughts and feelings. Now, at one point this inclination, this inborn love which by nature is very strong and burning, encounters mystery, and when their effects commingle in the human soul with the idea of mystery (that is, an obscure and confused idea), the thoughts and feelings that result from this commingling of supreme desire and natural tendency . . . must be very obscure and very confused, wavering, vague, indefinite, a hundred times less sensual and carnal than before . . . , and ultimately almost mystical. Thus, from such a material circumstance, like the matter of dress . . . , there occurs in man almost the most spiritual result that can ever occur in his soul: the most sublime thoughts and feelings, the most noble and proper for the spirit. . . . Out of such a real, visible, and determined circumstance are born in him the greatest illusions, the most vague, uncertain, and interdeterminate thoughts, the major operation of the most fervid, delirious, and dreamy imagination. . . . Finally, from an unnatural circumstance is born an effect that is considered universally the most natural, the most proper to man, the most absolutely inevitable, the least obtainable, the least realizable, the least productive . . . [of human experiences]. (Z, 3305–9).

Back to philosophy: again, the pessimistic evaporation into illusion. There is certainly little evidence of the romantic self-indulgence in the delightful furies of passion in Leopardi. Aleksandr Pushkin, the Goethe of *Werther,* Percy Bysshe Shelley, or Alfred de Musset do not inform the notebooks in this context. Even when they allude to the down-to-earth man-woman relationship, the *Zibaldone* entries, early or late, do not sound like fond confessions; he approaches love with a classical, analytical mind, almost as if, given his personal deceptions, he is not comfortable with the direct subject and prefers the indirect manner of philosophizing about it, doing exactly what he criticizes Virgil of doing in his "guarded, indeed disguised" (Z, 3609) way of treating Aeneas during the amorous Dido episode.

The same dichotomous contest between reason and illusion affects the "love" poetry: on the one hand, the exhilaration of love, without which "life has no worth"—that "divine" dream that "can resist reality" ("Il pensiero dominante") by creating through private fantasy a "celestial loveliness" that causes the poet to "gaze and smile at sea and earth" ("Aspasia"); and on the other hand, that "bitter [and] brutal" illusion ("A se stesso"). If "a life bereft of sweet illusions and of love is like a starless night in winter's midst" ("Aspasia"), its natural susceptibility to love also points to its "infinite vanity" ("A se stesso"). The synthesis of this dialectic turns out to be that "quiet and sweet melancholy" whose pain produces that "shadow of happiness." The easy association of the writer's illusory basis of love with the notion of Idea in the sense of Plato and the Neoplatonists, whom he knew well, leaves out the fact that the Greek philosopher referred to an actual, heavenly world while the Italian poet could only think in terms of the human imagination devoid of extraterrestrial realities. Though he might insist on its illusory quality, indeed its deception, in the long run love remains for Leopardi the poet as enigmatic as it has been over the ages. The poem "Il pensiero dominante" expresses it: love is

a dream and plain illusion. Yet your nature,
mid all our fair illusions,
is divine; for it is so vital and strong,
that with resolve it can resist reality . . .
And surely you, my thought, O you alone
the life-source of my days,
[are the] beloved cause of endless woes. . . .

As a philosopher, however, the poetic enigma finds an explanation in the phenomenology of self-esteem. Echoing François, Duc de La Rochefoucauld and Claude Helvétius, self-esteem, for Leopardi, is the basis of passion (*Z, 293*); like self-love, it is "innate" (*Z, 4242*), a man's only really innate attribute, and it is the measure of an individual's vitality, of his desires, hence it is also the cause of unhappiness. But it is not egoism. Self-esteem enables the individual to love outside of himself, and here Leopardi leaves the narrow, self-serving confines of the two French moralists; self-esteem directs itself often not to definite things like food or clothes but to indefinite objects, like freedom, friendship, and love. This constitutes "well directed self-esteem"; egoism is ill directed (*Z, 671*) and constitutes a base and cold form of this attribute. Into the well directed kind flow the vivifying qualities of illusion and imagination whereby it feeds other illusions ("No sweet and noble and lofty and strong illusion can survive without the grand illusion of self-esteem" [*Z, 4499*]—a statement of 1829 at the end of the notebooks that echoes 1820). Love for a woman may well be an extension of self-love, but it may also contain sufficient altruism to belie the cynical moralists. "La storia del genere umano" ("The History of the Human Race") clearly states how "man loves others as others and not himself in others or through others." Thus, while every egoism may derive from self-esteem, not every expression of self-esteem is a form of egoism.[36]

The matter turns psychoanalytical when self-esteem is conjoined with the theory of pleasure. Our inability to realize desire means our inability to realize pleasure which, in Freudian fashion, Leopardi relates to the senses. Self-esteem is rooted in "man's infinite inclination for pleasure" (*Z, 179*). "[The inclination] relates to no transcendence," in the words of one critic, "but only to this mental image which is simultaneously an impulsive force, and which a few

decades later psychoanalysis was to remove once and for all from
the conscious and compact stature of the ego, then to place it . . .
in the subconscious."[37] For Leopardi, the sense of universal nothingness, the insufficiency of all desires to fulfill us, and our tendency
toward an infinite we do not understand, stem from a material
rather than from a spiritual reason.

Although man always desires an infinite pleasure, he really desires a material and palpable pleasure, however that infinity or indefiniteness may
try to spread a veil to make us believe we are dealing with something
spiritual. What is spiritual in what we conceive confusedly in our desires,
or in our most vague, indefinite, vast, and sublime sensations, is nothing
else, one might say, than infinity, or what is indefinite in materiality.
Thus our desires and sensations, even the most spiritual among them,
never extend beyond matter (more or less definitely conceived), and the
most spiritual, pure, imaginary, and indeterminate felicity that we can
taste or desire is never—nor can it ever be other than—material. For every
faculty of our mind ends absolutely on the last boundary of matter, and
is entirely confined within the limits of matter. (Z, 1025–26)

Despite this declaration, Leopardi's materialism was not reductionist, nor would it lead him in the direction of the dialectical materialism of Karl Marx, since material nature is not propelled by
intention or predisposition, only by chance. Once again, it was
through the interaction of contrasts that he ultimately revealed his
posture, for a certain panpsychism inevitably creeps into his thinking. While he would deny the existence of spiritual principalities
or powers, he would also deny deterministic postulates, as "La
ginestra" clearly suggests. In addition, his sense of the infinite plays
a part in dulling the edge of the materialistic principle. Therefore,
we might associate his thinking less closely with Leucippus and
Democritus and more closely with Empedocles and Lucretius in
antiquity, and with Pierre Gassendi and Thomas Hobbes, or par-
ticulary Descartes, as opposed to Baron d'Holbach in more recent
history. Leucippus had developed the principle that all qualitative
differences in nature may be reduced to quantitative ones, while
Democritus, the first important materialistic philosopher of nature,
had evolved an atomic theory of the universe that involved human
perception. Intellectually, these would represent positions too extreme for Leopardi to acknowledge. Empedocles, however, who
introduced a theory of value into his explanation of nature—the

varying mixtures of the four elements (earth, water, air, and fire) which account also for love and hate and, by extension, good and evil—he would more readily count as a precursor of his own way of thinking, as he would Lucretius with his Epicurean modification of the atomistic determinism of Democritus in favor of chance and his opposition to the limitations of metaphysics and religion on the freedom of pleasure. Leopardi does not mention Gassendi in the *Zibaldone,* and Hobbes is alluded to only once. Though he would have objected to the former's metaphysics, to his orthodox views in theology, he would not have discarded his Epicureanism, and though he would not have welcomed the latter's notion of state, sovereignty, and government ("The corruption of mores is fatal for republics and useful for tyrannies and absolute monarchies" [*Z,* 302]), he could only have agreed, given the prevalence in this world of conflict which militates against pleasure, with the Englishman's first law of motion, in the context of self-preservation, which states that the primary condition of all organic and inorganic bodies in the universe is one of collision—which Leopardi would read as unhappiness.

Descartes, whom he admired as one of those "who truly changed the face of philosophy" (*Z,* 1854), not only encouraged his skepticism ("Descartes' precept: 'The friend of truth must once in his lifetime doubt everything' " [*Z,* 1720]) but also, through his dualism of body and soul, mind and matter, put proper stress on the universe conceived as a mechanical system. Furthermore, his theory of sensation, though the weakest link in the Cartesian explanation of cognition, and his notion of the will (in Leopardi's terms prompted by desire for pleasure) often overreaching the intellect and causing error or unhappiness, fitted the Leopardian understanding of human dynamics as well. This ontology diverged considerably from Holbach's rigid determinism, from his materialistic synthesis of nature and the physical and moral worlds, identifying matter and spirit and absorbing all sensations, including pleasure, into its orbit. Holbach spoke only of matter and movement, but this was too reductionist for Leopardi. If everything were matter, then pleasure might conceivably be obtainable; but it is its spiritual, "infinite" dimension that elude man. By the time of the first edition of the *Operette morali* (1827), Leopardi, we know, was firmly convinced of the impossibility of felicity.

Pleasure, then, becomes the subject for a material metaphysics. "The human soul . . . always desires fundamentally, and aims

uniquely toward, . . . pleasure [which is the same as happiness]"
(*Z*, 165). Just as the mind never stops thinking, so it never stops
desiring pleasure, thereby contributing to the process a sense of
infinity. In its effects, it resembles hope; what Iscomachus said
about his father and Socrates about Xenophon, Leopardi declares in
his notebooks: that all human pleasure consists in hope and the
expectation of something better (*Z*, 4126, 183, 2527).

This makes of pleasure a kind of withdrawal rather than a participation, "an abandonment or oblivion of life," for it is an "imaginary" quality of reason, something universally sought but never
conceived, "not even for a single instant," since man is really not
capable of it (*Z*, 4074, 2629, 1017, 2884, 3824). It exists continually in the future. Even so, it is vacuous, seeming more attractive
from afar than up close, where it appears arid and empty because,
without distancing, illusion cannot work its charm (*Z*, 271). One
must look beyond it: "If you seek only pleasure in something, you
will never find it, and you will only experience boredom, often
disgust" (*Z*, 4266). Yet our craving for it is infinite. Tilgher sees
another Leopardian contradiction, claiming that the author of the
Zibaldone had not one but two theories of pleasure: the first relating
to man's love of self and therefore the love of pleasure is innate and
limitless—an optimistic construct, and the second relating to pleasure's deriving from sorrow and pain, as eighteenth-century French
and Italian thinkers like Pierre Moreau Maupertuis, Pietro Verri,
or Giammaria Ortes had said—a pessimistic construct.[38] It should
be pointed out, however, that the contradiction is apparent and not
real, for the concepts that the absence of pleasure begets sorrow and
that the cessation of sorrow begets pleasure are not mutually incompatible. For even as Tilgher points out alluding to *Zibaldone*
pages 2599–602, the dialectical process obtains once again, in that
the neutralization of pleasure and sorrow, namely indifference—
things "neither good nor bad"—is "the cause of boredom," and
even "evils come to be necessary for happiness itself" (*Z*, 2600–
2601). Craving for the illusion of pleasure, then, constitutes a life
force.

The conceptual step between desire, infinite or not, and self-
preservation is short for Leopardi. Self-esteem and self-preservation
lie at the root of desire. In what might be considered a summarizing
statement, he wrote:

The infinity of man's inclination toward pleasure is a material infinity, and one cannot deduce from it anything great or infinite in favor of the human soul, any more than one can in favor of brutes in whom it is natural that the same love exist on the same level, since it is an immediate and necessary consequence of self-esteem. . . . In fact, it is noteworthy how that feeling which on the surface seems the most spiritual thing in our soul is an immediate and necessary consequence (in our present condition) of the most material thing in living beings, that is, of self-esteem and self-preservation—those very things we have in common with brutes, and which, as far as we know, may be in a certain way proper to all existing things. (*Z*, 179–80)

Love of life operates as a necessary consequence of self-esteem, which is analogous to self-love. When the latter is wounded or deceived—a common occurrence—deep pessimism taints one's world view. In this context, Leopardi's most depressed moment came with the resentment of "A se stesso." Love of life (like fear of death) is not inborn; "self-love is." Man is his own end, and nothing he undertakes is separate from that goal (*Z*, 4242, 4108). There is a difference, however, between self-esteem, which can be altruistic, and self-love, which equates with egoism. The latter is a species, or variant, of the former, but not its core. Self-service excludes the social capacity to do good, whereas the greater the sense of life or vitality in a person—the greater, in other words, the strength and activity of his mind—the greater his self-esteem. "All human affects derive from self-esteem which shapes itself in a variety of ways" (*Z*, 3282, 150). Though in its variant form it may loom as "the universal principle of human vices" (*Z*, 57), it remains a necessary and unlimited psychodynamic factor in our lives, because it invigorates that essential component of living, hence of self-preservation: illusion. "No sweet and noble and lofty and strong illusion can do without the grand illusion of self-esteem, the illusion of one's esteem of one's self and of hope. Remove this, and all the others will fall apart, and you will then realize that this one was the basis and the nurse, not to say the root and the mother, of all the others." (*Z*, 4499).

A desire for self-preservation does not imply a contradiction with a coexisting impulse for death (again, Sigmund Freud—and Jacques Lacan—come to mind). Fate created love and death together, Leopardi writes in the poem appropriately entitled "Amore e morte"; one gives pleasure, the other erases pain. An almost Heideggerian "being-for-death" preoccupied him from childhood, if his early poem "L'appressamento della morte," with its five cantos and cold conclusion ("May a slab cover me, and my memory perish") is any indication. The life of the universe "hurries indefatigably toward death," we read in the *Operette morali's* "Cantico del gallo silvestre" ("Song of the Wild Rooster"). Ernest Jones might have compared its author to Freud, in this respect—or to Michel de Montaigne, or to Sir Thomas Browne, whose fixed concerns with death color much of their thought. Philosophically, Eros and Thanatos interrelate simultaneously. Their reciprocity, like an impulsive force, underlies most of the *Canti.* One of Leopardi's most conscious poetic activities consists in a desire to transcend our ignorance of the dual phenomenon through a fusion of the two parts into a conceptual unit, "a reduction of the vital instinct to the death instinct, a life-death identification through thought's meditation and the deceptiveness of illusions. . . ."[39]

Death, like sleep, is a point in time; in the hereafter, Ruysch recalls the sweet sensation of falling asleep ("Dialogo di Federico Ruysch e delle sue mummie" ["Dialogue between Frederick Ruysch and His Mummies"]). We cross into it not gradually but instantly (*Z,* 292–93). Unless he suffers from extreme unhappiness, a person's reason, like nature, finds termination—anything that curtails the teleological process or anything that contradicts self-preservation— repugnant (by defeating our illusions, reason is always our capital enemy [*Z,* 816–17]). Death's function aims at the destruction of the human species, and it triumphs over the world ("Dialogo della moda e della morte" ["Dialogue between Fashion and Death"]). Hence, as natural and rational beings, we have learned to fear it. Indeed, in olden days the more we had to lose, the less we were repelled by it, but in modern times, Leopardi believed, when unhappiness prevails, it distresses us: "Love of life and fear of death have grown in the human species and continue to grow in every nation according to the lower value placed on life. . . . Death, which for the ancients, who were so active or otherwise full of life, was often the greatest good, is deemed and more commonly called the greatest evil the more miserable life seems" (*Z,* 3030).

Yet, the other side of the coin, that of the thinking man, whom he might have listed under the "suffering élite," anticipating Friedrich Nietzsche, reveals that life's unhappiness causes any cognitive creature to desire it. Since our psyche is such that something like death seems more tolerable at a distance than at close range, we may discover a self-preserving love of life when faced with the ultimate reality (*Z,* 137–38), but the fact remains that the meditator with a philosophical grasp of existence can only prefer extinction to continuance. This is the advice given the physicist/physician in the "Dialogo di un fisico e di un metafisico" ("Dialogue between a Physicist and a Metaphysician"). Even nature acts compassionately toward man in the advent of death:

The Neapolitan [Domenico] Cirillo opined that death has something delectable about it. I agree with him entirely and have no doubt that man (and any kind of animal) experiences a certain comfort and a certain pleasure in death. Not that its causes, and therefore the moments farthest away from it, are pleasurable, but rather the moments immediately preceding it, that very imperceptible and unsensed point or space of which it consists. And this holds true in any sickness, even the most acute, about which [Georges Louis Leclerc, count of] Buffon seems to agree that death can be painful. Indeed, the torpor of death must be all the more pleasurable as the pains preceding it are sharp, and from which, as a result, death frees us. As for those illnesses which extinguish a man little by little, someone fully conscious up to the very end, it is certain that there is no moment so immediately near death in which even the least illusioned man is not giving himself at least another hour of life. . . . So death is never too close to a dying person's thought, through one of nature's usual acts of compassion. (*Z,* 291)

The need for compassion even in nature—for Leopardi has told us frequently that nature is not "usually" solicitous—points up the brutality of the phenomenon. Hence the statements by Sophocles, Bacchylides, and Cicero concerning the misfortune of being born and the fortune of dying, a seeming gift of the gods (*Z,* 2672), for if all tends to nothingness, one may as well make one's passage into it not as brutal but as serene as possible, and thereby endow life itself with some equilibrium. "Human life was never happier than when it was believed that even death could be beautiful and sweet" (*Z,* 3029). Not to be bemused unduly by the notion of serenity in life, however, Leopardi does not allow us to forget two of the most distinctive characters of the *Operette morali:* Tristano ("Dialogo di Tristano e di un amico"), who interrupts his discourse on happiness and perfectibility with his declaration that he envies only the dead, and Malambruno ("Dialogo di Malambruno e di Farfarello" ["Dia-

logue between Malambruno and Farfarello"]), who is made to admit
that "not living is always better than living." In this sense, life too,
then, through self-esteem or self-preservation or otherwise, looms
as a towering vanity. Only death, it can be said, is not an illusion.

Pessimism

These considerations pave the way for Leopardi the moral philosopher. He does not have a clear perception of the autonomy of
morality, given the authority of his relativism. If not contradictions,
there are juxtapositions in his "moral system" or ethics that shift
freely in the *Zibaldone* (and later) between agonism and resignation,
skepticism and noble illusion, depending on time and place, subject
and context. Nonetheless, the variances do shape themselves into a
reasonably coherent picture, perhaps because his most telling utterances, apart from the *Pensieri,* came in the cluster of years 1821–
23, and perhaps, too, because the concept of morality never informed
his philosophy in a central way. At times, "one is tempted to believe
that Leopardi considered morals—insofar as they relate closely to
circumstances, conveniences, and customs—a functional superstruc-
ture over the positive 'conditions of fact' of a group or individual."[40]
He was attracted by the eudaemonistic siren, the one that evaluates
the morality of actions in terms of their capacity to produce happiness, but in the long run had to resign himself to the awareness
that felicity is like perfection, something unobtainable by mortals.

Gleaning from the *Zibaldone,* we note that Leopardi's approach
to the question begins along epistemological lines. Only "habit and
accustoming circumstances . . . transform disposition into faculty": "At origin, our mind merely has a greater or less delicacy
and susceptibility of organs, that is, a facilitiy to be affected in
various ways—a capacity and adaptability to all or some determined
type of apprehension, habit, conception, concern. This is probably
not a faculty but simply a disposition. No faculty exists in our mind
at origin, not even that of remembering. On the contrary, being
disposed, it acquires these faculties, some more quickly, some more
slowly, by practice [*esercizio*] . . ." (*Z,* 2162–65). Leopardi's es-
timate derives from John Locke's views on the formation of ideas,
though he places a special, and modern, emphasis on the Greek
semeiotiké, the relationship between language and conscience. First
of all, he saw the opposition between "terms" (*termini*—the exact

referents of the object, clearly denotative signs) and "words" (*parole*—allusive and subjective signs, variously evocative) (*Z*, 1700–701). Further, he speaks semiotically about "universal language" as neither language (language being signification of ideas achieved through words) nor writing (writing representing words and language, and where there is neither word nor language there can be no writing) but as the "algebra of language," recognizable "through a system of signs which . . . cannot be [considered] strictly universal" (*Z*, 3255–56). Signs of any period evolve and change, become corrupted, as it were, and no such system even retains a universal character for long. It subdivides into multiplicity—hence the formation of idioms and languages.

Considerably Lockian, at least in derivation if not in inspiration, is the denial of preexistence. "Nothing preexists things. Neither forms nor ideas, neither necessity nor reason for being, or for being this way or that way. . . . *Everything* is posterior to *existence*" (*Z*, 1616). And, as Prete notes, two consequences ensue: on the one hand, the assumption that sensation provides the only basis for judgment and the dismissal of any notion of absolutes, since our thought process is not innate or, in Leopardi's words, not "independent of things as they are, or of existence," and on the other, the questioning of the concept of man's perfectibility, not to mention that of increasing perfection, "modeled on false notions of absolute good and evil . . ." (*Z*, 1616–19).[41] "By geometric progression" (*Z*, 1767), the exercise of dispositions produces differences—in the body physical as well as psychical. Mutability is therefore a law of existence; any disposition is "susceptible of infinite and very different faculties" (*Z*, 1803), and just as we note change in the production of one author we should recognize the same phenomenon in man as a whole, and his language. We should never need to marvel, and we should be "truly disposed not to marvel at any strange and unexpected and new inclination, character, quality, faculty, or act of any known or unknown human being" (*Z*, 3468).

Difference derives from change: both are natural. What is unnatural is that society transforms difference into inequality and makes it appear to be natural. In every country, he notes as an example, human and social vices and evil "are regarded as particularities of the place" (*P*, 31). Fashion receives his sharper indictment. "The working of fashion, which joins up with death ["Dialogo della moda e della morte"] calling her 'sister,' while it replaces the classical coupling of Love and Death in the 'modern' mind, reproduces modern man's strategy of uniformity, of superficial equality, making of the body a 'spiritualization' of his knowledge, which is a knowledge of death."[42] Fashion spells uniformity, the root of *ennui* or tedium, which spells death. It becomes civilization's false facade parading under the shibboleth of equality, while difference means variety, the vitality of what resists classification and the notion of limits: "Leopardi's natural history is not modeled on Linnaeus nor on Buffon."[43] But variety by itself falls short of Leopardi's interest; it is how the various elements affect one another that captures his imagination, for through their interaction we learn to appreciate the passage from nature's order to society's disorder and from difference to inequality. Society has manipulated difference into an acceptance of inequality, calling natural a social order inconsistent with its constituency and holding aloft a theatrical banner of unity—false unity. A striking example of this concerns blacks, "who are believed today to be totally different from whites racially and in origin, yet who are totally equal to them in what concerns human rights," whereas in the sixteenth century they were believed of common stock with whites, yet in terms of human rights "far inferior to us; and in both centuries they were bought and sold and made to work in chains under a whip. So much for ethics . . ." (*P, 66*). Much more bitterly than Shakespeare's Macbeth, Leopardi saw life as "a theatrical performance" (*P, 23*), and society a monument to pretense and pettiness. "Conformity, a disposition for habit, the acquisition of dress, customs, languages—all that constitutes diversity among individuals and in the history of a simple individual, has become the mortar of society. Society was born where there was no disposition for society. Leopardi's thought . . . approximates Hobbes's and comes close to recognizing the absurdity of the social contract. And by moving along a Rousseauan line, it prepares the destruction of possible escapes into optimism. . . . The outlines of the nihilistic background become clearer."[44]

So that, even by considering man in nature, we may conclude that, less so than any other, his species is not very disposed to society, because it is made up of individuals naturally more different among themselves than are those of any other species. But as society introduces and pushes to the limit that inequality that we consider among states, riches, professions, and the like, so it increases a thousand times over and promotes inevitably—and by its very nature pushes to the limit—diversity that is physical or moral relating to the faculties, inclinations, character, strengths, bodies, etc. of individuals, nations, times, the various ages of an individual, and so on. It increases the natural and inborn differences between one man and another, and still more differences that are infinite and very large and that would not have existed in man's natural state; these it introduces and causes, necessarily and by its very nature. (*Z,* 3808–9)

These thoughts are of 1823, considerably before he mitigated the Rousseauan influence, but he never altered their focus. Thus does society accomplish inequality, and "just liberty," so dear to political philosophers, is nothing more than a return to "what nature had already found out for itself in primitive society" (*Z,* 118).

Leopardi twists eighteenth-century optimism around so that moral philosophy, for which the *Pensieri* provide striking disclosures, tends toward nihilism. He recasts it, indicating the failure of our most cherished principles and institutions: justice, society, freedom, virtue, love, equality, honesty, and of our most cherished perceptions and realities: faith, nature, joy, hope, beauty, reason. Neither original sin, which incorrectly presupposes our guilt, nor any religious hereafter which, if blessed, cannot ever make up for mortal misery, obtains. Compared with this misery, even Platonic idealism fades, as it must in a world of matter. Apart from Art, what spares Leopardi from total nihilism is that he questions as much as he affirms, and the questioning, eudaemonistic in nature, aims at finding plausible ways to *act* in the throes of failures and miseries. O. M. Casale refers to the possibility of relating this posture to nineteenth-century Anglo-American pragmatism—an open possibility not recently studied—and correctly alludes to Karl Vossler's framing of some of the essential Leopardian queries: "Why do men sympathize so much with each other while at the same time they hate each other? How is it they are sociable while each seeks his self-interest? Why are they so bold while each is so attached to life? Why is life so monotonous when once it was so varied? Why are joy, art, poetry, love, faith, and hope receding from this world? Why is happiness always more rare while everything tends toward it?"[45] There is in Leopardi's moral philosophy a human anguish that goes beyond the cool analyses of, say, Pierre-Jean Cabanis's *Rapports du physique et du moral de l'homme* (*Relations between Man's Physical and Moral Properties*).

Man is not about to regain paradise, not through religion, not through the social sciences; the word "perfectibility" is vacuous, above all because "everything is uncertain and lacks a model, since we keep getting farther and farther from nature's, which represents the only form and reason for a manner of being." Only Nature gives anything its "reason" for being the way it is. Leopardi ties perfection to the plain existence of things; the way they are *is* their perfection. "They all have their reason for being as they are . . . , and all are equally perfect" (Z, 1615).

So much for the natural side of the concept; civilization, however, has given it a moral side, having made the thought of perfection a category of its thinking. Existence implies necessity, Leopardi agrees (hence the need to find plausible action), but this does not necessarily need to imply any absolute category, like absolute being, or perfection. In "La ginestra," he satirizes bitterly "humankind's *magnificent progressive destinies.*" This is not a case of provincialism, as some have said, as opposed to the Europeanism of his contemporary Manzoni. It is a philosophical question of pointing up the theoretical fragility of such pious attitudes in a world in which it seems most logical to ask: "What would this perfection of man look like? when and how will we be perfect, that is, real men? in exactly what will human perfection consist? what will be its essence?" (Z, 1612–13). We must not be traduced by "false ideas of absolute good and evil" (Z, 1618–19), and if we are not, then the "idea of absolute perfection" will vanish, leaving no possibility to conjecture utopias. Clearly, as the "Dialogo di Tristano e di un amico" elaborates, "perfectibility" is a social deception. With inequality as our context, all we do is move from one barbarity to another in a vicious circle. For if we strive for reforms, we are also aware that reforms cause their own evil: the reduction of passion and vitality. If we strive for order, we are also aware that order ultimately means uniformity, which is a form of fashion, and which is very different from order in nature. The more Leopardi tries to widen his horizon of sensibility and thought, the more his mind apprises him of the illusory qualities inherent in his would-be order of the universe and the more his posture becomes anthropocentric, stressing man's unhappiness at the core of nature's indifference.

One would imagine that Leopardi's nihilistic thrust might involve him sympathetically with the idea of suicide, so prominent in romantic thinking from Mme de Staël to Schopenhauer. He noted its frequency in antiquity among older people rather than younger and how the reverse was true among the moderns, or its relative absence among the ancients who did not commit it as often as the moderns, out of tedium. He even noted its recurrence in England (*Z*, 484–85, 2988–89, 177). But while in the context of a bleak existence it may be considered normal or not abnormal (he disagrees with Holbach [*La morale universelle (Universal Morality)*] that "suicide cannot take place without a kind of madness" since hope bespeaks sanity [*Z*, 183]), he regarded it as "the thing most opposed to nature that one can imagine," the thing "nature repells with all its force" (*Z*, 66, 815). Yet, if nature finds it repelling, society works to make it acceptable. "Suicide, a disorder contrary to the whole of nature, to the fundamental laws of existence, to the principles and bases of being of all things . . . —what is it born of if not society?" (*Z*, 3883). Understandably, the protagonists of "L'ultimo canto di Saffo" and "Bruto Minore" are attracted to the idea not only as an act of relief from misery but also as an act that slices through a central contradiction: "The present condition of man that forces him to live, think, and operate according to reason, forbidding him to kill himself, is contradictory. Either suicide is not against morality (albeit against nature), or our life, being against nature, is against morality. If this is not true, then neither is that" (*Z*, 1979). Leopardi would have found Schopenhauer's view acceptable, that suicide is an act directed against that accidental portion of unhappiness which creeps into human existence; it therefore provides no answer, even though the "portion" may represent near totality. Leopardi's view is recorded in "Dialogo di Plotino e di Porfirio," where the former argues from a background of tedium and is countered by the latter's reliance on Plato's argument that suicide is against the will of the gods, and by his own concern with the pain it causes our loved ones and with the succor we can give one another while enduring our hard destinies—a foreshadowing of the brotherhood of "La ginestra." This foreshadowing is important, indeed this final stance by the poet, for it helps to modify the similarity between Leopardi and Schopenhauer that the critic Francesco De Sanctis tried to establish in 1858.[46] It shows that, while on the surface of pessimistic premises the two thinkers resemble each other, they differ in the quality of the outcome of their ideas: *fraternità* is not *Mitleid*. Fraternity, or brotherhood, involves compassion, "the only human passion not tied in with self-esteem . . . but [that] always stems from the self

. . . almost like an abnegation of one's self, a sacrifice of one's own egoism" (Z, 108, 4488, 3168). Pity, or *Mitleid,* on the other hand, involves a certain condescension (despite Baruch Spinoza's equating it with commiseration), and it is interesting to note in passing that, though it represents a prime ethical impulse, there is sufficient coldness and calculation about it to have been put aside as an essentially ethical principle in modern moral thinking. It is also interesting to note that the *Zibaldone* does not talk about *pietà,* but many are the pages that discuss *compassione.*[47] And it does not stem from "fear lest we experience ourselves an evil similar to the one we see," for, affirms Leopardi, there exists a spontaneous compassion, totally independent from such fear and entirely directed toward the wretched" (Z, 1674).

When all the pieces are put together, however, Leopardi's aggregate thought remains pessimistic. Logically, he denies the good any autonomous existence, as the *Pensieri* indicate. He does not see "good" in intrinsic terms, as something valuable in and of itself, but rather in nonintrinsic terms, as something related to a condition outside itself, say to a custom or opinion. This makes it immediately assimilable into his long category of illusions: "Evil . . . is real; good . . . is nothing more than imaginary; . . . [it] is not absolute but relative" (Z, 717, 391). And it causes us great infelicity in the sense that if we lack something good, our whole life is pained, whereas a partial evil afflicts only a part of it (Z, 1554). Therefore, "All is evil"; life is "an imperfection, an irregularity, a monstrosity": "Not only man but humankind was and will always of necessity be unhappy. Not only humankind but all the animals. Not only the animals but in their own way all other beings. Not the individuals but the species, the genera, the kingdoms, the globes, the systems, the worlds." (Z, 4175). As an empirical datum, evil does not require metaphysical or transcendental explanation. To demonstrate, as philosophers have attempted to do, why it must exist shows arbitrariness and solves nothing. The only recourse remains the Stoic's retaliation with dignity, proud resignation, silence, and scorn. Of what value is life, he asked, except to despise it? Endurance denotes nobility.

Leopardi's pessimism, his fundamental awareness of the purposelessness of existence, acted like a pedal point above which drifted the changing harmonies of all man's undertakings, aspirations, and pleasures. There is in him something of an ancient tragic Greek or Hebrew "come again to speak in modern yet timeless terms."[48] His universe excludes numinous conjectures or Kantian categorical imperatives. He left that to other romantic poets. Having "fallen" to the civilized state dominated by reason and science and by all kinds of denaturing factors, man faces daily nothingness *(nulla)* and tedium *(noia)*. The experience, as Unamuno noted in analyzing the tragic seriousness of life's contradiction between reason and the vital urge,[49] creates an existential landscape in which *noia* represents the old *taedium vitae* magnified into "the psycho-spiritual paralysis which makes all physical, moral, and intellectual activity or affirmation impossible and undesired, a kind of becalming reminiscent of Thomas Carlyle's 'Center of Indifference,' "[50] and in which *nulla* represents the final emptiness of meaning, the ultimate absurdity.

The whole question of *noia,* of course, is part and parcel of the romantic sensibility, the illness of a generation that did not feel at home in the world and felt the deception of the "magnificent progressive destinies" promised by the older generation. It is the frustrated world of the romantic protagonists, Adolphe (*Adolphe,* by Benjamin Constant) and Obermann (*Obermann,* by Sénancour) in France, Werther (*Die Leidungen des jungen Werthers {The Sorrows of Young Werther},* 1774) in Germany, and in Italy Jacopo Ortis, Foscolo's young suicide who had suffered disenchantment in love and disillusion in politics (*Ultime lettere di Jacopo Ortis {The Last Letters of Jacopo Ortis},* 1798). We should be wrong, however, in limiting its origin to a reaction against the *philosophes'* optimistic estimates of man, for it is as old as *Ecclesiastes* and as modern as Alberto Moravia, occurring after periods, like the Enlightenment or the age of positivism, of rationalistic and scientific confidence in man's abilities. Leopardi's sense of *noia,* however, is less vague than that of his contemporaries and more imbued with a modern awareness of *Angst* relating to concrete problems which he identifies throughout the *Zibaldone* and which have to do with an incomprehensible world. Indeed, its *noia* owes much to Pascal, as do many tenets of his thought in general: the physical and intellectual disproportion between man and nature, rational principles that warp judgment, the world moved by public opinion, reason's inability to arrive at truth and justice, doubt as the background of indifference, custom as tending to supplant nature and becoming a second nature, and perhaps even the method of proceeding from a particular event to a generalization—these are attitudes that the seventeenth-century philosopher did not teach the nineteenth-century poet, but they

surely encouraged his thinking, for Pascal is "worth reading" (*Z,*
382). As far as the matter of tedium is concerned, as one critic
suggests, "One cannot say that *noia* was born in the eighteenth
century, but it is quite certain that the word entered the everyday
vocabulary at that time thanks to the sensationalism of Locke and
even more to that of [Etienne] Condillac, who provides a psychological explanation of *ennui.* To this feeling Leopardi will add a
metaphysical dimension of Pascalian origin."[51] Psychology here
compels the philosophical premise, for Condillac had underscored
how tedium can be a powerful mover to action—Leopardi's agonistic
search of how to act. And Pascal contributed the metaphysical concern relating to man's misery on earth (for Pascal mainly because
of the absence of God, for Leopardi because of the failure of reason).

Echoing the *Zibaldone* (3714), the poet in the "Dialogo di Torquato Tasso e del suo Genio familiare" ("Dialogue between Torquato
Tasso and His Friendly Spirit") states: "*noia* has the nature of air:
it fills all the spaces between all material things . . . , all the
intervals of human life between pleasures and displeasures. . . ."
It is, alas, "the most sterile of human passions," the "desire for
happiness left, so to speak, pure," unsatisfied; it is "life fully felt,
experienced, known . . ." (*Z,* 1815, 3715, 4043). This was 1824.
But in *Zibaldone* 4306, that is, four years later, the phenomenon is
less pervasive, afflicting primarily those "for whom the spirit is
something," for those who "have no occupation . . . , [who] are,
for the most part, like animals, . . . are not bored by doing nothing." Thus—again, not the contradiction but a refinement of concept, distinguishing between those who exist in a state of
consciousness and those who exist in the opposite state. This is the
situation of the sheep in the "Canto notturno di un pastore errante
dell'Asia." The year is 1830. But the refinement hardly means that
noia does not fill the interstices of all life inevitably. The sheep are
"fortunate" because they are not conscious of it. Like death, it is
certain, a truth ascertainable primarily by those with the deepest
and most sensitive perceptions, "in whom spirit is something," and
in this sense may be regarded as "the most sublime of feelings" (*P,*
67–68). "The sorrow or despair that is born of great passions and
illusions or any misadventure in life is not comparable to the choking
feeling that comes from the certainty . . . of the nothingness of
all things. . . . All is nothingness in the world, even my despair
. . . , even this sorrow of mine that at a given time will pass and

become nothing, leaving me in a universal void. . . . We know this from the few who have felt it, like Tasso" (*Z*, 72, 140–41). More than Pascal, who headed toward a mystical purgation, Leopardi felt, through "L'infinito," the terrifyingly vast nothingness of interstellar space, analogous to that of the soul. In expressing it, what he stressed was the philosophical negation of life, in both its effectiveness and false felicities. Only this way can one demonstrate moral consistency: through the affirmation of a negative totality.[52] This turn of mind was admired by Schopenhauer, who at one point had to exclaim: "No one in our time has ever treated the argument of nothingness and of life's sorrows in a more accomplished and profound way than Leopardi."[53]

It has been pointed out, of course, that Leopardi reflects the typical romantic poet's recognition of his alienation and his creation of a personal mythology around it. Leopardi, however, delves far deeper into his own "myth" than anyone else (perhaps this was the basis of Schopenhauer's admiration); the abundant explorations contained in the *Zibaldone* assume a universal character and remove him from the private categories of a Byron, a Wordsworth, or a John Keats, a Charles Baudelaire or an Aleksandr Pushkin, as he elevates his analyses of alienation to a broad and insightful existential level.

Art

In moments when he simply had to contradict, at least partially, his pessimistic convictions, he fondled his illusory thoughts, proposing them as "remedies," as actions to push temporarily aside "the infinite vanity of all things." A remedy for *noia*, for instance, is to give oneself "a goal, more or less determined, more or less serious or imporant" (*Z*, 347), something Wallace Stevens might have called a "supreme fiction." This makes his melancholy sometimes less acrid, particularly when, as in "La ginestra," he promotes a fraternal contemplation of existence. In a sense, pessimism leads to a knowledge of the value of human life (though life itself remains a useless misery), and tedium gives us the greatest indication of the grandeur and nobility of human nature. Thus the positive value of illusion offsets negation; a valuable deception, illusion turns into man's only justifiable pleasure. Because of it, Leopardi can adjust his moral philosophy to embrace brotherly solidarity and compassion (his compassion, though not as central to his ethics as *Mitleid* was to Schopenhauer, is still less condescending and more empathetic than Schopenhauer's).

For the poet, as in this case for Schopenhauer, the major such illusion is Art. Art is genius.

They have this in common . . . , that when they disclose the nothingness of things, when they demonstrate with evidence and make one feel the inevitable unhappiness of life, even when they express the most terrible despair, still, even for a great mind that finds itself in a state of extreme dejection or in the most bitter and *deadly* of misfortunes . . . , they always serve as consolation, rekindle enthusiasm, and, while not treating or representing anything other than death, they endow that mind at least momentarily with the life it had lost. . . . The author who described and felt so strongly the vanity of illusions yet harbored a great reservoir of illusion. . . . [And] in the same way, the reader, however disabused on his own and through his reading, is still drawn by the author into that same deception and illusion that are concealed in the most intimate folds of the mind and that he himself felt. And the very knowledge of the irreparable vanity and falseness of anything beautiful and great has in itself a certain beauty and greatness that fills the mind, when this knowledge is found in works of art [*genio*]. . . . Its vivacity prevails in the reader's soul over the nothingness [of things], and the soul receives life (though ephemeral) through the same force by which it senses the perpetual death of things, including his own. (Z, 259–61)

It is not so much that Art partakes of the twin illusions of Beauty and Truth. The affirmations of the seventeenth-century moralists, Nicolas Boileau ("Only truth is beauty") and the earl of Shaftesbury ("All beauty is truth") or Leopardi's contemporary Keats ("Beauty is truth and truth is beauty") carry little weight in a context—as the philosopher David Hume, for whom such a causal inference was not certifiable, would have agreed—in which the symbolic knowledge that Art represents tends to undermine the primacy of truth as an absolute category. Indeed, more Platonically, though with praise instead of rejection, Art validates "the false," for Leopardi, if falsehood is related to the imagination, the élan vital of Art.

Leopardi saw Art as strengthening human bonds on the one hand, through its communicative spiritual value, and on the other as providing eudemonically the grounds for action in the search for answers, which, however confounded, gives us a temporary feeling of nonfragmentation, of wholeness. Art saves from *noia,* among other things, so ultimately there was perhaps less tedium in Leopardi's life than he might lead one to believe. The search through Art integrates our faculties. Life is what the imagination creates, and if there is a living reality (as opposed to that of death), it is the poetic dream. "The poet," writes De Feo, "when he is such, does not exhaust his mission in one despairing song; deep in his soul always resides the knowledge that nothingness itself is a reflection of our conscience, giving it a content and a color consistent with his own desires. Therefore, even the poet of sorrow is a demiurge, a creator of phantasms that live in an ephemeral and eternal world made to calm our torment and give existence a meaning."[54] Foundering in the infinite of "L'infinito" produces a desire which, through the art of the "algebra of language," shapes itself into an affirmation of life. So what Leopardi finally did was to negate negation, developing what he called an ultraphilosophy, in today's terms a metaphilosophy.

An ultraphilosophy cannot have a system because, as a philosophy about philosophy, it rejects reason. Leopardi notes that Bayle, too, recognized "that reason is more an instrument of destruction than construction" (*Z,* 4192) and that in metaphysics and morals it cannot edify, only destroy. Art transfigures reason as it transfigures sorrow, and becomes thereby the most important postulate of ultraphilosophy; it becomes the only valid measure of what is.

Chapter Three
Poetic Myths:
The *Operette morali*

Leopardi's dismay, observes one critic, is the gauge of his affirmation; "no statement [of his] is greater than its opposite, and if the tragedy in which man is involved is immense . . . ., it is because the stature of man partakes of that immensity."[1] In partaking of it, he fashions dreams, and these dreams through Art vitalize life, somehow making it all worthwhile. The vitality of poetic feeling that dislodges the ascendancy of philosophical negativism provides the impetus that gives shape to those "hard and sad truths" which, the "Dialogo di Timandro e di Eleandro" ("Dialogue between Timander and Eleander") would have us believe, underlie the world view of the *Operette morali.*

This idea of presenting his whole "system" and world view through brief essays or narratives had begun to take shape in 1819 when Leopardi wrote what might be called a few anticipatory exercises, "Senofonte e Niccolò Machiavello" ("Xenophon and Niccolò Machiavelli"), the story of two rivals for the post of tutor of Pluto's and Proserpina's son who was destined to rule on earth, and the "Dialogo tra Galantuomo e Mondo" ("Dialogue between Gentleman and World"), in which the former, in the service of the latter, must learn the worldly ways of ruse, hypocrisy, adulation, conformity, and the like in order to succeed.[2] From 19 January to 16 December 1824, that is, from the "Storia del genere umano" to the "Dialogo di Timandro e di Eleandro," he wrote twenty of the *Operette morali,* published in a first edition by Stampa in Milan in 1827, followed by a second of twenty-two by Piatti in Florence in 1834, then by a third (sequestered by the Bourbon government) by Starita in Naples in 1836. Ranieri put out the first complete edition of twenty-four in Florence in 1845, after Leopardi's death.

Leopardi wished that the whole remain an integrated structure. He did not want the dialogues "published piecemeal in some newspaper."[3] It was Giovanni Gentile who in 1916, after De Sanctis's rehabilitation of the *Operette morali*,[4] saw a veritable conceptual design extending over the first twenty pieces (after the "Dialogo di Timandro e di Eleandro" Leopardi supposedly inserted the four new ones as he wrote them).[5] He insisted on an organic approach to the work that would blend its philosophic dispositions and poetic inclinations. The first third would depict life as unhappy because through civilization and reason man has withdrawn from nature and deprived himself of the illusion of pleasure, in the face of death and nothingness, to such an extent that not living is better than living. The next third would consider man and nature, and the latter's cold indifference to his sorrow, enough to produce tedium and a desire to end one's life. In the final group would emerge the need to occupy life with action, even risk and hope, hence a reaffirmation of illusions like fame and love. While Gentile's symmetrical outline may have stretched the point a bit, his premise has remained valid and allowed subsequent commentators to stress the work's unified structure while assessing it from varying points of view—as a fantastic satire, a mythicizing of concepts, or a stylistic exercise swinging between serious argument and sharp irony.[6] Whatever the points of view, the notion of structure in the *Operette morali* is distinctly arguable, more so than in, say, Giovanni Boccaccio's *Decamerone*.

To follow their evolution, from the original "short satirical pieces in prose" (*prosette satiriche*) in the manner of Lucian to the versions included in the *Operette morali* and their placement in it, accounting for reordering, discardings, and replacements, brings into relief many pages of the *Zibaldone* out of which they grew. But more significantly, they underscore the author's artistic consciousness through his desire to give his philosophy the force that only the aesthetic dimension could provide. As they evolved, the *Operette morali* expanded thematically and stylistically, so that in the long run the emphasis shifted from the analytical notation of the *Zibaldone* to the more poetic tenor of the finished product. The style of the *Zibaldone* is unadorned and demonstrative, as compared with the more "literary" style of the *Operette morali* or the lyrical and moving style of the *Canti*. By "literary" here is meant a more complex and elaborate use of language, varying according to topic and type (essay or dialogue), sometimes solemn, sometimes suggestive, sometimes lighthearted, frequently ironical, and usually fluid. The work constitutes a genuinely creative effort. And creative writing, especially of the poetic variety, constitutes an act of affirmation.

The "poetry" of the *Operette morali* has been recognized repeatedly.[7] The reason is understandable, since Leopardi himself called attention to his intentions when he claimed to his father that he had wanted to write "poetry in prose," allowing the philosophy to become absorbed and diffused by the poetic quality: "I assure you that my intention was to put together *poetic prose* . . . , to follow one mythology and then another, arbitrarily, as one does in writing verse. . . ."[8] Indeed, Tristano tells us as much in the "Dialogo di Tristano e di un amico" when the main speaker describes his work as "a book of poetic dreams, of melancholy inventions and caprices, or an expression of the author's unhappiness." This does not mean that Leopardi saw his book in terms of melancholy dreams from the outset, or as a source of moral inspiration. In fact, what is meant by "moral" here needs to be addressed. In the words of one commentator, "The title, *Operette morali,* points to his philosophical intention, but it can in no way be understood literally. The *operette* are 'moral' in the sense that they proclaim the true nature of life itself and ultimately advocate facing it for what it is. They are also 'moral,' therefore, in the sense that every real work of art is moral: a translation of the perpetual desires and disappointments of man into images of permanent value and thus an exalted, universal objectification of such desires and disappointments."[9] With some ingenuousness, no doubt, he first saw his "short satirical pieces in prose" as personal, neo-Socratic meditations which he might share with his contemporaries, but as it became clear that these contemporaries either would not understand the thrust of his arguments or would condemn their negativism, he penned the conclusion of his collection in 1832, the "Dialogo di Tristano e di un amico," with the emphasis on the aspect of dreams and whims.

Leopardi's style received good reviews, but not his subject matter. The Accademia della Crusca denied him its prize in 1829, for example, and even after his death the Roman curia placed it on the Index in 1850. However he tried to conceal the pessimism under the veil of fantasy, of "the natural illusions of the mind" ("Dialogo di Timandro e di Eleandro"), his real *modus cogitandi* was well known. His "poetic prose" was in fact a series of intellectual premises, discussed in the *Zibaldone* with reference to the dialogues themselves: "I have considered . . . , I have demonstrated . . . , I have explained . . . , See my [dialogue] . . ." (Z, 4079, 4131, 4248, 4099, 4130). The perennial, dialectical opposition between illusion and reality dominated his state of mind, and during the years immediately preceding the *Operette morali,* the struggle had assumed hard, pessimistic proportions. Hence Luigi Blasucci's assertion that the essays and dialogues do not represent Leopardi's pessimism but more precisely one of its phases, the one that emerges between 1822 and 1824, whose beginnings can be traced to 1820–21.[10] This was the "historical" phase, when Leopardi argued that the ancients found more happiness than the moderns and ancient virtue and liberty shone, and when he wrote "Ad Angelo Mai" (1820) and "A un vincitore nel pallone" (1821). Pessimism had not yet reached that final stage in his thinking, called "cosmic" and resulting from more radical, materialistic convictions—convictions holding that mankind experienced unhappiness at all times in history because felicity is congenitally and spiritually unattainable. Blasucci calls our attention to a transitional document by Leopardi: the "Comparazione delle sentenze di Bruto Minore e di Teofrasto vicini a morte" ("Comparison of Sayings of the Younger Brutus and Theophrastus, Both near Death," March 1822), revealing that the Greek's disillusion with life was not historical but existential.[11] There is something of the "vanity" lament of *Ecclesiastes* in it. Thence Leopardi's statement to his sister: "Human happiness is a dream; the world is neither beautiful nor bearable. . . ."[12] His disillusionment with living in Rome at this time, as expressed in this same letter ("Besides, it's no good to live in a large city"), constitutes only a small part of a broadening picture. The bitter views of the early 1820s had rested on his various elaborations of the theory of pleasure, whose basis was sensationalist and whose point of departure was coincident with self-esteem (*Z,* 2410–14; May 1822). Here reason crushes illusion at every turn, for the amount of pleasure naturally demanded by the human being is limitless (*Z,* 646; February 1821) and consistently belied by the vagaries of reality, one of which is man's innate inability to govern himself equitably (*Z,* 2644; November 1822). The end result is a world view that ranges from "dark and silent," in the opinion of one interpreter, to "absolutely negative," in that of another.[13]

Again the caveat needs mentioning: that of too easily ascribing Leopardi's pessimism to the miserable state of his health. "The ill that pains us," as he says in "Ad Angelo Mai"—and the illness, physical or metaphorical—he considers accidental, in 1820 and 1822 (*Z,* 2552–54; July 1822), but he began to refine this view in the fall of 1822: "while they are accidental taken individually, perhaps their genus and universality is not accidental" (*Z, 2600–602; August 1822*). Later, the same materialistic view of human unhappiness removed the qualifier "perhaps." The moment infelicity was universalized in his mind, his private, physical ailments could no longer inform his world view; in fact, what happened was that man's infirmity spurred him to declare and react against the insensitivity of stepmother nature. His infirmity sparked anything but desperation.

Now, because the *Operette morali* move toward the "cosmic" order of pessimism, the style of the work eschews concrete narrative in order to attain the quality of poetic myth.[14] Hence Leopardi's convincing intermingling of mythic times and themes, as in Dante, with historical events and ideas, in order to give his "melancholy inventions" a more universal quality: the origin of the world, its death, the beginning of love, the questions of time and space, pleasure and pain, fame and tedium, nature and destiny. While often pointing at history, the work always points to a "beyond," thus becoming, in its own mythical way, "a model of perpetual inactuality."[15] We read of the historical Tasso and Giuseppe Parini, Plotinus and Nicolaus Copernicus, Christopher Columbus and Friedrich Ruysch, Porphyry and Strato, or of the mythological or invented Prometheus, Hercules, Atlas, Momus, Malambruno, Farfarello, Timandro, Eleandro, Tristano, the Icelander—all of whom are heard alongside sprites and gnomes, nature and birds, the earth and the moon. Out of it all emerges, as from biblical parables, a sense of timelessness and poetic legend, leaving with the reader the aggregate impression of a vast metaphor of reality. This was the private *Zibaldone* come to public, artistic fruition; Leopardi was so close to it that, fearing the evil blade of censorship, he asked that it be treated with full precautions: "I should much prefer to lose my head than this manuscript."[16]

Until recently, the tendency has been to emphasize either the ideological content or the stylistic performance. This is unfortunate. To see the *Operette morali* as brief narratives thought out poetically and then translated into prose, as Flora does, is stretching the notion of poetry a bit far at the unfair expense of their content. This notion, which denies Leopardi his philosophical intention by insisting that the conceptual side has much less validity than the play of images, fantasy, and irreality hovering between what is dreamed and what is lived, has had many adherents. True, "The *Operette morali* were primarily essays in good writing. In their period structure, the intimate nexus that binds the discourse, the clarity of exposition, the musicality of the words, they reach one of the highest peaks of Italian prose. Some of them may not even be thought of as prose, but as free and pure verse, dominated by chords that are not less beautiful for being unusual."[17] But rather than aesthetic exercises, or would-be versifications of thoughts derived from the *Zibaldone,* they represent a point of convergence of these thoughts with the spirit of the *Canti* he was composing around that time (ca. 1820–22). His youth early spent, he found in his maturity that he could turn to meditate with melancholy and feeling on caducity and nature, tedium and illusion, and to do so in a way that would formulate a concept of what life is in a new and satirical blending of both content and form. The dialogued fantasies were aimed at deriding present civilization and "modern philosophy,"[18] and therefore, "though written with apparent lightness," they were "the true harvest of my life . . . , dearer to me than my own eyes."[19]

They exhibit a true narrative flair in pointing up the mystery of the universe, the enigma of human life and human destiny, the nonsense and evil of this existence in the face of nonbeing, and our recourse for ephemeral happiness in illusion. The *Canti* remove our rose-colored glasses more gently; in the *Operette morali* we see with more precise immediacy the reality of human unhappiness, whether in sharply negative terms (as in the "Storia del genere umano," "Dialogo di Malambruno e Farfarello," "Dialogo di Torquato Tasso e del suo Genio familiare," and "Dialogo di un venditore d'almanacchi e di un passeggere") or in more positive hues (as in the "Dialogo di Cristoforo Colombo e di Pietro Gutierrez" ["Dialogue between Christopher Columbus and Pedro Gutierrez'] and "Dialogo di Plotino e di Porfirio"); we feel with the chill of a *Dies Irae* the condition of death in the "Dialogo di Federico Ruysch e delle sue mummie"; we confront the vanity of fame in "Il Parini, ovvero della gloria" ("Parini, or Concerning Glory"), and the logic of extreme materialism in "Frammento apocrifo di Stratone da Lampsaco" ("Apocryphal Fragment of Strato of Lampsacus"). The beauty of these dialogues and essays is that philosophy and poetry go hand in hand, not to illustrate a simple doctrine of evil, suffering, vanity, and nothingness as a reflection of the author's own bitterness, as Croce would put it, but to express almost symphonically a meditation concerning what it means to live and think and feel. The cosmic meditation does not excel where "the poet has vanquished the philosopher," as Origo suggests,[20] but as an experienced totality, as a single work which, through its interrelation of ethics and aesthetics, shapes a coherent and moving, albeit pessimistic, mood about the human condition.

And one can speak only of the human condition, not of the characters who animate it. There is no characterization as such: Leopardi was not a novelist like Boccaccio or Manzoni. The protagonists are his thoughts, which, unlike the sentient human beings of *I promessi sposi* or the *Decamerone,* do not move us with their historical predicaments. They move us through the philosophies they embrace. Descriptions themselves—very stimulating especially when they relate to nature (as in the "Elogio degli uccelli" ["Eulogy of the Birds"])—serve more to corroborate ideas than to fix moods. Therefore, the manner most suited to the intellectual and artistic purpose is that of simplicity, of the spoken word (hence the preponderance of dialogues), anything that does not invite fanciness and obscurity. The poetic quality itself must hold to this tenet, which carries over into the *Canti* as well. But it fashions or dresses the message, gives it tonality and visibility, and shapes the prose, simple on the surface and unornamented, into a sterling vehicle of communication. For the *Operette morali,* Leopardi chose the vehicle of prose, not verse; E. Bigi correctly refers to a passage in the *Zibaldone* to make the point:[21]

Not only in French (as Mme de Staël observes) but also in other modern languages, it seems that prose suits modern poetry better than verse. I have shown elsewhere what this must consist of, essentially, and how it is more prosaic than poetic. In fact, while reading ancient prose we sometimes almost wish to get the number and the measure because of the poetic quality of the ideas it contains . . .; the reverse is true when we read modern verses, even the best among them, and all the more when we try ourselves to put our thoughts into good, modern verse: we want freedom, looseness, abandon, fluidity, facility, clarity, placidity, simplicity, unornamentation, sensibleness, seriousness and soundness, composure, the sound of prose which harmonizes better with those ideas that hardly have anything transferable to verse. . . .[22]

Leopardi was sensitive to the movement of harmony, and proved through the *Operette morali* how prose can often claim a greater affinity with music than her sister art of poetry. The work's "musical" quality has elicited comments from various scholars of stylistics, though the term must be used with utmost prudence. It is just as useless to refer to "Beethoven-like effect[s]" sounding from a poem's disconsolate review of mankind's disabilities in an alien universe,[23] as it is to allude to a dialogue's "Mozartian designs and arabesques" rising rhythmically from the sadness and despair of the ideas.[24] There are assonances and dissonances, slower and faster rhythms, and there are "freedom," "fluidity," and "clarity" which make not for music but for musicality, and in this sense Leopardi is right in speaking inferentially of a harmonizing sound of the prose. It has "a constant vibration, remote and even," a contained emotion; hence "echoes, delicate modulations, notes that are never high and shrill" but usually moderate or *mezza voce*,[25] which means a Greek, or at least *Trecento,* quality (Leopardi deemed the *Cinquecento,* with its aesthetics of stylistic composure, verbal symmetry, circumlocutions, subordinate clauses that do not jar the conceptual flow, etc., the apogee of Italian prose).

This, too, contributes to the poetic effect of the *Operette morali.* In addition, their "placidity" and "composure" make possible still another tonality whose subtlety has even invited occasional denial of its existence. Irony, it has been variously said, especially when Lucian serves as the model, could not find its way into Leopardi's prose since it was not in his nature to maintain a necessary detachment from reality. Yet his very attractiveness lies in his balanced posture between philosophical aloofness and poetical commitment. This middle road does not preclude irony in any way; on the contrary, it welcomes it, and in the process makes it gentle and unobtrusive. Perhaps the word is sarcasm, or merely comedy. Whatever the case, Leopardi was surely aware of it: "I should have liked to write a preface for the *Operette morali,* but it seemed to me that the ironic tone that dominates in them and their very spirit absolutely excluded any preamble."[26] The *Zibaldone* reports: "In my dialogues, I shall try to inject comedy into what has been proper to tragedy up until now . . . [using] the arms of ridicule."[27] The "Dialogo di Ercole e di Atlante" ("Dialogue between Hercules and Atlas"), "Proposta di premi fatta dall'Accademia dei Sillografi" ("Announcement of Prizes by the Academy of Syllographs"), "Dialogo dell Terra e della Luna" ("Dialogue between the Earth and the Moon"), and "La scommessa di Prometeo" ("The Wager of Prometheus") are cases in point. The tone of the *Operette morali* varies considerably, and if Carducci noticed above all their solemn sadness, the sentences of this sadness are punctuated with irony as often as they are with elegy. If at times they seem to some a bit on the cold side (this, too, has been charged: the metaphysical modes, the one-dimensional characters, the author's nonparticipation in their lives, the sense of unreality, the lack of dramatic intellectual commitment, and so on), it is because, purposely, the subject matter is cosmic more than private, the characters move in a timeless and spaceless world of abstractness more than in an immanent context of quotidian concerns, and the emphasis of the poetry is more on affirming philosophical postulates than on engaging us with personal emotions. There is a remote calm—that "beyond"—about them, a sentimental distance. This makes the *Operette morali* and the *Canti,* apart from their obvious formal or generic difference, fundamentally distinct creative productions. In the former, Luigi Russo would say that Leopardi's ironic smile proceeds from his mind, not from his heart.[28]

I. **La storia del genere umano** (The History of the Human Race, 1824).   All people were created at the same time, in a state of childhood and in a uniform world without stars or oceanic pools between the land masses. "Delighting insatiably in contemplating the land and sky," they had reason to be happy. But as the years went by and they reached adulthood, their happiness became habit, and when boredom set in, a number of them ended their lives. Not being able to start all over again, Jupiter decided to modify the world, making it bigger and more variegated, granting people dreams and illusions that would deceive their reason, but this state, too, did not last long, so that when unhappiness encouraged immorality, the universal flood was the only possible divine reaction. From this cataclysm, only two survived: Deucalion and Pyrrha,[29] who reconstituted the human race. In order for good to be better appreciated, the gods chose to inflict real evils: hard labor, natural disasters, changing seasons, a plurality of races, and various figments of the irrational imagination, like Country, Virtue, Glory, Justice, and Love, which served to give people something to cling to, even if they ultimately caused more unhappiness than ever before. Tedium, however, set in again, when another figment of the imagination, Knowledge, promised Truth and all it would deliver—and did not deliver. Jupiter could not stand the people's whining any more, and banished Truth. At this point, most of the gods pitied the plight of humans, so that to alleviate matters somewhat, Jupiter agreed to send Cupid, the son of Celestial Venus, to earth every now and then to contact the gentler and nicer people.

As noted before, the quinquennial prize of the Accademia della Crusca was denied Leopardi for the *Operette morali* partly because of this initial myth, and the author's disclaimer, in the 1834 Florence edition, that it had nothing to do with biblical history did not mitigate the displeasure of the clerics. Leopardi's cosmographical allegory about man's nature and destiny, seen in inner rather than outer, "historical" terms, was lost in the throes of literal interpretation, though, to be sure, through the story, man, created with desire and dreams, with a need for happiness and hope, and punished for having them, seems very much the victim of divine ill-planning. Suffering, growing progressively as his days evolve in an unjust universe, looms as his irremediable fate, whatever the effect of the momentary vision of spiritual or sentimental love (always at odds with Truth) accorded by the son of Celestial Venus. If something is recaptured on occasion by the imagination (and something must be, for Leopardi, since the allusions to Cupid conclude the *operetta*), there is a latent sense of divine condescension, as we finish the myth, in the gods' allowing man to have at least that bone of ephemeral consolation. These ideas are accompanied by a number of other favorite Leopardian themes, presented in a polished, somewhat solemn, literary idiom that reminds us of predecessors in the attempt to recreate the mythical ages of man, like Hesiod, Plato, and Ovid: the theme of wonder before nature—stars, winds, meadows, hills, forests, echoes, valleys, seas—and the infinite, or the theme of childhood when illusions provide life with a sense of Beauty that "the harsh domination of Truth" will later dissipate. In this respect, the first *operetta* serves the dual function of a thematic and a tonal introduction to the ensuing pieces.

II. Dialogo di Ercole e di Atlante (Dialogue between Hercules and Atlas, 1824).   Hercules offers to help Atlas support the weight of the earth, but the latter refuses, since the earth has become lighter "than this cloak which I use to protect me from the snow" and very still. "I rather believe she is sleeping." To awaken her, the two toss the earth to each other as they would a ball, but at one point Hercules misses and "the ball" falls to the ground. Yet silence continues to reign. Before asking Jupiter's forgiveness for the mishap, the giant, recalling Horace's dictum that the just stand firm even when the world collapses, determines that all men must have become just "since the earth fell and no one moved."

Through its caricature and frequent humorous nonsense, the dialogue reveals Leopardi's original Lucianesque inspiration and suggests sardonically, with ironic erudition, the lifelessness of this world we live in, the absence in it of any moral fiber, of any idealism, and its overall sleepy indolence. The world is light because men here become fatuous, sleepy because they live in ignorance. They have become nonachievers and are on their way toward destruction and death, as some coming *operette* will show. Hercules would not touch the globe with his club for fear of making it "a waffle." The mythological background puts into relief the "new defects" it has acquired, while the jesting tone stimulates the author's ironic fantasy. In the astral setting, the puniness and ineffectualness of the dormant earth—particularly the modern one, for the ancient one was not as sleepy and empty—are comically obvious.

III. Dialogo della Moda e della Morte (Dialogue between Fashion and Death, 1824).   Fashion (or Custom) and Death, as daughters of Caducity, realize that their function, each in her own way, is to destroy humanity: "their nature and common cause is to renew the world continuously" in order to erode it continuously. Death attacks "persons and blood," while Fashion deals with things, from hair to houses, or from skin-burning to childrens' skull modification. Thus Fashion "increases [Death's] estate on earth," and Death triumphs.

This funereal conversation invites more erudite attention than the previous jocular situation. Through the prescriptional conventions of custom, which weaken health, consume life, and make people inflict torturous practices upon themselves, Leopardi tries to chastise his century's vanity, its indifference to ideals, to things that should count more in human life, like virtuous acts (one of the motifs of "Ad Angelo Mai"). Implicitly, he bemoans our vanities, gullibility, and lack of seriousness of purpose. There is something of the poet Parini's satire in his veiled argument, in that it is more sociologically than cosmically focused. Not the most successful of the dialogues (Death appears too traditionally as blindness, deafness, incapacity to stay put and always on the move, and Fashion too patly as

loquaciousness, fickleness, and chatter—though the contrast between the laconism of the first and the naturalness of the second is
effective), it nonetheless highlights the centrality and irrevocability
of Death.

IV. Proposta di premi fatta dall'Accademia dei Sillografi (Announcement of Prizes by the Academy of Syllographs, 1824). For
progress and the common good, the Academy of Syllographs[30]
launches a contest to seek to implement man's already machine-
dominated activities with automatons that would address his spiritual needs. First prize (a gold medal with the weight of 500 florins
stamped with Pylades and Orestes on one side and on the other the
winner's name with "First Verifier of the Ancient Fables") will go
to whoever invents a machine that will substitute for a loyal friend,
since humans do not produce such a person. Second prize (a gold
medal with the weight of 450 florins, stamped on one side with an
abstraction of the Golden Age and on the other the winner's name
with Virgil's "Eclogue IV" 's "under whom the iron brood shall
first cease, and a golden race spring up throughout the world") will
go to whoever invents a vapor robot that can accomplish virtuous
deeds. Third prize (a gold medal with the weight of 500 florins
stamped with [Pietro] Metastasio's Arabian phoenix on one side and
on the other the winner's name with "Inventor of Faithful Women
and of Domestic Happiness") will go to whoever invents a robot-
perfect woman, like the one in [Baldassare] Castiglione's *Il Cortegiano*
(The Book of the Courtier) or the one created by Pygmalion. To finance
the competition, recourse will be made to Diogenes's purse or to
the sale of one of the three golden asses of Academy members
Apuleius, Firenzuola, and Machiavelli.

More than distrust, Leopardi shows contempt for the notion of
material progress, here represented by our scientific—today, tech-
nological—worship of machines to improve man's lot. If the targets
of the competition remain in the realm of traditional satire, the
spirit of distrust for applied and experimental sciences the piece
exudes leaves no doubt as to the bleak prospects Leopardi had for
the misguided aspirations of man and the progress of civilization.
There is even an implied criticism of governmental or institutional
economics, since the financial means of rewarding the winners does
not rest on any reliable basis.

V. Dialogo di un Folletto e di uno Gnomo (Dialogue between a Sprite and a Gnome, 1824).   Suspicious of the calm and silence of Earth's people, who are usually troublesome and cantankerous, a Gnome is sent up by his father to investigate and is told by a Sprite that "they are all dead . . ., their race has died out. . . . Some fought with each other, some died at sea, some devoured each other, some killed themselves, some rotted in idleness, some racked their brain over books, some indulged in debauchery and a thousand disorders. . . ." Both Sprite and Gnome believe solipsistically the world to have been created for their own species, the former emphasizing the values of the upper air, the latter those of his underground. Though without people, natural life has continued without disruption: moon, land, rivers, seas, stars and planets—all have continued their normal functions. "And the sun has not plastered its face with rust as it did—according to Virgil—when Caesar died, for whom I think it cared as little as Pompey's statue did."

The setting is again remote, the mood again one of surprise, though the topic dates as far back as Xenophanes. This time a sylph and an imp contend a globe which proud yet insignificant man has always insisted was his. The dialogue adds a strong dose of artistic, lighthearted fantasy to Bernard de Fontenelle's equally readable but somewhat more ponderous *Entretiens sur la pluralité des mondes*. Just as the Frenchman had inveighed against the notion of final causes, so Leopardi satirizes man's anthropocentric self-image as an end in himself. Most critics concur that this is one of his most successful dialogues.

VI. Dialogo di Malambruno e di Farfarello (Dialogue between Malambruno and Farfarello, 1824).   Malambruno, a magician, conjures up an infernal spirit who would "put all his powers . . . at his service." Farfarello appears. Malambruno seeks to satisfy only one desire—not nobility, riches, power, love, honors, but to "make me happy for just one moment of time." The devil declares this to be impossible, and in defending his declaration with logic forces the magician to admit that "nonliving is always better than living." So if Malambruno will agree, Farfarello is ready to make off with his soul ahead of time.

Often quoted, this airy dialogue illustrates Leopardi's philosophy of pleasure, that illusory goal that can never find fulfillment. Again he pities mankind's cruel lot. In a world characterized by the conflict between self-esteem or self-love and the repeated nonsatisfaction of desire (what self-esteem engenders), one can know only unhappiness and sorrow. Logically, the sole conclusion one can reach, therefore, is that nonbeing is preferable to being. If it were not for this cheerless climax, which the infernal spirit argues with the training of a lawyer, the similarity between this story and the Faust legend, indeed Goethe's drama with its central motif of "Stay, Oh moment, thou art so fair!," would invite closer attention.[31] As it is, the avenue is identical, but then it bifurcates, Leopardi's leading in a direction of deception and vanity with no thought of salvation.

VII. Dialogo della Natura e di un'Anima (Dialogue between Nature and a Soul, 1824). Why, asks the Soul of Nature, is she condemned to the punishment of "Live, be great and unhappy"? Must Nature decree such misery? Nature argues that according to the laws of fate, universal misery necessarily is proper to the human condition. Only great souls, who instinctively suffer more than others, receive glory as compensation, "the major good conceded to mortals." But despite the examples of [Luiz de] Camões and Milton, the Soul rejects the offer of immortal glory, asking Nature instead to accelerate her death and place her "in the most imperfect" of beings, to make her "conform to the most stupid and foolish human spirit."

The bitter though resigned tone of this dialogue echoes many pages of the *Zibaldone* (for example, 2410–14) where fame and unhappiness, in symbiotic relationship, plague especially those who have fine sensibilities, feelings, and a genuine disposition for magnanimity. Self-esteem again lurks beneath the unfortunate workings of things as they are; desire again generates human misery. It is better to seek an insensate condition whose brutishness precludes expectation and fame and their inevitable disillusion. Therefore, the Soul asks to be rid of her faculties and be reduced to an unsentient state.

VIII. Dialogo della Terra e della Luna (Dialogue between the Earth and the Moon, 1824). Ancient and recent philosophers "from Orpheus to De la Lande [Pierre-Antoine Delalande]" claim to have discovered that the Moon is inhabited, and the Earth wants to know, should this information be correct, if men live there with their besetting intrigues and wars. Men have always coveted the Moon, hoping to reach it somehow, but failing so far. The Moon replies that not men but beings unknown to Earth live there. Recalling the poet Ludovico Ariosto's *Orlando Furioso,* Earth asks if lost things (beauty, youth, sanity, intellectual labor, etc.—all except folly, which remains down here) reach there and clutter the landscape. The answer is negative. What there is, however, is vice, misfortune, sorrow, old age—all the evils. These the Moon shares with all the other planets.

Leopardi's sarcasm over popular beliefs and scientific opinions regarding the moon—which means regarding most things—is clearly shaped around a simple dialogue between the two spheres, whose allusions to other planets (Uranus, Saturn, Mercury, Venus) suggest the broadest possible cosmic coverage for the presence of sorrow, especially with reference to humankind's material evils, as adumbrated in the "Storia del genere umano." Indeed, the sun and the stars, too, partake of universal suffering in the wake of disintegrated illusions. One hears Lucian in the background and the pessimism concerning vices, defects, and misdeeds remains basically social. The coming "Dialogo della natura e di un islandese" and the "Cantico del gallo silvestre" will broaden the perspective. The style's simplicity does not have the liveliness of many other *operette,* and betrays a certain sluggishness in intellectual mood. Speeches are often long, and by their length militate against the spirit of the dialogue form. However, the pessimistic ascertainments, though they fall typically within Leopardi's world view, are balanced at times by a sense of fable that breaks through the torpor.

IX. **La scommessa di Prometeo** (The Wager of Prometheus, 1824).   According to the College of Muses, a crown of laurels awaits any inhabitant of Hypernephelus,[32] divine or human, who puts together "a praiseworthy invention." Bacchus for his wine, Minerva for her oil, and Vulcan for his economical copper pot are selected, but each finds a reason to refuse the laurels. Prometheus surprises the judges by stating his disappointment at not having been selected, for he had entered "the clay model that he had made and used to form the first people." One day he mentioned the unjust verdict to his skeptical companion Momus and, to implement a financial wager, proposed to visit all five continents with him to observe the praiseworthiness of his invention. In the New World, they see savages cooking and eating human flesh; in India a widow, following local custom, burns on her dead husband's pyre—which leads Prometheus's ironical companion to ask if such was the intended use of the stolen, heavenly fire. Prometheus is sure that civilized areas of the world, like Paris or Philadelphia, would prove his point, but in London they learn of a wealthy but bored man who committed suicide with a pistol after killing his two children. Momus was about to remind his companion that no other animal outside of man kills himself volontarily or his children out of despair, but Prometheus prevents him; "and without bothering to see the other two continents, paid off his bet."

Some of Leopardi's favorite themes dominate this narrative/dialogue: man's supreme imperfection, abetted by the evil of civilization which, instead of improving his condition, makes it more terrifying. Unlike Rousseau's primitive, man is selfishly self-serving. The experiences mount in intensity, from the primitive Colombian cannibalism through the vicious practice of immolation (*suttee*) in Agra to the horror of the results of tedium in advanced societies, in this case England. Boredom dominates the mood of man, suspended as he is between desire and disappointment—a condition that leads to suicide, a theme with which the Romantics were highly preoccupied. The sweeping movements across the continents, the ingenuous encounters with the natives, and the sarcastic adventures have much in common with *Candide;*[33] Prometheus does remind us of Voltaire's jejune wanderer, and Momus has at least biting wit or surly criticism in common with either Cacambo or Martin. The *operetta* is a Lucianesque fantasy, structurally weak in spots but poignant in its sober message describing the human condition.

X. Dialogo di un Fisico e di un Metafisico (Dialogue between a Physicist and a Metaphysician, 1824). An ecstatic physicist/physician (a scientist) has found the way to prolong life, but a sobering metaphysician (a philosopher) advises him to keep his finding locked up in a lead box until man finds a way to live happily. So long as he believes that life means happiness, all is well; the moment this is belied, he prefers death. Many are the examples adduced from mythology and history to illustrate this view. Longevity is not what is desired, rather an existence of activity, of "actions and sensations," anything to dispel tedium. "Let each think and act according to his ability." Life must either be "true life, or death will outdo it in merit."

As Fubini notes, this dialogue stands out speculatively as one of Leopardi's most important. It derives from a page in the *Zibaldone* in which he comments on a German scientist's (Christoph Wilhelm Hufeland) publication of a work concerned with increasing the human lifespan. Again, the problem of happiness lies at the core. Here is made a distinction between life as simple duration and life as intensity of sensations. Leopardi says that he "never knew that someone who taught the public to prolong life helped the public and was considered laudable"; princes should endow university chairs for those who endeavor to make life happier, "and then we would be grateful to someone who taught us how to prolong it" (*Z*, 352). This, from Leopardi, was not an unexpected reaction. What strikes the reader, however, is a possible modification of his gloomy world view in a eudemonistic direction. Rousseau's *Emile* had proclaimed at one point that to live is not simply to breathe; similarly, for Leopardi, the human being's happy life is not the "pure" one but the active one of "efficaciousness and sensations."[34] The pessimism remains, but the concept of life is broadened.

XI. Dialogo di Torquato Tasso e del suo Genio familaire (Dialogue between Torquato Tasso and His Familiar Spirit, 1824).   Like Socrates, during a period of mental trouble, Torquato Tasso thought he spoke at length with a friendly spirit; in his Ferrarese prison,[35] they conversed about women and how they affect the imagination of men with "such strength as to renew my soul, so to speak, and make me forget so many misfortunes"; about what they really are like and how when "present . . . [a woman] seems a woman, and when distant . . ., a goddess"; about love and how, despite the divorce between the real and the imagined, "I die from a desire to see her again and speak with her"; about dreaming and how "between truth and dream the only difference is that the latter can sometimes be more beautiful and sweet than the former ever can"; about pleasure and how "it is always past or future, never present"; about tedium, having "the nature of air," and its remedies; and about habit and solitude. Where does the spirit live? "In any strong wine."

The author of the *Gerusalemme liberata* (*Jerusalem Delivered*), an ideal poet for the romantics before whose tomb Leopardi had experienced deep emotions, Torquato Tasso, offered him a likely occasion to spin a lyrical reverie around his favorite themes: life, its purposelessness, its core in boredom (like the airy state between pleasure and pain), the unavailability of pleasure (pleasure belongs only to dreaming, not to living) in the context of the present, and the conflict between hope-producing illusion and hope-dashing reality. The background is psycho-sensationalist and existential—hence basic to the whole of the *Operette morali*. More than the substance of the theories, which may be described as sincere though not always compelling, the essence of the dialogue, one of Leopardi's best, lies in their poetic presentation, through which they enjoy a special liveliness and emotional importance. It is the virtue of "strong wine" to produce *veritas*.

XII. Dialogo della Natura e di un Islandese (Dialogue between Nature and an Icelander, 1824).   An Icelander, wandering in the heart of Africa "in a place where no man had ever visited before," sees a large stone bust (as he thinks at first) in the distance which turns out to be a gigantic woman resting against a mountain. She was "both beautiful and terrible": she is Nature, whom he had tried to escape. He accuses her of enmity toward the human race. She, however, retorts that she has never bothered about man's happiness or unhappiness, as she evidences in her "perpetual circle of production and destruction." While the Icelander is asking her fundamental questions like why we were born and why pain and evil exist, two lions burst forth from the forest and devour him. (In another version, he is buried in a sand storm, mummified, then placed in a European museum.)

From a kindly force that protects children from the ills of reason and civilization, Nature here becomes unfriendly, inflexible, the cruel "stepmother" or "harsh nurse" of "La ginestra," indeed the real source of human suffering, apart from the sensationalist argument. Regardless of the slightly ironic close, the narration/dialogue represents an acute, anti-Rousseauan indictment which here once more gains power through stylistic and poetic subtleties. Nature's terrible indifference and cryptic manner outdo her beauty, and in her inescapable presence only one destiny awaits the traveler. In a curious way, the variant endings seem to underscore the idea that, whatever the climate, this type of destiny prevails, and the possibility that the gigantic figure stands for God adds considerable poignancy to them. Along these lines, one commentator goes as far as to establish a parallel with Herman Melville's *Moby-Dick*: "Al-

though the Icelander is passive compared with the raging Ahab and
desires escape instead of confrontation or mastery, in both works
the force encountered blends beauty with terror, cruelty with indifference, and is, above all, inscrutable."[36]

XIII. Il Parini ovvero della gloria (Parini, or Concerning Glory,
1824).   The great writer Giuseppe Parini turns to a promising and
gifted disciple to discourse on glory—not the glory of heroic action,
which no longer obtains, but the one which is more "private" in
nature and less frequent, the glory of literary and philosophical
accomplishment: "No intellect is created by nature for study, nor
is man born to write—only to act. Therefore we note that most
excellent authors . . ., like Vittorio Alfieri, were at first inclined
to great actions, and when the times rejected them . . ., they
switched to writing great things." But literary fame meets many
obstacles: too few people can judge, readers are often ill disposed,
many books have no value. And in the case of philosophical and
scientific study, prejudices, fears, faulty perspectives, and many
more difficulties stand in the way. Frequently, if recognition comes,
it comes posthumously and inadequately, and even if glory is achieved
during life, suffering and heartaches are attendant discomforts, and
it is at best uncertain and tenuously maintainable, "similar to a
shadow."

A long and tightly reasoned piece in twelve chapters, *Il Parini*
rings with the subjective concerns of an author who had longed for
fame from an early age and who, some would say, undoubtedly saw
in it compensation for his unprivileged physical state. It is Leopardi's
more than Parini's literary credo. It reads, not very poetically, like
a treatise on glory's inconsistency by someone who still longs for
it; this may explain the length which stretches out with many
pertinent digressions, such as an important one on stylistic "perfection." "Very often it happens that, if you remove quality of style
from a famous piece of writing most of whose merit, you thought,
resided in its ideas, then you so denude it as to make it appear
insignificant." Then comes the matter of glory. So "limited in its
usefulness, difficult, and uncertain," glory cannot "be felt or grasped
. . . when you have it in your very hands." Yet, though an illusion,
what is he to do whose nature locks him on such a course? Leopardi's
reply that ends the *operetta* contains its most vibrant, personally felt
words that warn against self-deluding beliefs: "As much as times

permit, other persons act, and as much as our mortal condition can bear, they enjoy. Great writers, by nature or habit incapable of many human pleasures, or even deprived of them (many voluntarily), not unusually neglected in human society except perhaps by those who engage in the same type of study, are destined to lead a life similar to death, and, provided they make it, to live after they are buried. But our destiny, wherever it drags us, is to be followed with noble and strong heart—something required especially of your virtue, and of those who resemble you."

XIV. Dialogo di Federico Ruysch e delle sue mummie (Dialogue between Frederick Ruysch and His Mummies, 1824).   Everywhere on earth the dead awaken with the arrival of the "great mathematical year" (a special cycle in the universe's chronological existence). Friedrich Ruysch, the Dutch physician and naturalist, who had embalmed and preserved mummies in his studio,[37] hears them sing in chorus (the dialogue opens with the verses of a hymn to death). During the fifteen minutes they will be alive, he asks them what sensations they experienced—pleasure or pain—as they were about to die, to which their spokesman replies that he never noticed the moment of death, just as living man does not notice the moment in which he falls asleep. Besides, everyone hopes he has "at least an hour or two left . . .," as Cicero, too, recognized. But no answer comes forth to the naturalist's query: "How did you know that you were dead?" The fifteen minutes were up.

The macabre poetry of the beginning suggesting that to the dead life is just as perplexing as death is to the living, yields gradually, when the prose takes over, to a brilliant fantasy, tinged here and there with gentle humor, in a rare tour de force in which Leopardi keeps the reader uninterruptedly "engrossed in the absurd, the unspeakable and the unthinkable, in an absolute of fantasy and images."[38] The subject, reminiscent of passages in Buffon's *Histoire naturelle de l'homme,* is Leopardi through and through, nourishing the Epicurean belief that body and soul both perish. Death, a painless and even pleasurable sensation when it approaches, extinguishes our life in an infinite sea: "Every created thing devolves in you." Sleep and death become synonymous. It is to the living as life is to the mummies, "something arcane and wondrous," only it is also a "profound night in the confused mind." A languid feeling of nothingness beyond pleasure and pain permeates the story; the sensation of timelessness is not mitigated by the realistic, almost comic, touches of Ruysch's fright and annoyance when he first hears the weird music. And the inconclusive ending could not underscore mystery more effectively.

XV. Detti memorabili di Filippo Ottonieri (Memorable Sayings of Filippo Ottonieri, 1824). The ironic philosopher Ottonieri,[39] like Socrates, left no writings, deeming conversation to be more significant. Accordingly, he discussed frequently and widely with friends "whatever subjects the occasion presented": man and destiny, unhappiness, vices and virtues, desires and passions, egoism and self-esteem, love and pleasure, paradoxes, slavery, truth and beauty, old age, negligence, books, and in the end the author adds a few famous mottoes and witty retorts of his. Rousseau, Cicero, Socrates, Epicurus (Ottonieri thought of himself as an Epicurean, "perhaps more jokingly than seriously," for he "condemned Epicurus," even if his doctrine was "most suited to the modern age"), Horace, Xenophon, Homer, Donatus, Virgil, Gaius Melissus, Diogenes Laertius, Plato, Plutarch, Lorenzino de' Medici, Tasso, Lucian, Emperor Havius Claudius Julian, Jacques Bénigne Bossuet—Ottonieri was a man of vast intellect who discoursed on all these personalities and more, and by his own epitaphed admission was "born . . . to glory . . . and died without fame. . . ."

The long, intellectual biography, speckled with humor, is in seven chapters; its importance lies in the fact that they focus not on Ottonieri's beliefs but on Leopardi's own. It is—to whatever extent this is possible—a stylized compendium of the *Zibaldone's* essential disclosures and has often been referred to as a cento. More precisely, it is the material of the *Pensieri* presented with selectiveness, consistency, order, and amplification, and above all without the harshness of their pessimism. Elements of existential sensationalism permeate the discussion of man's infelicity (see especially the beginning of chapter 2). But the style of the "sayings" is gentler. "Everything is more graceful, picturesque, and human."[40] Some consider it out of character with the *Operette morali* because it contains no story line as such, but the topics echo sympathetically those found in the companion *operette,* giving each of them, if only by virtue of being singled out, a special relief of its own. No longer buried in the thousands of pages of the *Zibaldone,* they breathe a fresh life—through their form as well as through their attribution to a different historical figure, albeit a skeptical moralist and kindred spirit.

XVI. Dialogo di Cristoforo Colombo e di Pietro Gutierrez (Dialogue between Christopher Columbus and Pedro Gutierrez, 1824). On the deck of the flagship, Columbus and a shipmate, Pedro, meet one night; both admit to each other their fatigue. "Speaking frankly," says Columbus, "I confess I have begun to doubt a bit" about the success of the venture, though he will see it through. Even if no glory should await or usefulness should reward the outcome of the leader's "speculative opinion," the voyage including all its risks was profitable "because for a period it freed us from boredom, made life dear to us, and made us appreciate many things we took for granted otherwise." If the signs are correct (the plummet's soundings, the shape of clouds around the sun, the softer air, the varied wind, the floating cane, the birds), they will soon touch land, which "for a few days will seem blessed."

Though historical,[41] Columbus is as much a Leopardian creation as the Icelander. The central concept reflects the author's view of the active life—here the sense of risk that constantly menaces the sailor—as the best way to counteract tedium and make us feel, in the lap of worldly despair, that this existence means something to us after all. Danger, as "La quiete dopo la tempesta" also suggests, endears us to what we have, and many of the positive overtones of the dialogue derive from the genuine attachment to the manners and voices of nature Columbus expresses to Pedro on that quiet night under the stars. Stylistically, words and poetry intermingle. Fascinated by anything dealing with the New World, partly because of the wonder and mystery of it all, Leopardi establishes a wondrous mood in this dialogue, one of his most captivating and one that grows into a tribute to the Genoese admiral, who in "Ad Angelo Mai" discovered "an unknown, immense land."

XVII. Elogio degli uccelli (Eulogy of the Birds, 1824). The solitary philosopher Aemilius (actually Gentilianus) sits reading when birds interrupt and "he gives himself to listening and musing." He takes to writing their praise: "birds are by nature the most joyful creatures in the world. . . ." They sing, and this denotes gayness. They fly from place to place, and this means that they cannot be bored. "It was surely a wise provision of nature to assign both song

and flight to the same creatures, so that those who had to bring
joy to other living beings with their voices should usually be in a
high place, from which their song could extend over a wider space
and reach more listeners, and so that the air, the element made for
sound, would be peopled with vocal and musical creatures. Truly,
the song of birds brings much comfort and delight to people no
less, to my way of thinking, than to other creatures. And I believe
that this arises mainly not so much from the sweetness of the sounds,
however great they may be, or from their variety, or from their
mutual suitability, as from the sense of gladness naturally contained
in song generally, and in the song of birds specifically. A bird's
song is, so to speak, a form of laughter which it intones when it
feels pleased and well." Birds possess "great strength and vitality,
and a great deal of imagination," not of the "fervid and tempestuous"
variety like Dante and Tasso, "but the rich, changing, light, un-
stable imagination of children" in which they themselves delight.
"In short . . ., [Aemilius] should like for a while to be changed
into a bird, to savor their contentment and joy."

The description is a poetized Buffon (*Discours sur la nature des
oiseaux* [*Discourse on the Nature of Birds*]), a prose poem making its
own musical sounds in a swooping flow of images that translate the
spontaneous joys and carefree movements of birds (recurring images
in the *Canti*). Because of their internal and external vivacity, as
compared with other species in the animal kingdom, birds seem
less subject to boredom. Aemilius is here less the student of Plotinus
than Leopardi himself, in line with the ancient and medieval avian
traditions, putting down his book to seek out the birds with his
eyes, actually the eyes of his mind which takes to meditating, or
better, to rhapsodizing—see the comparison between a human's
laughing and a bird's singing—on something the human condition
lacks (at least as experienced by Leopardi in this perhaps special
lyrical moment): festive spontaneity.

XVIII. Cantico del gallo silvestre (Song of the Wild Rooster,
1824).   Hebrew masters had advised that a giant rooster, "its feet
on the ground and its head and beak touching the sky," had the
use of reason and could communicate with words. The author has
come across a parchment written in a mixture of "Chaldean, Tar-
gumic, Rabbinic, Cabalistic, and Talmudic," and translated it,
albeit in a style that necessarily reflects the original text of the

canticle entitled "Morning Song of a Wild Rooster." The rooster informs men that sleep is like death; it is given to them to prolong life (lest continuous toil exhaust their strength). They should awaken. But the happy thoughts at awakening are immediately replaced by sad ones, just the way the morning of human life is serene and its dusk is sorrowed as it proceeds from the confidence of youth to the discouragement of later years. Great human empires disappear without trace; so "of the infinite trials and calamities of created things nothing, not even a vestige, will remain but a naked silence, a very deep quiet that will fill the immense space."

The dialogue could be called the emotional climax of the collection of the *Operette morali;* man's unhappiness is dramatized in a universe of fallen illusions where "nature directs every work of hers toward death." Here cosmic and materialistic pessimism merge. The emotion reveals itself with particular tension and stress, using Leopardi's own words, through a certain stylistic choppiness and inflation "consistent with . . . Near Eastern expression" and abetted by the device of pretending to have discovered an ancient manuscript. If it is a morning hymn, supposedly deriving from Psalm 50 and the Book of Job, it chills us by virtue of the contrast between this hopeful time of day and the lugubrious speculation, through the disparity between the solemn poetry of an elegy and its philosophical substance. The universe drives toward destruction, as toward a black hole. Hence the wild rooster "promises the indecipherable silence of centuries to come."[42] After this kind of ancient Hebrew wisdom, the reader is gripped with speechlessness, less because of the message itself than because of the cosmic tone it has now assumed.

XIX. Frammento apocrifo di Stratone da Lampsaco (Apocryphal Fragment of Strato of Lampsacus, 1824).   A preamble followed by two chapters, "On the Origin of the World" and "On the End of the World"—this is the fragment the author came across in the library of Mount Athos's monks and translated. How much is directly attributable to the peripatetic philosopher Strato of Lampsacus and how much of it is apocryphal? "Let the erudite readers judge." Chapter 1 states that material things, since they have an end, once also had a beginning; but matter itself is eternal. In chapter 2 we are informed that the constant reproduction of things does not imply endless duration for the world. "We know that, because it keeps turning around itself, the earth, fleeing from its

center and areas near the equator and yet pushing toward the center
those areas near the poles, has changed configuration and continually
changes it, becoming ever fuller around the equator and ever more
depressed around the poles. From this, after a certain time . . .,
the result will have to be something of a flattening here and there
around the equator, so that having lost its global roundness, the
earth will look like a thin round table," eventually like a ring around
Saturn, until it will dissolve in space, winding up in the sun or
some other planet. This will happen to all the asters. And yet matter
will survive to give rise to "new orders of things and a new world."
But we can only guess about their quality.

Through its scientific emphasis, Leopardi gives his pessimistic
outlook broader configurations than would have been possible without it. Matter, Strato avowed, is the center of everything eternal.
The dry style, perhaps necessary for—indeed consistent with—the
materialistic creed, stands out in contrast with, say, Plato's *Phaedrus*,
which is livelier. Leopardi had no reason to be lively, since the
reality of universal matter and its ultimate course gave him little
cause for rejoicing. Somewhere in the *Operette morali* he wanted to
use his early interest in astronomy to shape a statement that seemed
to emanate not from the world of abstract ideas but from the scientific world of fact. Hence the language not of a poet but of an
analyst who has come to certain geological conclusions about global
pressures and shapes. Although with some modifications this view
can still hold its own in various sessions of astronomical congresses,
the importance of the statement lies less in its scientific truth or
falsehood than in its metaphorical impact. The outcome of the
pressures and shapes fulfills our (Leopardi's) expectation of final
nothingness, the same destiny in store for the coming "new genera
and new species" of the next "new world."

XX. **Dialogo di Timandro e di Eleandro** (Dialogue between
Timander and Eleander, 1824).   Eleander has written a book deriding mankind, for which Timander reproaches him. Eleander may
be compassionate, but Timander esteems men and wonders how his
friend could have been so abused as to show such hostility. "Listen,
my friend," says Eleander, "I was born to love and have loved . . .,
[but] today I am not ashamed to say that I love no one outside of
myself, given the nature of things." What makes him inveigh against
men is his desire to reveal "the necessary unhappiness of all living

people." Unfortunately, ancient and modern philosophers claim the contrary. "Let people remove their masks." One learns by experience more than books that have sought the "truth," "that miserable and cold truth." "Philosophy, hoping and promising at first to cure our ills, in the long run is reduced in vain to find a remedy for itself." Eleander is thus constrained to recall "some hard and sad truths." He will continue to condemn the study of other, exalting "truths," and to praise the "beautiful and joyful flights of the imagination which, though vain, give life some merit: the natural illusions of the soul. . . ."

This *operetta* ended the first collection of the *Operette morali,* serving as an apology against optimists like Timander who cannot stomach bitter truths. Leopardi/Eleander wishes to disabuse his contemporaries of their false beliefs. Despite his utterances elsewhere that the truth can help mankind, philosophy in the normal sense of the word is here humiliated by the poet who recognizes art as the only beneficial reality available to the human spirit. Eleander underscores his creed: "If this unhappiness is not true, then everything is false, and we may as well forget about this or any other conversation. If it is true, why should it not be permitted me to lament it openly and freely, and to say: I suffer?" Through these words, and the calm yet intense rhythmic movement of the style, Leopardi, while justifying his book, demonstrates once again his genuine compassion for man and his unhappy lot.

XXI. Il Copernico—Dialogo (Copernicus: A Dialogue, 1827). Four dialogued scenes constitute the mini-drama: The First Hour and the Sun, Nicolaus Copernicus on His Balcony, The Final Hour and Copernicus, and Copernicus and the Sun. In the first, the Sun refuses to ascend to bring light to "a handful of puny little animals that live on a handful of clay." Let them burn their own fires in some way, perhaps by hunting "fireflies and glowworms." First Hour fears that they will "all die in the dark, frozen like pieces of rock crystal." But the Sun suggests that poets and philosophers will eventually convince the Earth to move. In fact, the Sun urges First Hour to go fetch from the Earth one of those philosophers who speculates about the heavens, in order to convince him to get the Earth to start running. In scene 2, Copernicus scans "the eastern sky through a roll of paper, for telescopes had not yet been invented." He is perplexed that the Sun has not yet appeared. Perhaps those unscientific legends are true that have the Sun rise out of certain lakes, and the like, and "reason and science are not worth a pin." Scene 3 finds Final Hour inviting Copernicus "at once to the house of the Sun, my master." After some hesitation, the astronomer mounts upon its shoulders and they take off. In the fourth scene, Copernicus informs the Sun of the difficulty of convincing the Earth to get moving, since its inhabitants have always thought of themselves as lords of the universe. Then too, other planets will have to follow the Earth's lead and start moving also, and the stars will imitate the Sun, if the Sun will stay fixed. Last but not least, he is afraid that he would be "roasted alive, on this account, like the Phoenix," without, however, rising from his ashes. But the Sun prophesies that other philosophers will be burned after him, but not himself, especially if he dedicates his book on the subject to the Pope. "For thus I promise you that you will not even lose your canonry."[43]

As in several previous dialogues, man's misplaced pride in himself forms the subject of this one, though Leopardi summarized it with more acerbity when he referred to it as being concerned with "the nullity of the human race."[44] His mood, however, was not acrimonious; the dialogue is jocular, sparkling with humorous phrases in the spirit of a Mozartian divertimento, especially when they enliven some of the author's more polemical attitudes. Philosophers—meaning here scientists—for example, are people who have been "climbing into power, every day a little more," and have made the Sun quite lazy in his old age because now he wants the Earth to get to work and go running around him; but in a sense poets might be better for the job, "because poets, by indicating with one fable or another that the things of the world are valuable and important as well as pleasurable and very beautiful, and by creating a thousand happy expectations, often stimulate in others a desire to work, while philosophers unstimulate them." Yet it is the astronomer Copernicus—and a very unhistorical Copernicus, of course, yet someone the effects of whose discovery Leopardi deeply appreciated—one of those "who keeps cool outdoors," who receives the sign, because "today on Earth no one listens to poets any more than I do," muses the Sun, and whereas "they once held sway," they would now "not be effective even if listened to."

XXII. Dialogo di Plotino e di Porfirio (Dialogue between Plotinus and Porphyry, 1827). The dialogue concerns suicide. Porphyry's biographer Eunapius confirms the story that Porphyry, Plotinus's disciple and author of *The Life of Plotinus,* was dissuaded from killing himself by his master. They talk. Porphyry's attitude stems "from the tedium I feel so violently that it resembles a pain and a spasm . . ., from the vanity of everything that happens to me during the day, so that not just my mind but also my feelings, even my body, are filled with this vanity. . . . Only tedium, which is always born of the vanity of things, is never a vanity or deceit; never is it founded on falsehood." Plotinus recalls Plato's injunction: "It is not permitted to remove oneself, like a runaway slave, from this prison the gods put us in." But his disciple would rather leave Plato aside; though the laws of nature impose on all living things the need "to look to self-preservation," nature also "granted us death as a medicine for all our ills. . . . It would be strange, if nature prohibits my killing myself, that she also had the ability to force me to live when she has neither the will nor the strength to make me happy and to free me of my misery." Tedium is sufficient reason to end one's life, especially those of us living "in a so-called civilized state" (the idea of suicide never crosses a savage's mind). Plotinus rebuts that though he agrees on many points, the ills of life are bearable; indeed, they must be borne, lest we cause added sorrow to our friends and dear ones: "You should help us to endure life rather than abandon us without giving us a thought. Let us live, my Porphyry, and comfort each other; let us not reject to bear that part of our species' ills which destiny has prescribed for us. Let us keep each other company, keep encouraging each other and giving each other a helping hand in order to accomplish in the best way possible this labor called life—which without a doubt will be brief. And when death comes, then we will not grieve, and our friends and companions will comfort us even in that final hour; and the thought will gladden us, after we are gone, that they will remember us often and will still love us."

The understanding and more humane Plotinus has the last word, though he and the coldly rational Porphyry represent two sides of Leopardi himself, like the "Moi" and "Lui" of Denis Diderot's *Le Neveu de Rameau* (*Rameau's Nephew*). Yet the importance of the final utterance, by virtue of its concluding position, suggest an imbalance in favor of the master. It goes well beyond what the *Zibaldone* has to offer on the issue of suicide, or the poem "Bruto minore." No light touches enliven this solemn dialogue between two impressive—albeit unhistorically depicted—philosophers of antiquity; their speeches are often appropriately long, tending more toward disquisition than conversation. For this reason, the poetic quality of other *operette* does not surface in this one which involves us with its pervasive seriousness (though not heaviness) and the moving nobility of its closing message, a decade before "La ginestra."

XXIII. Dialogo di un venditore d'almanacchi e di un passeggere (Dialogue between an Almanach Vendor and a Passer-by, 1832). A wayfarer meets a peddler of almanacs and engages him in a conversation about happiness. The past and the present hold none, since, even if one could, anyone would not opt to relive years gone by—a sure sign that they contained more evil than good. "No one would like to be born again." The only happiness is a vain one: the hope for a better future: "The life that is a fine thing is not the life one knows, but the life one does not know." The almanac peddler agrees.

A passage in the *Zibaldone* reports that Leopardi, the dialogue's wayfarer, "asked a number of people if they would be happy about reliving their lives with the understanding that they would relive it exactly as it was lived the first time." All would have been happy to live again, "but with that understanding, no one." Only our ignorance of the future and the illusion of hope make us want to keep on living, for happiness is a matter of future anticipations, not of past realizations.[45] "With the new year," suggests the wayfarer to the peddler, "Fate will begin to treat us well—you and me and everyone else—and a happy life will begin for us. Isn't that so?" The tone is lighthearted, the subject depressing. The irony in Leopardi's Socratic manner is particularly evident in the way the modest peddler answers the wayfarer's queries about happiness in the coming year with enthusiastic affirmatives (hoping to sell his calendars), not knowing he is dealing with a philosopher, trained in the Athenian's method, who will lead him from sad admission to sad admission until he reaches an unenthusiastically negative conclusion. It does not take the wayfearing philosopher of the dialogue, the inquiring writer of the "Dialogo di Torquato Tasso e del suo Genio familiare," or the inspired poet of "Il sabato del villaggio" (which also treat the impossibility of happiness) to arrive at this verity, which is accessible, alas, to the humblest of vendors.[46]

XXIV. Dialogo di Tristano e di un Amico (Dialogue between Tristan and a Friend, 1832). The Friend finds Tristan's book "melancholy, disconsolate, despairing," as usual. But Tristan has changed his mind. "I believed that my sad voice, describing the common lot, would find an echo in the heart of every man . . .," but this was not the case. "It is best for all men everywhere"; unhappiness is an error of the mind, and "knowledge and enlightenment are on the increase . . .: long live statistics!" Happiness is one of the great discoveries of the nineteenth century; man possesses endless perfectibility, and the human race improves by the day. Note how many "learned men, true scholars," existed a century and a half ago, and compare them with the smaller number today; as the wish for knowledge increases, "there is a proportionate reluctance to study. . . . Knowledge is not like riches, which can be divided and put together again, and always come to the same sum. Where everyone knows a little, little is known; for knowledge follows knowledge, and will not be spread out. A superficial education cannot be divided among many, but is merely common to many who are not learned. . . . Now, except perhaps in Germany, where scholarship has not yet been uprooted, don't you think that the existence of very learned men becomes less possible every day?" The Friend is not at all sure that Tristan has changed his mind, though Tristan reassures him: "Certainly," this century is superior to all those of the past. But Tristan does not care to keep up the irony and finally informs his Friend that indeed he has been joking. "But as for me, by your leave and that of this age, I am most unhappy and know it . . ., and I dare to desire death above all things with such ardor and sincerity as few men, I believe, have ever felt in desiring it. . . . I have an inner feeling that almost makes me sure that the time of which I speak is not far off. I am too ripe for death, it seems too absurd and incredible—being spiritually dead as I am, with the fable of my life already told—that I should linger on. . . . I shudder at the thought. . . . Now I no longer envy either the foolish or the wise, the great or the small, the weak or the powerful. I envy only the dead, and with them only would trade places."

"Palinodia al marchese Gino Capponi" ("Retraction for Marquis Gino Capponi") and "Amore e morte" echo in the background of the noble grandeur of this dialogue which modulates from tongue-in-cheek to stateliness. It is a hymn, a serious "poetic dream," as the *triste* (sad) Tristan describes his book which he advises his Friend to burn, "an expression of the author's unhappiness." Death is the pedal point, striking even the final note: "If, on the one hand, I were offered the fortune and the fame of Caesar or Alexander unsullied, and, on the other hand, death today, I would say, death today, and would need no time to make my choice." The desire for love has modulated to a yearning for death (Porphyry had said that death was good, and Ruysch that it was pleasurable). In this last *operetta*, Leopardi writes a compendium of the *Operette morali* and of himself—he being Tristan—the poet who derides man's silly pride, man's ineptitude yet overconfidence, his faith in progress despite his unhappiness, his negligence in education toward his own body (an echo by Leopardi of a recently aborted love affair), and his foolish trust in the social sciences; Tristan observes the human condition with compassion while he confronts fate with heroism. "I tell you frankly that I do not submit to my unhappiness, nor bow my head to destiny, nor come to terms with it, as other men do." Five years later, on his deathbed, Leopardi entertained an identical attitude.

The *Operette morali* stand out as a felicitous creation containing a wealth of sayings about the human condition, each inviting close attention, and each capable of inspiring sympathetic echoes in succeeding generations. One might venture to say that their overall pessimism dissolves in the mixture of irony and humor, fancy and imaginativeness, insight and nobilty that mark every page. Or if it does not dissolve, it is subjected to diversified coloration, a kind of variegation that creates by itself its own poetic mood. For these reasons, critics like to pour over the work today, sifting out its multiple aspects, and trying to arrive at a comprehensive or integrated critical view. There are many colors, or tonalities, depending on the topic and Leopardi's imaginative disposition, all relating to a particular weltanschauung with reference to the problem of human happiness. Though the problem assumes cosmic proportions, still modern man, more than ancient man, is particularly smitten by the inability to attain felicity due to his greater expectation of himself and to his escalated difficulty in translating expectation into reality. Moreover, there is the more intense suffering of him who feels and thinks more sensitively. In addition, there is that plethora of ills

that besets any individual's simple act of living under any circumstances. And finally, there looms, like a cosmic cloud above all else,
a sense of the exiguity of man in front of the infinite reality of
being, accompanied by the certainty of ultimate decimation and
therefore of the vanity of all things. Thus Leopardi's scenario gets
broader and broader, and the philosophical and the poetic merge in
such a way as to produce a human, life-bound chain of complementary myths. Giovanni Getto presents quite convincingly a description of the *Operette morali* in terms of a tonality that intensifies
the poetic: the religious sense "in which, if God is absent, His
attributes remain intensely operative: the infinite and the eternal;
and if Leopardi's demeanor shies away from any certainty and from
any commitment with reference to a positive religion, it still partakes of that deep emotion that characterizes great mystical experiences. . . . The *Operette* . . . remains a book of disquieting religious poetry."[47]

Chapter Four

An Advanced Poetics

Scattered throughout Leopardi's writings—one thinks of the *Zibaldone,* the *Discorso di un italiano intorno alla poesia romantica,* the *Epistolario,* the *Operette morali*—lies a solid and consistent, perceptive and advanced poetics that makes him one of the leading theoreticians of poetry in the Western world. Within the context of romantic poetry, one reads much about Wordsworth and Coleridge, Keats and Edgar Allan Poe, Théophile Gautier and Baudelaire, Goethe and Schlegel, but in most instances, as has been pointed out by G. Singh who finally pieced the theoretical picture together,[1] the poet from Recanati surpasses them. In an unusual and remarkable way, Leopardi's philological scholarship, steeped in antiquity, made him a modern theoretician. True classicists, of course, would hardly be surprised at this. Out of Leopardi's vast store of knowledge grew a critical awareness that perceived the importance of style, language, manner, freedom, the lyric, and the intimate relationship between psychological and poetical experience. While Singh may engage in some wishful thinking when he claims that Leopardi's thought is often compared today with that of modern or contemporary writers and critics, he is correct in referring to his "almost incredible modernity," and to him as "the most pioneering, the most liberal-minded, and the most original of all the poetic theorists of the nineteenth century."[2] The composite ingredients of Leopardi's theory include the cardinal principles of imagination, memory, and imitation, working together with personal notions of melancholy, sincerity, inspiration, and imagery, in order for both the poet and the reader to arrive at an inner possession of the poem, as it were, for only then does it become a work of art, something whereby one experiences "thousands of movements and images, wandering at times in the sweetest delirium, almost transported beyond oneself,"[3] or something that produces "marvel and delight, that excites the mind, the passion, and motivates to great deeds" (Z, 287).

On the question of poetic theory, some pages of the *Zibaldone* exist in dialectical relationship with other pages, but it is a complementary and not a contradictory relation, in which the would-be synthesis emerges in the form of an evolution. As noted before, the *Zibaldone*, corroborated by numerous references in his correspondence, bears witness to a maturing accumulation of concepts more than to a shifting of premises. It is true that, as N. J. Perella warns us at one point in his sensitive study, we must not confuse earlier and later views. The passage concerns Leopardi's idea of poetry: "We must not confuse Leopardi's later conviction that the only poetry possible for modern man is poetry of sentiment and melancholy with his earlier idea of poetry as the expression of the natural pathetic. His later view sees poetry as the expression of the human spirit no longer able to wander freely in a richly illusory world and so reduced to a poetry that has more in common with 'philosophy' than with what poetry, according to the earlier view, was supposed to be about, that is, the untutored and happily ignorant picture of an anthropomorphically animated nature and/or the expression of feelings—'pathetic' or sentimental—that nature arouses spontaneously in a spirit undefiled by reason."[4] We would simply add that the critic should also be on his guard against hasty conclusions of contradictoriness.

What endears Leopardi to many modern critical minds is the fact that, despite his familiarity with all the classical and neoclassical *artes poeticae* of the past—Aristotle, Horace, Antonio Sebastiani da Minturno, Giulio Cesare Scaligero, Lodovico Castelvetro, Philip Sidney, Pierre de Ronsard, Boileau, etc.—he recognized the danger of measuring the product against a formula. As in philosophy he deemed perfection to be how the object is and not how some a priori concept would have it be, so in poetry he saw each poem liberally as an expression of itself, of its own spirit, capable of offering the receiver no more than what it is, or of yielding no more than what it itself engenders, and not as a composition to be matched against past models. Poetry is life, he insisted, in the sense that it grows organically out of life (material life) and assumes an artistic shape—a notion which, though common enough, leads Leopardi to speculate on the indivisibility of aesthetic pleasure and ethical cognition. It is the product of an intellectual and emotional unity which perforce changes with life, with the evolutions of culture, and therefore cannot be subject to previous formulations or rules.

The question of Leopardi's supposed romanticism or classicism has received wide treatment, though necessarily inconclusive, due largely to the poet's personal blend of attitudes toward both modes of expression. After perusing Leopardi carefully, anyone would have to admit that he emerges as a partisan of neither school.[5] In the context of a poetics, his commitment to clarity and restraint was too pronounced to be confused with romanticism, and his emotional attachment to personal themes ran too deep to be congruent with classicism.

Croce exaggerates when he reduces him to a mere creator of sentimental idylls, just as Luporini does in focusing on his neo-classical rationalism, while Timpanaro, on the other hand, wisely places the poet in a distinctive lyrical-philosophical dimension, whereby the Enlightenment idea of progress must be jettisoned, since the nature of the universe, for Leopardi, is such as to render impossible man's self-removal from the hostile consequences of his condition.[6] Early on, Leopardi had seen nature classically as protective, concealing this condition from her children, but by the time of "La ginestra" the protectiveness changed to the cruelty of allowing the intolerable condition to persist. In its own primitive way, antiquity, too, provided some escapist illusions, but by the late 1820s when he completed the *Operette morali,* he deemed happiness pessimistically (some would say romantically) as the axiomatic reality of life, not subject to social permutations.

These attitudes, which can be made to reflect equally romantic and classical tendencies, enter the question of his poetics, and in the aggregate shape only the Leopardian profile and not that of any "—ism." One can see him as a classicist, for example, in his negative reaction to the enormous popularity of Byron's "The Giaour" of 1813 (translated into Italian in 1818), the first "Byronic" hero, preceding the Corsair, Lara, Cain, and Manfred. Leopardi reacted against its romantic extravagance: the Giaour's sorrow-ridden pallor combined with his satanic smile that veils occasional vestiges of nobility. The quest, he wrote in 1821, for originality ("a quality one must have without seeking it") has "plunged" his contemporaries into "a thousand excesses" (Z, 1672); this continues the thought of several years before, that through improper liberties the romantics "give birth to monsters" (Z, 10). Hence his taking Byron's admirer, Ludovico di Breme, to task in his *Discorso di un italiano intorno alla poesia romantica,* an unpublished work that ultimately transcends polemics in order to formulate a few—antiromantic—poetic principles.

In the *Discorso*, Leopardi enunciates the following: the poet must create illusions, and through his illusions imitate nature, and by imitating nature delight. Romantic poets may have engaged in creating fantasies, but, not unlike Balzac's visionary meanderings, they grew out of what they saw as reality; hence the results came under the heading of "realism," that is, a form of truth, however subjectively apprehended. These illusionary realities and Leopardian illusion have nothing in common; the latter was known consciously in advance to be different from truth, though because they emerged as beautiful they were deemed valuable. Similarly, Leopardi's stress on the hedonistic experience did not blend with romantic emotionalism and its appurtenant moral messages. Romantic realism, he believed, lacked that sense of the sublime "which elevates the imagination, inspires profound meditation and intimate, enduring sentiments" (Z, 87). In fact, speculating on the arts, he inveighed against the Germans and their gift of romanticism, "a very false system in theory, practice, nature, reason, metaphysics, dialectics" (Z, 1857).

The weakness of the *Discorso* is that it tends to reduce the classicism-romanticism confrontation to a simplistic opposition between illusion and reality, that is, classical illusionism and romantic realism. This weakness, based on a polarization of concepts that in aesthetics are not mutually exclusive, merely points up Leopardi's uneasiness with both schools. For we as readers of Leopardi must feel constrained to modify the work's apparent antiromanticism, even while romanticism is being condemned for its gloomy and obscure imagery, or especially for its abstruseness and metaphysical quality which he found disproportionate to the intelligence of the common people. Conversely, as one critic observed, "When did it ever happen that a classicist was concerned with 'the intelligence of the common people?' "[7] Romantics claimed democratic views that Leopardi thought were more consistent with his own and that the romantics, if anything, betrayed: "it almost seems that I oppose the romantics by maintaining that poetry must not be popular, when in fact we [in Italy] want it to be most popular, and the romantics instead would make it metaphysical, reasoned, learned, and proportioned to the level of knowledge of our age in which common people hardly participate."[8] Again, no alignment with any school. And it is principally because of Leopardi's poetics that we can say that it was not in his nature to be formally conscious of any "ism" with reference to his own work.

Given the historical juncture during which he lived, there is bound to be in him something of the so-called romantic spirit, though not necessarily of romantic practice. He did, for instance, nod to the Schillerian distinction between "ingenuous" and "sentimental" poetry. He also placed considerable emphasis on feeling and unrealistic fancies, indeterminateness and pensive reflection, not to speak of the notion of love, not simply as exhilaration but especially as suffering. Still, in the long run, his participation in the romantic movement was more by historical association than by adherence to its tenets. Sapegno aptly summarized the constituent elements of his romanticism: his sensibility and sense of humanity, his view of poetry as pure lyric, "a palpitation of the heart in its momentariness and immediacy [which] precludes any incursion of the intellect," the pessimistic solution of his meditation, "though born and developed in the context of Enlightenment rationalism and materialism," and his polemical, rebellious (within limits) opposition to destiny which reminds us of "fraternal souls like Goethe, Friedrich Hölderlin, Byron, Shelley, and Vigny."[9] But since these attitudes do little more than scratch the surface of literary romanticism or conjure up associations that turn out to be un-Leopardian, and since Leopardi generally broke through commonplace attitudes and left on what he said a distinctive imprimatur of his own, we must conclude that he was a "modern," not of his generation, in fact ahead of his time, with a nonclassifiable—that is, nonpartisan—view of poetry.

He repeatedly condemned the modern age as incapable of poetry; without illusion, he maintained, no poetry is possible, and science, as Blake too had warned, being inimical to the development of illusion, is inimical to the development of poetry. Such was not the case with the ancients, who benefited by belonging to the early stages in society's discovery of knowledge because there was room then for reason to corroborate illusions. The role of modern reason, mightily ensconced atop the intellectual accumulation of centuries, was instead to squelch them. In this sense, reason is an extension of knowledge, and, says one critic, "'Knowing' man is a denaturalized man."[10] Illusions are themselves a form of reality, "dear and delightful appearances," as Leopardi called them, which "can only be deprecated by deluded people" (Z, 1715). As Wordsworth too would say, children make the equation instinctively. Blake earlier and Giovanni Pascoli later would agree. Antiquity, the childhood of Western civilization, did just that; it had no reason to fear the corrupting influences of habit, time, and custom. Sentiment, one ventures to say, develops with experience and physical maturity, whereas imagination lies in the province of the child who does not distinguish between the worlds of fantasy and reality. Hence Leopardi ascribes to the ancients the poetry of imagination, and to the moderns that of sentiment. Romanticism, with its heavy personalization of all experience, held that the closer one is to nature, the more likely the growth of sentiment—a disposition which could only go so far with the earlier Leopardi who looked more simply, or more "purely," to nature, like the ancients:

[Lodovico di Breme] (like all romantics) wants modern poetry to be founded on the ideal, which he calls pathos and is more commonly referred to as sentiment, and he correctly distinguished between pathos and melancholy, since pathos, as he says, is that depth of feeling that sensitive hearts experience through the impression that something in nature makes on the senses—for example, the bell in your place of birth (says he), and I add the sight of a landscape, of a ruined tower, etc. This, in short, is the difference he finds between ancient and modern poetry, for the ancients do not experience these feelings, or less so than we do; wherefore we, according to him, are superior to the ancients *in this,* and since, again according to him, true poetry consists really *in this,* we are infinitely more poetic than the ancients. (This is the poetry of Chateaubriand, of Delille, of Saint-Pierre, etc., not to mention the romantics proper, who may differ in a few things. And this pathos is what the French call *sensibilité,* and we could call *sensitività.*) Well now, this pathos, this depth of feeling in hearts, must find excitement, and it is of this, as is natural, that the poet's supreme art will consist. And it is in this sense that di Breme and all the romantics and followers of Chateaubriand, etc. go astray. What is it that excites these feelings in people? Nature, purest nature as she is, as the ancients saw her: natural circumstances, not contrived artificially but spontaneously occurring: that tree, that bird, that song, that dwelling, that wood, that mountain. . . . In brief . . ., nature . . . awakens these feelings. Now, what did the ancients do? They depicted nature simply, and they knew how to depict and imitate her so that we see these very objects in their verses . . . as they are in nature, and as they awaken those feelings in the state of nature [if we could isolate them], so they awaken them in us when depicted and imitated with perfection. The poet selected the objects, placed them in their true light, and through his art prepared us to receive their impression, while in nature all kinds of objects are shoved together: though we see them very often, we pay no attention to them. . . . Thus did the ancients obtain their great effect, the one the romantics seek, and they obtained it in a way that captivates, sublimates, and immerses us in a sea of sweetness. . . . (Z, 15–16)

Though the benign focus on nature changes tonality with the later Leopardi, the basic verities of the above passage remained unchallenged. A few pages later he pursued that the romantics demean art and preach nature, yet they do not notice that the less the art the less the nature (Z, 20–21). These are the thoughts of a classicist. Homer recurs as the prime example of his theory, also because of his language: the Greek bard never had to rely on mystical or emotive emphases. Consummate philologist in the old sense, Leopardi had, more than most figures in the history of literature, a religious respect for the word, not just for the word in isolation but for words in combination. Their poetic validity derives from appropriateness, association, and juxtapostion, and the vocabulary of one poet represents a significant, distinguishing trait—the same as the vocabulary of one period when compared with that of another. Artful manipulation produces new effects, ultimately becoming style, so that the basic poetic art relates more to the magic of words than to the expression of ideas. In a way that would have pleased Wordsworth and Coleridge, though more "lucid" (says Singh)[11] than they, Leopardi noted:

[The poet's] art consists in selecting the most beautiful among known things, in arranging the known things . . . in a new and harmonious way, adapting them to the capacity of the majority, newly clothing, adorning, and embellishing them with the harmony of verse, metaphors, and every other stylistic splendor, in conferring light and nobility upon obscure and ignoble things and novelty on those that are commonplace, in changing the aspect of anything he is handling, as if by some magical incantation; for example: in taking persons from nature and making them talk naturally, but even so in such a way that the reader, by recognizing in that language the language he is used to hearing from similar people in similar circumstances, may find it at the same time new and incomparably more beautiful than the ordinary language because of the poetic adornments, the new style, in short, the new form and new body the poet gave it. (Z, 3221–22)

Imagination

To evolve a poetic language means to activate the imagination, if only because, even historically, the formation of language and the imagination went hand in hand (*Z*, 4367–68). In a modern, philosophical sense, Leoparadi's view concerned itself with the productive rather than the reproductive imagination, that is to say, with the creative rather than with the perceptual function. In this category, he differed radically from someone like Hugo, perhaps one of the most "imaginative" poets on the European scene at the time. Hugo was optical, or, as Hippolyte Taine liked to say about him, he used the imagination of the eyes. Leopardi, rather, used the imagination of the mind. We might adopt the phrase of one critic who alludes to his "poetry of the look" (*poesia dello sguardo*)[12] as the secret of the (mental) pleasure it generates. His sensory impressions produced intellectual visions, not pictorial visions. In so doing, he necessarily opposed the long tradition of diffidence toward the linguistic power of shaping mental images that dated as far back as Plato's attack on art. For the ancient philosopher, epistemologically, imaginative activity was unreal and untruthful. Descartes had referred to the imagination as a mistress of falseness that had to be watched and controlled, and David Hume had feared its dangerous effect of error on philosophy. Yet Leopardi could only have agreed with the same Hume who seemed to grasp nonetheless the cognitive power of the mental image and who defined understanding in terms of the established properties of the imagination.[13] Leopardi, too, saw this relationship with philosophy, but he stressed the poetic attributes, indeed making the imagination the springboard not only of reason itself, but, on the aesthetic side, of feeling, passion, and poetry as well (*Z*, 2133–34). And poetry is the ultimate form of knowledge.

Kant stressed this productive nature of the imagination, putting the faculty of forming images, verbal or otherwise, at the service of the cognitive powers of the mind. Along analogous though not identical lines, Leopardi refused to link fancy, or invention, with imagination (*Z*, 257–58). So did Coleridge, in the *Biographia Literaria*, who instead linked fancy to a mere mode of memory, stimulating only an awareness of superficial resemblances. This is quite different from the imagination which shapes and unifies, underlying true poetry by reaching into the deeper truths. One must be cautious, though, in the Leopardi-Coleridge comparison, for when the latter spoke of the two types of imagination—the primary one (similar to productive imagination) and the secondary one (the source of art)—he made distinctions that the former did without, or expressed differently: "almost all the pleasures of the imagination and of feeling consist of recollection" (*Z, 4415*). Memory, in other words, goes beyond fancy. And if Coleridge saw the imagination significantly as a shaping and modifying power, he also saw fancy less significantly as an aggregative and associative power, something on which Leopardi preferred to put more emphasis. For him, the most glorious attribute of the imagination is that it *is* associative, the identifier of inner relationships, without which the poet's intellectual vision flounders. It leads the poet even beyond Wordsworth's praise of the imagination as the "source of untaught things" or Shakespeare's "forms of things unknown." Imagination, wrote Leopardi, "is the most fecund and marvelous discoverer of the most hidden relationships and harmonies" (*Z, 1836*); the poet, to be a poet, cannot in any way ignore what the imaginative mind fashions by way of rapports. It creates images to illustrate our concept of the present and past and our vision of the future. But—more important—it creates conditions out of present reality that have not been associated with that reality and that presage future conditions not generally supposed to be potential in that reality.

It makes sense that the encompassing nature of the imagination demands, for its proper exercise, a condition of freedom (hence, among other things, what is known as poetic license); the liberty of the imagination is the *sine qua non* of any poetics worthy of its name, the very element, to Leopardi's way of thinking, scientific truth or mathematical rigor tends to kill. Poetry, then, must perforce appeal directly to the imagination, not to reason. A phenomenology of perception is involved. Leopardi lauds the ancient poets for their ability to manipulate indefiniteness, a fundamental device for poetic expression, for they cast their sights beyond normal limits in attempting to reach the extremities of time and space (what else does he himself do in "L'infinito"?). "Not only elegance," he wrote in 1821, "but nobility, grandeur, and all the qualities of poetic language, in fact poetic language itself, consist . . . in an indefinite way of speaking, or in a not well defined way, something always less defined than prosaic or common speech. . . . All that is precisely defined may find its way at times in the language of poetry, since poetry can only be considered as a whole, but properly speaking such language is not poetic" (*Z*, 1900–901). Nothing suggests that the ancients were less capable of employing reason than the moderns, but they knew where to draw the line and allow an aesthetic measure of vagueness to color the idea poetically. In concrete terms, reason alone militates against indefiniteness and is therefore the instrument of disillusion (so common, Leopardi believes, not only in aesthetic matters but also in the civilized state), whereas imagination, a primitive impulse, by knowing how to employ vagueness, cultivates hope, and if its growth is inevitably concomitant with a tragic sense of life (the knowledge that all illusions are, after all, just that, illusions), the resulting melancholy is at least honest and contributes significantly to artistic expressiveness, to the truthful beauty of the poem and to how it is received. Hence, "whoever has never had imagination" can never know the beautiful; whatever we do, in poetry and knowledge, resides in "natural illusions, in the imagi- nation," embracing the entire system of nature and of the universe (*Z*, 1833): "Only the imagination and the heart can feel and therefore know what is poetic; only for them is it possible, and only they can enter and penetrate the great mysteries of life, of destiny, of both the general and particular intentions of nature . . ." (*Z*, 3242– 43).

For this, a controlled kind of poetic vagueness—today we would prefer to say ambiguity—is central, especially in what concerns the unraveling of natural secrets. Leopardi's aim reminds us of what Poe would have called suggestive indefiniteness. Vagueness, like ambiguity, allows for the infinite, and for the reader to discover connections. "It is the duty of poets and writers to cover the nudity of things as much as possible, as it is the duty of scientists to uncover it for us. For this reason, precise words suit the latter and not really the former. . . . For the scientist the most convenient words are those that are most precise and express a bare idea, whereas for the poet and man of letters the best are vague words which express either uncertain ideas or a [simultaneous] number of ideas" (*Z*, 1226). A precise language like French, for instance, despite its reputation, is not deemed poetically good by Leopardi; its exactness gives it a dullness and uniformity that erases any distinction between prose and poetry: "its poetic style is not distinct from its prose style [and] it has really no poetic language as such" (*Z*, 373). Italian, on the other hand, possesses such a distinction, and therefore is, Leopardi believed, "of all the illustrious modern languages, the one most distinct from and the least dominated by usage, especially today . . ." (*Z*, 3749). Reminiscent of Hume's "Of Simplicity and Refinement in Writing," Leopardi's ideas also revolve around the notion of simplicity, an important "device" in his poetry, and the difference between Italian simplicity and French naiveté (*Z*, 1415–20). The basic consideration, however, encountered more briefly in Coleridge's *Biographia Literaria,* is the question, in the English poet's words, of "modes of expression . . . in a serious prose composition [that] would be disproportionate and heterogeneous in metrical poetry." Leopardi expounds:

The poetic style and language of an already formed literature . . . distinguish themselves from prose and pull away from vulgar speech not only through their use of phrases and expressions which, though understood, are no longer used in familiar discourse or in prose—phrases and expressions which are no more than ancient dictions and locutions that have fallen into disuse except in poetry—but also through the different material inflection of the same phrases and expressions still in use in vulgar speech and prose. Hence very often a certain phrase or expression is poetic if pronounced or written in a certain way, and definitely prosaic, indeed totally ignoble and vulgar, if pronounced or written in another way. . . . This way of distinguishing and separating the language of a poem from that of prose and vulgar speech, by inflecting or conditioning differently from normal use a familiar prose phrase and expression, is most frequently adopted in any language that has a distinct poetic idiom of its own—Greek always had one, and Italian now. (*Z*, 3009–10)[14]

What gives Greek and Italian "distinct poetic idioms" is, among other things, their great potential for artistic indistinctiveness, which means that they invite the imagination to exercise its productive powers more freely and more widely.

Melancholy, Antiquity, and Originality

The question of poetic melancholy, for Leopardi, relates to various percepts of his which include, besides the imagination, antiquity and originality. For him, ancient mythology provides a good example of reason and imagination in perfect balance (which does not necessarily imply equal proportions), of the communication of truths not through the limited appeal of abstract logic but through the livelier and broader appeal of the free imagination. And the element of melancholy is central in our time-spanned way of appreciating antiquity and all it produced; chronometric remoteness, we might say, infuses our perception with a sense of vagueness that goes psychologically hand in hand with melancholy. Perhaps this is one reason why, for Leopardi, modern melancholy, unless anchored in memory, tends toward superficiality: "The way the mind conceives the space of many centuries produces an indefinite sensation, the idea of an indeterminate time in which the mind loses itself, and though it realizes that limits exist it does not discern them. . . . This is not the case with things modern, because here the mind cannot lose itself, for it sees clearly the whole extent of time . . ., and the limit" (Z, 1429); melancholy functions less well where things are concrete.

Nonetheless, the moderns make melancholy equate with poetic feeling, lamented Leopardi, now that the ancient poetry of imagination has been superseded by sentiment, by the heart-felt "pathetic" (*patetico*), or what the French romantics call *sensibilité* (Z, 15):

Around Homer's time, what is called heart today was of little consequence, whereas imagination was used very much. Today, on the contrary (and so, too, in the times of Virgil), imagination is usually alloyed, frozen, torpid, extinct, and it is difficult to revive it even in the great poet. . . . If the spirit of cultured people is still capable of any impressions, of any live, sublime, and poetic feeling, this properly belongs to the heart. In fact, today among verse and prose writers the heart has crept in universally and almost completely replaced the imagination; that is what inspires them, that is what they aim to move. . . . Today's poets of imagination reveal labor, effort, and research, and since it was not the imagination that moved them to write verses but they themselves as they wished to express their brain and their *genius*—and thereby created and fabricated an artificial imagination—they seldom or never succeed in resuscitating and rekindling the true imagination, which is already dead in the readers; no good effect is produced this way. (Z, 3154–55)

As in poetic practice there is artificial imagination, so is there also artificial melancholy. Leopardi considered very few poets of the eighteenth and nineteenth centuries, like Alfieri and Foscolo but not Parini, for example, endowed with sufficient passion and feeling to be genuinely melancholy (Z, 2364). He is referring only to poetic melancholy, of course, not to the gloomy pensiveness induced by despondency and depression. The melancholy involved here is pleasurable because it plunges the mind in vague and indeterminate thoughts (*Z*, 170). His romantic contemporaries went awry, he believed, by confusing melancholy with *sensibilité*, when instead, honestly and philosophically conceived, it is "the friend of truth, the light by which to discover it, and the least subject to error" (*Z*, 1691). As Singh points out, poetic melancholy need not spring from calamity or unhappiness, and "is often compatible with the pleasure one finds in the discovery or even the very pursuit of truth, even though one knows about the utter incompatibility between truth and illusions, on which, when all is said and done, a large part of the unhappiness of most people, according to Leopardi, depends." He adds that this partly moral and partly aesthetic pleasure can coexist not so much with the way some romantics like Chateaubriand or Byron expressed it (since so much of theirs is a pathological kind of hedonistic gloom for its own sake), "as [with] the one that arises from the contemplation of one's relation with oneself and with the universe. In a word, the Leopardian concept of poetic melancholy is more philosophical than romantic—a melancholy, as he says regarding the one produced by music, that 'rather than pour itself out loves, on the contrary, to curl itself up, to gather within itself, and thus to confine the spirit as much as possible within itself.' "[15]

But on the other hand, poetic melancholy, according to Leopardi, is only necessary today, and at best can only remain second in importance to the imagination. The pathetic, however pure, cannot dislodge the sublime, just as our emotion *about* things cannot replace the things themselves—the things themselves in their natural, primitive state. In this, Leopardi is close to Giovanni Battista Vico and Schiller, at times Novalis, not to mention Rousseau; he related primitivism to childhood and antiquity, seeing in it a unique and genuine expressiveness that stimulates the imagination through uncorrupted, youthful, and fresh inspiration. The question intimated is that of newness. Poetry is a question of novelty, not of originality; the romantics confused the two, misled by the latter into thinking they were fashioning the former. The quest for originality leads to self-consciousness, which is antinatural. According to Leopardi, the poet needs not to copy nature but to discover it, or rediscover it; novelty consists in this. And this the ancients did better, because they looked at things naturally, not self-consciously. The poet discovers by "sharpening his eyes in order to perceive what we are not used to see, though it exists all around us, [and then by] removing the objects that conceal it, so that by uncovering and unearthing it, removing the mud . . . of civilization and human corruption from it . . .,"[16] he may draw into view a new, though not necessarily original, experience. So is the imagination finally abetted by poetic melancholy, which creates the "light" by which to discover newness.

Newness invites a caveat, for originality frequently results in obfuscation and abstruseness. Leopardi demanded simplicity and naturalness; only clarity, he averred, can be eloquent, and a poem becomes risible if it needs footnotes. Actually, as in philosophy, so in poetry: clarity concerns not so much the object described as the speaker's state of mind: "For the effect of clarity is not really that of making the reader conceive a clear idea of something in itself, but rather a clear idea of the precise state of our mind" (*Z*, 1372). Affectation and sophistry corrupt the eloquence of poetry (*Z*, 100). Indeed, they falsify the imagination itself, not to speak of the purity of memory, and thus cause the poem to degenerate through insincerity.

Sincerity, Enthusiasm, and Wonder

For all his learnedness—and no one would deny that Leopardi was one of the most erudite literary figures of his day—he remained the poet who never waivered in his allegiance to what resists analysis. Learnedness did not produce in him the narrow rationalism that would give illusion and other "irrationalities" short shrift. He did not have the reservations of Coleridge, who feared to become philosophically learned in Berlin because he would then lose his poetic spontaneity. A poet-philosopher, Leopardi retained, through his sense of the appropriateness of language to bridge the object to the expression of it, a continuous sense of wonder in his verses. It has been pointed out that illusions, for him, are similar to William Empson's essential "fantasy-gratifications and a protective attitude toward one's inner life."[17] The delight they produce depends "not only on the qualities of the imitated objects, but beyond that, especially and essentially on the wonder born out of seeing such objects almost transported to where one did not think possible, and represented by things which one would not have thought could represent them, so that an infinite number of objects that by nature do not delight us at all delight us totally when imitated by a poet or painter or other artist, and other objects that delight us in their real state do so now all the more."[18] The rigor of study and the magic of wonder are not incompatible. Indeed, if study acts as a means and not an end, it acts as a source of inspiration—we need only refer to T. S. Eliot—not only for the poet, but for the reader (of whom Leopardi was forever conscious) as well. Since the poetic act must be shared by the receiver, as Leopardi would have it, the poet's imagination re-creates with wonder for the reader's own, personal re-creation. Both move in the context of enthusiasm, and through the language that expresses and communicates, both are involved in the poem's uniqueness, in seeing an object, thinking a concept, or experiencing a feeling in a unique way. The notion of enthusiasm, however, requires a word of caution; the psychology of the creative process is such, for Leopardi, that a sense of wonder cannot be obtained except through a certain distancing by the poet from the motivating event. Few things are more important, in Leopardi's poetics, than to keep the manner of sincerity—honesty in feeling and candor in expressing—in perspective, for excessive enthusiasm invites blatantly the dangers of insincerity or overpersonalization, and in the process the effect of wonder is left behind.

Poetry can express many things, but for Leopardi, in its most serious, philosophical, and intense moments, it deals unavoidably with the theme of human suffering. Only detachment communicates it effectively, lest the universal consciousness of mankind's sorrow be reduced to a merely personal concern. And no one was more aware of such potential "reductionism" than Leopardi, who knew he was "consecrating" [his] pain with poetry."[19] Critics have often used a passage from one of his letters, written at an early age, to underscore his overpersonalization and deny him his philosophical universality: "My travail derives more from the feeling of my own unhappiness than from the certainty of universal and inevitable unhappiness."[20] By so doing, they place him in the category of scores of romantic poets who claimed they suffered, or even cultivated their suffering, in order to arrive at the pseudophilosophical posturing of the sensitive soul afflicted with *Weltschmerz*. They do not see the difference, in Leopardi's case, of someone of whom the universal and the personal blended naturally and instinctively; his "travail" may have stemmed from intimate causes, but these causes were part and parcel of a larger "certainty," one of "inevitable" cosmic magnitude. More to the point is the passage from a later letter: "People have liked to consider my philosophical opinions as the result of my particular suffering, and they insist on attributing to my material circumstances that which I owe only to my understanding. Before I die, I shall protest this gratuitous assumption by the weak and the vulgar, and beg my readers to go about confuting my observations and my reasoning rather than blaming my diseases."[21]

The poet must not wallow in suffering or unhappiness but control it, in order for the poem to achieve artistic form. Leopardi's great diffidence regarding overpersonalization did not mean that he would have praised the so-called impersonalism of Flaubert, whose assiduous constraints over his style in *Madame Bovary* uncovered his presence behind every sentence. The writer, Leopardi believed, cannot conceal his personality, and the more conscious he is of doing so the more he reveals it. Yet the gushy romantic outpourings characteristic of Wilhelm Wackenroder's *Herzensergiessungen eines Kunstliebenden Klosterbruders* (*Outpourings from the Heart of an Art-Loving Cloister Brother*) or of Byron's "bleeding hearts"—*"continuous excesses"* (*Z,* 3823)—are morbid sentiments that cheapen sensibility and falsify intimacy. In other words, they impair sincerity. Leopardi does not indulge in pathetic fallacies whereby his contemporaries with pronounced sentimentalism identified the outer world with their own feelings and thought to distinguish themselves in the process. When he looks at the moon, he sees in it not a pathetic extension of himself but a soul of creation that he can engage in discourse through the magic of illusion, perhaps even a kindred spirit, but never a self-reflexive image. Keats's "negative capability" applies, the quality that enables the artist to avoid making the poem the expression of his personality. If the style is the man, as Buffon averred, in this sense, too, Leopardi is not a romantic. Indeed, he always showed how his lot *differed* from that of the world around him. And he differed from his fellow poets in his high degree of emotional control, his shunning of effusiveness, which always tends toward insincerity. Thus, whatever the subject, traditional or contemporary, the poet is able to present his essential (private as contrasted with social) personality, that is, his individuality.

To express enthusiasm and create wonder thereby does not demand that the poet escape inside himself; rather, when filtered through the control of sincerity, it demands a blending of the personal with the universal. Such control is achieved through language, of course, and Leopardi fashions his langauge at a distance, after the heat and fury of the initial excitement. If poetry was for Wordsworth a form of emotion recalled in tranquillity, so it was, too, for Leopardi:

In the matter of the fine arts . . ., one does not need [to create during] a time of enthusiasm, heat, and a fired imagination. In fact, such a time harms. One needs a time of intensity, but of tranquil intensity, a time of real genius rather than of real enthusiasm . . ., an impression of past or future or habitual enthusiasm rather than its actual presence—let us say its twilight rather than its high noon. Often the most suitable moment is the one which follows an excitement or an experienced emotion when the mind swells calmly like a wave after a storm, and recalls the past sensation with pleasure. That is perhaps the aptest time for conceiving an original subject or its original ingredients. And generally we might say that in the fine arts and poetry, demonstrations of enthusiasm, of imagination, and of sensibility are the direct fruit of the author's memory of the excitement rather than of the excitement itself. (Z, 258–59)

The effect of memory is crucial. One can only poetize in recollection, in the wake of spent ardor. To do so enhances candor.

For Leopardi, poetizing, therefore, came down to a question of honesty, of naturalness in the treatment of the subject matter and the avoidance of affectation which touches only on externalities. There are genuine poetic styles that intrinsically have something genuine to express, and superficial—insincere—ones that extrinsically are cultivated for their own sakes. Leopardi never thought in terms of rhetorical techniques or devices; they induce expressive dishonesty. He preferred to believe that the poet's craftsmanship and self-conscious artistry resulted from study and educated training. He studied Virgil, "the *non plus ultra* of poeticalness" (Z, 3719) to fertilize the imagination, and Petrarch, who "makes the heart talk" (Z, 113), for lyrical candor and tenderness. Every poem of his reflects his dictum: "It is not enough that the writer should be master of his own style. It is also necessary that his style should be the master of things; in this do the perfection of art and the excellence of the craftsman consist" (Z, 2611). The poet cannot accomplish this, however, in the absence of sincerity.

Inspiration and the Lyric

Leopardi recognized that, given one's normal inability to sustain emotional intensity—ethical or aesthetic emotion—after distancing especially, inspiration is short-lived. Such is its nature. It stems from an electric concordance between personality and object. From this view of the abbreviated duration of inspiration, he concludes that the epic as a genre is "against the nature of poetry" and not, as for Keats, a test of invention. Leopardi emphasizes the "impetus" or élan of the poetic act, which cannot be prolonged without weariness—something even Virgil showed when he got to the last six books of the *Aeneid,* without "the impetus of the soul" (Z, 4356).[22] What emerges, then, as the highest form of poetry is the lyric, because it coincides most intimately with the very nature and timing of poetic inspiration: "What is not of itself authentically lyrical in poetry was not much esteemed in Leopardi's view. In a way, therefore, Leopardi may be considered to be the spiritual father *malgré lui* (since in his own poetry he is something quite different) of what is termed 'pure' poetry."[23] René Wellek comments that Leopardi's "poetry is conceived in a flash of inspiration lasting two minutes, but even the shortest poem takes two or three weeks to elaborate and revise. Yet without inspiration he could not have written ["If inspiration does not spring in me by itself"] 'Water could sooner flow from a tree trunk than a single verse from my brain.' Thus, Leopardi says, anticipating Poe, the 'labors of poetry desire by their very nature to be short.' "[24]

Wellek also finds in Leopardi's *Zibaldone* "a series of most remarkable pronouncements on literature which should change any superficial first impression of Leopardi's conventionality and neoclassical orthodoxy," the work of a thinker who "asserts more radically than anybody else in contemprary Europe" the cause of the lyric, which Leopardi designates as "the summit of poetry," "true and pure poetry in all its extension," "the eternal and universal kind because first in time."[25] Of all poetic modes, it attracts the most because of its intimacy (a better word, in this case, than subjectivity) or personalism, which, in guarded use, communicates more immediately with the reader. Intimacy, Leopardi understood, draws the reader's attention psychologically as part of the artistic process; one can speak, therefore, of a psycho-aesthetic level for communication between poet and reader. So shaped, the lyric acquires a quality of honesty that cultivates a "receiver's" sensibility; it makes possible his proximity to and concurrence with the poet's response to the world, which, for Leopardi, we know to be synonymous with melancholy. Sensibility and melancholy are inspiration for "a superior capacity for feeling pain" (Z, 2630), and are most adaptable

to the expression of sorrow and suffering, modern man's due for
having lost those "dear and delightful appearances" of yesteryear.
So the Spirit in the *Operette morali* dialogue explains to Tasso.

Memory

Leopardi would have described the use of memory in poetry as
the conceptualization of an image to apprehend something past and
private to him—call it a content of his mind. St. Augustine conceived memory in terms of image; before him, for Aristotle, it was
impression, and after him, for Locke, it turned up as idea. The
terminology matters little. Leopardi's was an inward process that
resuscitated a bygone energy and endowed it with the hues of life.
More often than not, a present object or occurrence provided him
with what Bertrand Russell would identify as a sign, an indication
that refers back to a "remembered" thing or event. For example,
in Leopardi's "Le ricordanze," a poem built around the notion of
memory, the "Bright stars of the Bear" or "the hour's toll [from
the town belfry] borne by the wind" evoke recollections of the many
emotions and hopes, dreams and illusions of his childhood in his
ancestral home. So, too, his observation that "ordinary day follows
the feast" and conjures up the thought of life's caducity, in "La sera
del dì di festa," brings to memory the fame and fate of ancient
Rome, and in "A Silvia" the very factor of memory makes possible
the philosophical consequences of the poet's meditation about the
young lady's passing away and "that period in [her] mortal life when
beauty shone."

The resurgence of the past through the stimulus of something in
the present, known as the "representative" theory of memory, opposes "naive realism," according to which what presents itself *directly*
to the mind is the remembered thing itself, unstimulated by anything in the present. Of the two, "naive realism" obtains far less
often—though it is surely not absent—in Leopardi than the "representative" process. His conceptualizing the image in the context
of what one calls a throwback—which ultimately is what he means
by memory and how he uses it—is not idle reminiscing. Romantic
poets tended to delight in mere reminiscence, really a form of
dreaming—Gérard de Nerval, Clemens Brentano, like later Gustavo
Bécquer[26]—which Leopardi could not accept as a productive mental
activity for poetry. He needed the mind to revive actively perceptions

it once had, to help to shape a perceptual knowledge of the external
world, for memory, Leopardi would insist, is a retention of knowledge, not an acquisition of it. This is important, because if an
image of the past were never retained, the poetic emotion would
not occur.

All this has much to do with sentiment, which, for Leopardi, is
not immediate emotion. Wellek argues that it is reminiscence,
which means memory, the recollection of childhood and the past,
that made him worship antiquity.[27] Childhood and antiquity remain
synonymous in Leopardi's thinking pattern, like symbols of a pre-
history or lost archetypes.[28] To recall a vision is to be inspired. And
a vision is an image recalled, whose interplay with other images,
deriving perhaps also from other poems, generates the language of
poetry:

Remembrances that occasion the beauty of many many images in poetry
not only relate to real objects, but very often they derive even from other
poems, that is to say that many times an image turns out to be pleasing
in a poem because it mirrors remembrances of that same or similar image
encountered in other poems. . . . Perhaps the major number of images
and indefinite sensations that we feel even after childhood for the rest of
our lives are nothing more than a remembrance of childhood; they refer
to it, depend and derive from it, like an influence and a consequence. . . .
Many images . . . make an impression upon us and give us supreme
pleasure not in themselves but because they renew past impressions. . . .
(Z, 1804–5, 516, 4515)

The best poetic images, then, grow out of remembrances; memory
is an imitative virtue, without which no creative talent can develop
(Z, 1383, 1508). Indeed, the act of writing resembles literary recollection, reconstituted by new language and given new form by a
special nexus of images: "It is like one text producing another;
fiction grows out of repetition: the nature of symbolic mechanism
[dispositivo simbolico], as we are equipped to read it today, was already
noticed by Leopardi."[29] The following passage from the Zibaldone
has been taken as anticipatory of the symbolist theory of poetry:[30]
"For the sensitive and imaginative man who lives, as I have lived
a long time, feeling and imagining continuously, the world and its
objects are in a sense double. He will see a tower with his eyes, or
a countryside; with his ears he will hear the sound of a bell; and at
the same time with his imagination he will see another tower,

another countryside, and he will hear another sound. In this second kind of object lie all the beauty and the pleasure of things" (Z, 4418).[31] Again, on the cardinal principle of memory, Leopardi makes this telling biographical statement about idea-sensations in the *Discorso di un italiano intorno alla poesia romantica:*

I remember in my youth having apprehended with my imagination the sensation of a sound so sweet that it is not to be heard in this world; I remember, looking at some shepherds and sheep painted on the ceiling of one of my rooms, having imagined in my fantasy such beauties of pastoral life that, should such a life ever be granted to us, this life would not be an earth but a paradise, the dwelling not of men but of immortals; without fail (reader, do not ascribe what I am about to say to pride) I should believe myself a divine poet if I could bring to life in my writings and make live exactly in others those images I saw and those sensations I felt in my childhood.[32]

Leopardi puts aside metaphysical notions of ideal beauty, scientific notions of objectivity, theoretical notions of rule, and philosophical notions of innateism. These ideas pertain, respectively, to Plato, Locke, Poe, and Baudelaire. In creating superrealities through the use of memory, and in this case induced directly, Leopardi supersedes much of their speculation.

Mimesis

In the Platonic construct, the phenomenal world does not derive from originals but rather resembles or imitates originals, or ideal Forms, and is therefore inferior because it presents itself as an imitation. And Art, which imitates that world, becomes unreliably further removed from Form by being the imitation of an imitation. Leopardi is more Aristotelian in that his universals are immanent— which means that Art is not unreliable for being an imitation. The Aristotelian view obtained in the eighteenth century, making mimesis more or less a reproduction of things as one sees them, a copying of reality. And this, despite St. Augustine's attempt to make mimesis concomitant with an "imitation" of the spiritual world, a world in effect closer to a Platonic vision of the universal. The Renaissance reduced *imitatio* to an artistic representation of nature, but, as Larry Peer has shown (discussing Manzoni),[33] the concept was refined in two directions, with the first of which—

copying—Leopardi would not agree, and with the second of which—re-creating—he might, if, as a principle, it both synthesized reality and fashioned it into a motivator of poetic vision, into a creator of illusion.

If anything, imitation precedes imagination and must not usurp its function. It represents one of "the basic faculties of human intelligence," but it is also a finite experience, having natural limitations imposed by its dependence on actuality; it is "nothing more than minute and exact attention to an object and its parts . . ." (*Z, 1364–65*). This, at least, in its strictest terms. In its poetic application, it is also a selection, arrangement, and presentation, as Aristotle would say, which then allows the imaginative process to work and inspire wonder: for the more "imitation exceeds the limitations it is destined to have, which characterize and *qualify* it, the more it departs from its nature and propriety and diminishes wonder" (*Z, 977*). Hence even in imitating, as we know Chinese painters recognized so well, Leopardi favored the introduction, or selection, of a defective subject: "Because perfection is very rare in all things, those who imitate . . . blend a defect into their imitation, that is, they imitate rather by portraying or choosing a defective individual than a perfect one in order to make imitation more verisimilar and believable . . ." (*Z, 288–89*). Poetic mimesis, then, comes down not to mimicry or copying, certainly, but to verisimilitude and re-creation.

Leopardi's literary theory regarding mimesis did not admit, as it did for Horace and Boileau, the philosophical designation that separated the visual arts (painting and sculpture, in their case), which reproduce the object supposedly as one sees it, from the other arts, like poetry. Poetry is verbal imitation, he believed, in the spirit of *ut pictura poesis,* and as such it—imitation—could not become synonymous with inauthenticity. Of this he thought the romantics guilty, those for whom mimesis was at best an act of discovery but not a personal illumination or a private identification of a truth rendered verisimilarly. Here, Singh's statement obtains: "It is in connection with the imitation of nature that Leopardi makes the psychologically profound statement that 'the most ordinary things, especially when they are also very common, appeal to our thought and imagination much more strongly when they are imitated (in art) than when the are presented in their real form . . . [that] while reading poetry one is better disposed to feel the efficacy of things

than when the things are physically present.' "[34] Good poetry enhances a reader's appropriate disposition.

We know that Leopardi did not link imagination, a superior
creative process, with invention, a superficial one, but invention
has its place, in the context of mimesis, particularly in the way it
interrelates with imitation. Invention stems from imitation: "Man
imitates even while inventing, but in a broader sense; that is, he
imitates inventions with other inventions, and he does not acquire
the inventive faculty except by dint of imitations, and while he
exercises his inventive faculty, he imitates, and this invention is
quite imitative" (Z, 1697–98). Leopardi agrees with the theorist
Gian Vincenzo Gravina who associated poetic imitation with portraiture, referring to the pleasant surprise one has when one sees
the person portrayed more attractive on canvas than in reality; for
in reality we see the person in an ordinary way, while in a portrait
we see the person in an extraordinary way, in a way that sharpens
our seeing and our thinking (Z, 1302–3). Poetry, then, fosters a
fine tuning of the human senses and faculties. For this reason, "man
and the human spirit, his advancement, that of the individual and
of his faculties, manual or intellectual, the development of his dispositions, soul, talent, imagination—all, we might say, is imitation" (Z, 3950). It cultivates not just what we see, but also what
we think and feel; hence it becomes a form of expression. And its
raw material need not be beautiful, for ugliness, deformity, and
pain, if properly imitated (though it is, Leopardi claims, harder to
imitate than to invent), can be made aesthetically acceptable—not
by enhancing the appearance of the ugly, as in Baudelaire, but by
relating it to the sadness of the human condition, which is the basic
verity. Aesthetic beauty implies no advocacy; one should not assume
that any aesthetic representation of ugly actions condones evil.
Though possibly artistically pleasing, such ugliness remains morally
deplorable. But well imitated (meaning if the imitation adheres to
verisimilitude), things like baseness, cruelty, and sordidness—favorite subjects for the various generations of poets following Leopardi's—provide perfectly acceptable material for the work of art:
"Not the Beautiful but the True or the imitation of Nature in any
form is the object of the fine arts. . . . The perfection of a work
of art is not to be judged according to whether it represents the
most beautiful, but according to whether it is the most perfect
imitation of nature." Leopardi further notes that if only the finest

beauty were pursued in the arts, "instead of pleasing us [it] would nauseate us"; even Homer recognized the principle if only by making Achilles "infinitely less beautiful than he could have made him" (Z, 2). What is morally and what is aesthetically beautiful are not the sole objects of imitation. Here again, Leopardi demonstrates his emancipation from traditional values, though he would insist, against the notion of the utility of art, that the function of art is primarily to delight—and perhaps incidentally to instruct, and though he would also agree with Matthew Arnold, as paraphrased by one commentator, that "poetry divorced from morality is poetry divorced from life, inasmuch as the whole of life itself, and not three-fourths of it, is conduct, necessitating the presence and operation of moral criteria for its full and proper education."[35]

If we add these ideas to the previous ingredients of his poetics, we arrive at an extrememly salubrious perspective on Art, one which does much to modify and mollify his philosophical pessimism. For Leopardi, mimesis, in its broadest sense, implies a gathering of the fecund powers of the imagination and inspiration and an interplay of melancholy, sincerity, and memory, most effective when it adheres to verisimilitude, avoids sermonizing, and finds expression through indeterminateness. Vagueness means indeed a form of clarity, of poetic lucidity, ultimately of creative freedom, which enables the mind's eye of the poet, sustained by the other factors, to reach for the infinite, and in the process the poet becomes a seer, the visionary artist whom Arthur Rimbaud will later identify as a *voyant*. We may thus summarize Leopardi's theory of poetry as a sublime mimesis. It forms the counterpart of his metaphilosophy, for it, too, transcends reality, transfiguring reason and sorrow, and by not limiting its own strength and freedom, converts the poetic enterprise into an example of human greatness. "We need Art, and we need it to be studied extensively, especially in our own day" (Z, 20).

At this point, still under the heading of poetics, a glimpse at Leopardi's stance in the matter of the Italian language is in order, inasmuch as he shared an interest in the problem, related poetics to language and language to the life of a nation, spoke liberally of the need for modernity and contemporaneity, and yet denied that poetry "had to be contemporary, that is, adopt the language and ideas and depict the customs, perhaps even the events, of our times" (Z, 2944).

Unlike any number of his contemporaries—poets whose aesthetics still leaned in the direction of classical models and of poetic prescriptions—his guiding principle was liberty, not of the revolutionary variety, as we find expressed defiantly in Hugo's poem, "Réponse à un acte d'accusation" ("Response to an Accusation"), but, in his opinion, a delicate concept which, in language as in politics, needs gentle, not agitated treatment: "For liberty, both among nations and among languages, is good only when enjoyed peacefully, without contrastive actions against it, and legitimately, as a matter of right. But when it is conquered with violence, it is lawlessness, not liberty. *It is in the very nature of things human that after they have reached one extreme they jump over to their opposite, and then jump back to the first, never knowing how to stop in the middle where nature had placed them during their primitive stage, and whither nature alone can redirect them.*" Perhaps it was Leopardi's ability, following his own precepts, to draw new meanings from ordinary words that gave his language, through its own "lawfulness," the poetic luster and the expressive *freedom* of a master stylist.

Leopardi's focus on liberty applies, in relation to language, to the *vexata quaestio* of Italian from the Cinquecento onward: "la questione della lingua," the problem concerning the establishment of an official language, whether it should be a chosen dialect or an idiom independent of any one dialect. Of all his contemporaries, Manzoni looked upon the question with the greatest discernment and concern, not only because for a writer the luster of a work of literature depends on how words are used, but also because for an Italian the linguistic problem became fundamental to the political movement for national unity. Freedom in language could only have ideological implications closely linked with the Risorgimento.

The two debated theories had to do with the desired language's *fiorentinità* (Florentine quality) or *italianità* (Italic quality). In the first instance, was it to be modern Florentine or old Tuscan, the language of the Trecento, and in the second, was it to be what the writers produced by way of a combination of all dialects (an opinion influenced by Dante's *De vulgari eloquentia*)? Then there were the variants of the various positions: Vincenzo Collo Calmeta's claim for the *lingua cortese* (courtly tongue), which Pietro Bembo assumed disapprovingly to mean that of the Roman court in lieu of what he preferred (*Prose della volgar lingua,* 1525), namely, Tuscan of the Trecento—an opinion in turn opposed by Castelvetro. Baldassarre

Castiglione would have been content with the elegant language of aristocratic society, while Machiavelli favored the Florentine of daily living, for which Benedetto Varchi's dialogue *L'Ercolano* could serve as an example. Influenced by his friend Giordani, Leopardi veered away from *fiorentinità* toward Bembo's notion of Trecento Tuscan, a stance ardently proposed by the philologist Antonio Cesari in his *Dissertazione sopra lo stato presente della lingua italiana* (*Dissertation Concerning the Present State of the Italian Language*, 1809). We must beware, however, that Cesari and Bembo were not to Leopardi's liking as writers: "Bembo was a sixteenth century Cesari, and Cesari is a nineteenth century Bembo . . .: no spark of genius, . . . [only] aridity, sterility . . ." (*Z, 4249*). Besides, Cesari espoused too closely the notion of recapturing linguistic purity.

Leopardi's utterances on the subject tended to be more theoretical than practical like Manzoni's. However, he was aware of the realities—for instance, that France, Spain, and England had been nations for some time, and Germany, while yet ununified, was ruled by German-speaking princes, whereas Italy was governed by foreign nationalities, and their political and administrative presence inhibited the formation of a single language while allowing, consequently, considerable autonomy to the dialects. Even Manzoni wrote his early version (1823) of *I promessi sposi* in Lombard before setting the telling example of "rinsing his clothes in the Arno" and revamping the novel (republished in 1840, hence after Leopardi's death) in the more literary Tuscan which was ultimately to become the official language of the peninsula. During Leopardi's years, Italian did not possess expressive means, especially for romanticism's mystical and sensual thematics, comparable with those of French, German, and English. It was not a spiritual organism, as it were, that could handle unconventional material (romantic, more popular motifs, as compared with classical, more exclusive themes) without a poet's feeling discomfort. A national language and a common literary tradition were needed to mediate between the aristocratic and the popular. Both Manzoni and Leopardi recognized this. The elitist nature of Italian literature needed modification in a direction of contemporariness, of encompassing social realities along with cultural values, and this in turn required a freer and more individualized experience of those realities and values.

But Leopardi was more at home on the philological level of the problem. For him, the history of language is the history of the human mind (Z, 2591), and language reflects "the total image and history of the character of the nation that speaks it" (Z, 2847). A language that is free, that is, not codified by strict laws and not subject to academic rigidities or overly conservative qualms of purity, acquires a richness and a quality consistent with the temper of the people. And "liberty, a language's most beautiful and useful merit" (Z, 1954), functions more favorably in Italian than in other modern languages because it is anchored in a perfected and long elaborated base—"matured institutions," as Leopardi called them, that date back to Dante's time. Dante's Italian is our own, while other European languages are much younger, having evolved relatively recently from other languages called Old French, Old English, Middle High German, medieval Spanish, and the like. Only because of its "perfection" (in the classical sense of *per-fectus*) can Italian give evidence of the fresh vitality and sound novelty required by modern expression: "Originality and liberty coexist in Italian" (Z, 1955). Those who conservatively seek "a language's purity, character, and laws" are not "free" artists; rather they are the "slaves" (Z, 704) of a constricting concept. Indeed, only the liberal concept produces most of a language's "richness," for liberty "is the surest . . . safeguard of the [true] pureness of any idiom" (Z, 1046–47). And language freely shaped exists in conformity with the life of a nation (Z, 3863–64).

Eventually, Tuscan, as learned Florentine, established itself, not totally in the sense of Manzoni's "Arno rinsing," but not too far from it either. Graziadio Isaia Ascoli's *Archivio glottologico italiano* (*Italian Philological Archives*), published in 1873, would not have displeased Leopardi, for it implied a literary language that leaned heavily toward Florentine but which absorbed the influences of many Italian regions and separate Italic cultures. Like most of his contemporaries, Leopardi understood the need of a single language as preferable to a transcending combination of spoken dialects, and Tuscan, he felt (like Manzoni), had the literary tradition to evolve into the proper linguistic organism claiming both historical definition and development. Throughout, Leopardi remained quite modern, whatever his favorable disposition toward Trecento Tuscan. Usage determines communicability, he insisted, and vocabulary must be augmented in accordance with the times: "With the advancement of knowledge and the successive variations of usages, opinions, ideas, intrinsic and extrinsic circumstances . . ., the words and wealth of a language grow in its daily use, whence they must pass into writing, if language needs to speak to contemporaries . . ." (*Z*, 787). In his usual philological manner, Leopardi saw that new words and locutions evolve whose use no language ought to impede, unless it wishes not to grow and be reduced to impotence or dependence on foreign expression (*Z*, 780–81). At the same time, Leopardi agreed that the establishment of an official language both presupposed and required the existence of a fine (*perfetta*) corpus of literature, in *all* genres, to support it (*Z*, 1057): "No language is ever formed or established unless it is applied to literature" (*Z*, 1037). It is only through writing that a language acquires consistency and universality (*Z*, 1202–3), but at the same time, while a difference between the written and the spoken will—and should—always exist, the gap separating the aristocratic and the popular is reduced by elevating the latter nearer the former: "As the national language influences the writer, so does the written language influence the spoken" (*Z*, 854). Thus Leopardi ennobles the language of the *trecentisti* while injecting the *vexata quaestio* with a spirit of liberalism and modernity.

Chapter Five

The Poetry:
The *Batracomiomachia*
and the *Canti*

Leopardi the poet means the author of the *Canti* more than of the politico-satirical *Paralipomeni della Batracomiomachia* (*The War of the Mice and the Crabs*), which was written after most of the former, but which in no way illustrates his poetics as admirably as the former. The political satire, his longest poem, has nothing to do with the songs of solitude that made Leopardi the world-renowned poet he is.

Paralipomeni della Batracomiomachia shows an unusual side of even the ironic humor found in the *Operette morali,* inasmuch as in this continuation ("paralipomena" means "additions" or "things left out") of the homonymous pseudo-Homeric poem which he had translated into Italian three times, *Batrakomiomakía,* the humor is sardonic and sarcastic. He had thought about this work from 1830, when he conceived it in Florence, to the end of his life when he completed it in Naples. As E. G. Caserta points out, other possible models might have been Giambattista Casti's *Animali parlanti* (*Talking Animals*) and even, according to Moroncini, Byron's *Don Juan* or *The Age of Bronze* (if contempt of despotism be the point of comparison),[1] for the inspiration is political—or antipolitical. Indeed, many are the fabulists of the past, from Aesop and Phaedrus onward, who may have turned Leopardi's mind in the direction of talking animals to represent and mock the foibles of human beings in accordance with the near-Machiavellian indictment of mankind found in the *Pensieri:* "the world is a league of scoundrels against gentlemen, of cowards against the generous. . . . You will find only with great effort very few truly great men. . . . [Most are] prey to egoism, mutual envy and hatred. . . . Mankind is divided into two parts . . . , the one that uses abusive insolence, and the one that suffers it. . . . [People] promote [*si cattivano*] and preserve themselves through indifference and disdain. . . . There is nothing rarer than a normally bearable person. . . . They pretend to be what they are not. . . . They use cleverness to cover up their lack of intelligence."[2]

The oversatirical political poem begins where Homer's ended. The Olympian deities, seeing the mice defeated by the crabs, did not wish to see the extermination of the frogs. The mice have lost their king in battle: Ham-Eater (Mangiaprosciutti).[3] In retreat, they suddenly discover that the crabs have vanished, as Looker-Around (Miratondo) informs them. With a new lease on life, they elect a new chief, Chunk-Stealer (Rubatocchi). Alas, Italy's heroes do not compare with the ancient Romans, now that decadence has replaced glory! Anyway, the mice make the liberal patriot and knowledgeable optimist Count Bottom-Licker (Leccafondi) their messenger to the crabs, and his journey to them begins quietly and confidently, though not without reluctance, at night [canto 1]. Similar to Ulysses' experience, of which he is reminded, the count detects a good omen in the song of a bird—a cuckoo. The moon lights up the battlefield and the dead mice strewn across it, then at dawn the enemy camp comes within sight. The Count and his small peace party shake in fear, but their sense of honor pushes them on their way to General Strong-Claw (Brancaforte), to whom Bottom-Licker lays out the mice's liberal plan for self-governement, complete with voting and elections. Strong-Claw will have none of this and throws the legates in jail, chained. Emperor Without-Head (Senzacapo) intervenes and makes the General present the crabs' theory of government, as he arrogantly keeps spitting: the crabs police all the land because they are strong—their shells are hard. In Rat City (Topaia), thirty-thousand crabs will have to be hosted by the mice, given food and double pay, for a period of years: these are the hard terms of peace the Count agrees to take back to his mice for approval within fifteen days. Chancing upon a few frog acquaintances, and learning from them that life under the crabs is very unpleasant, the Count concludes that his fellow mice are better off after all [canto 2].

Back in Rat City, where Chunk-Stealer has taken refuge with his army, all are awaiting the legation's return. The city is underground, discernible only by the stench that issues upward from surface holes. Talk and newspaper communications of patriotism and liberal ideas renew, so that Chunk-Stealer foregoes the notion of absolute rule and listens to the people, thereby promoting another election. A constitutional monarchy is voted, with Bread-Muncher (Rodipane), who as son-in-law of the late monarch Ham-Eater possesses the qualifications, king. Free cheese and mush are distributed to the population [canto 3]. The poet takes time to criticize modern thinkers who think mankind primitive, and theoreticians in general like Lamennais and Joseph-Marie de Maistre who believe man has fallen from a golden age through sin, or like Rousseau who maintain that civilization is the cause of corruption, let alone those who harbor notions about innate ideas. The mice blame themselves, since Nature seems kind. Bread-Muncher is crowned King of Mice (not of Rat City) by his affectionate countrymen; he swears respect for the constitution. Then Bottom-Licker arrives with the crabs' terms, which seem harsh, but a desire for peace makes the Council accept them, and the enemy presidio is established. After a second mission to the fearsome crabs, Bottom-Licker is made Minister of the Interior, in which position he augments public education, industry, and commerce. A series of public buildings reflect the city's prosperity and progress, which makes the ferocious crab Emperor Without-Head, forever suspicious of constitutional regimes, dispatch an envoy to Bread-Muncher's court [canto 4].

Crab ambassador Ironed-Mouth (Boccaferrata) informs the mice that his king cannot tolerate a constitutional monarch and popular participation in government in Rat City. Only an absolute ruler, with legitimate successions, will do; barring this, the Emperor would send his terrible army against the mice. When Bread-Muncher refers the demand to his people, the latter, after long deliberations, reject it, preferring war to defend their liberty. Patriotic orations are delivered and rousing songs are intoned, while Chunk-Stealer, like a modern Achilles, takes command of his people's forces. But once on the battlefield in the presence of the formidable crab army, terror grips the mice (as it had before) and they scatter in panic. Only Chunk-Stealer, valorous and heroic until the end, fights the crabs, slaying many before he succumbs. The poet is moved to extoll his nobility, even if he is only a mouse [canto 5]. The crabs from the presidio help Strong-Claw's forces to seize Rat City, which is then sacked and put under military government. All constitutional guarantees are abrogated, Bottom-Licker is discharged, while Bread-Muncher is retained as puppet king. But he is assisted by an astute advisor, Crooked-Walker (Camminatorto), who promotes a dictatorial and obscurantist politics of closing down schools, factories, theaters, and the like, the result of which drives the mice into secret conspiracy. Again they start feeling bold in their exchange of views, in their newspapers, in their special hymns, and symbolically in their newly adopted mustaches and sideburns. Before long, Count Bottom-Licker is identified as the leader of the reborn patriotism and sent forthwith into exile. He wanders from court to court asking for assistance for his country, and after being disoriented during a storm, in the darkness he makes his way to a splendid palace whose lone master, Daedalus, prefers animals to men but still treats the Count, now reminiscent of Aeneas, to a fine dinner while listening to his story [canto 6].

Daedalus proposes to lead Bottom-Licker in a journey on wings to Atlantis and in a descent into Hell so that the Count might question the souls of dead mice about Rat City and how to liberate it. The problem of the mouse race must find a solution, though the gracious host with all his experience (like Virgil for Dante) cannot be of much further help [canto 7]. Bottom-Licker must go it alone, since Daedalus cannot fit into the descent hole (he will wait for him above ground). Among the souls, the Count recognizes Ham-Eater and Chunk-Stealer, to whom he asks how their race of mice will ever gain freedom. Will the promised foreign assistance help?—at which query the whole underworld bursts out laughing. All the advice he receives is to seek the wisdom of General Taster (Assaggiatore). Back on earth, though disconsolate, he asks Taster about Rat City's future; the General would have nothing to do with politics, but finally, after being implored, is about to answer Bottom-Licker, when the poet announces that the parchments have run out and that he cannot complete the tale [canto 8].

Paralipomeni della Batracomiomachia drew severe criticism, even from Leopardi's friends (Giordani, Vincenzo Gioberti, Giuseppe Giusti, and Gino Capponi); for them, the acid spoofing of the Italian nationalistic efforts of the Risorgimento went too far, especially since their interpretation remained purely and immediately political and they overlooked the underlying broader, philosophical posture of the poet. Indeed, the work enjoyed little and no popularity until this century, thanks to the inquiries of critics like Donadoni, Bacchelli, and Capucci of earlier years, and more recently like Binni, Brilli, and Savarese, through whom it has come to occupy, if not a place in the actual Leopardian canon, at least a position of visibility.[4] Though Gioberti labeled it "a terrible book," he nonetheless also labeled Leopardi's acrid sarcasm "quite justified."[5] Leopardi had in mind not only many persons and events, but also many ideas. On the first level, he mocked the Carbonari secret society, the way Italians went about their conspiracies and revolutions—lots of speeches and chest beating along with lots of ready music and posturing with mustaches and sideburns; he mocked the way they were not overly anxious to engage the foreigner man to man on the field of battle, and the way they talked up an idealistic storm in the squares and cafés. Focusing even more sharply, it is possible to identify, either through the poet's own revelations or through his suggestive touches, the retreat of the Belgians (Flemish) in 1831 or of papal army General Michele Colli in 1797 during the Napoleonic Wars; the supposed European balance of power after Bonaparte's defeat as maintained by the Holy Alliance on principles stipulated by the Congress of Vienna; the battles reflecting the revolutionary movements in Naples in 1820–21 and in Italy and Europe in 1830–31; the Austrians as the vicious and repressive, greedy and brutish crabs; the Italians as the woeful, decent but spineless mice who resort to any form of government in order to eat; Guglielmo Pepe's defeat at Androdoco in the flight of the mice—or even Joachim Murat's 1815 defeat at Tolentino—with some recollection of how the general (Chunk-Stealer) yet led his troops to safety; Bottom-Licker as the naive Prince of Canosa, or Capponi, or the educated daydreaming idealistic visionary Mazzini; Strong-Claw as Marshal Bianchi who vanquished Murat; Crooked-Walker or Ironed-Mouth as the famous (and notorious), above all cunning Austrian statesman Klemens von Metternich; not to forget regents like Without-Head as Emperor Francis I of Austria, and Bread-Muncher or Ham-Eater as Bourbon King Ferdinand of Naples or King Louis-Philippe of France; and, adds Caserta, a part of Daedalus as Jean-Jacques Rousseau personifying the philosophy of history, optimism, and idealism derided by the poet, or if not Rousseau, some German or Hegelian idealist.[6] Taster, of course, would be Leopardi himself, not without a measure of the other part of Daedalus. Had Leopardi lived longer, he might have been heartened by the sustained valor of the "mice" during subsequent decades of the Risorgimento in asserting their ideals for unification with the appearance of many a "Chunk-Stealer" to drive away the oppressive "crabs" once and for all. But by the end of the 1830s, Gioberti's comment about the justification of Leopardi's disdain was not off the mark.

If only on the satirico-grotesque level of historical allegory (the poet would not have used this term), the work appears involved enough. But on the more philosophical level, it gets even more complex. Leopardi's mock epic assails the optimism of social progress and all the idealistic, spiritualistic doctrines that were determining the cultural trends of his day. To him it was ludicrous that such animals should preach progress and utopia—crabs who exterminate mice who exterminate frogs. The misery of the human condition echoes in every corner of the poem, the very misery which drove that noble exception, Chunk-Stealer, into heroism and that only human being in the tale, Daedalus, into solitude, though cognizant of the need for brotherhood. The name "Daedalus," incidentally, meaning master craftsman, leads to conjectures similar to those one has about James Joyce's Stephen Dedalus in *A Portrait of the Artist as a Young Man:* both characters have rejected home, religion, and country, a rejection which the latter emphasizes with his exclamation "Non serviam" to all orthodoxies and conventions, even friendships, from which he flies across the sea into exile on wings on his own making. The palace and the labyrinth rise as well crafted monuments to seclusion.

The satire acquires conviction stylistically in its many fine poetic moments, correctly identified by one commentator in terms of three topics: the usual gift Leopardi had for describing nocturnal settings:

> The whiteness 'mid the greenery and brownish air
> Uncovered here and there more than just one
> Farmer's home, now o'er the fields remote,
> Now o'er the road and o'er the hills;
> And from each the dogs' barking
> Was heard now and then through the silence,
> The gardens permeating, and inside the stables
> Horses hoofing, sounding with their bonds . . .,

the usual polemic against nature, the "capital slaughterer and enemy"; and the unusual "grandiose fresco"[7] of the macabre scene depicting the Hell of the mice:

> In the depths are immense files
> Of seats where . . . / sit the dead

. . . .
No one glances at his neighbor or utters word.
If ever you have seen one of those paintings
That were done before the time of Giotto . . .
Gothic . . .
To look at them inspires fear:
Their faces long and somnolent,
Their limbs leaning and drooping. . . .

This Hell induced Binni to comment, in his not infrequent involuted manner, on Leopardi's tendency toward the macabre (we are reminded of the "Dialogo di Federico Ruysch e delle sue mummie"), "toward the grotesque charged with rationalistic sharpness and with a speechless sense of mortuary horror that lies silently under the domestic and divinely picturesque green turf of the idyll with its brief lives and youthful deaths. The 'terrible' book . . . envelops the most cruel barbs, mitigates the most fearsome light, but it also allows the reader to have an experience that is coherent and vital in itself, instead of offering him isolated and questionable prose like Poe's. . . ."[8]

It is the *Canti,* however, that constitute Leopardi's most outstanding poetic legacy. In them, he exercised what the Spanish-born American philosopher and poet, George Santayana, calls "a steady contemplation of all things in their order and worth," turning "his practised and passionate imagination on the order of all things, or on anything in the light of the whole."[9] Composed mainly during the two decades running from 1816 to 1836, the *Canti,* at their chronological outset, breathe the melancholy air of the turn of the century, pulsating with rhythms of romantic sadness, disheartening tones echoing delusions lurking in th depths of the soul. With Leopardi, however, the melancholy permeates the whole in a highly personal manner, because it stems from a universal or cosmic pessimism, like an open diapason echoing under the vaults of memory long after the reader has put down the book.

The echoes of sadness come early, before the *Canti,* in the "Appressamento della morte" ("Approach of Death": November–December 1816), four cantos in terza rima expressing life's delusion and ending with the invocation: "Let a slab cover me, and my memory perish." Then from the individual, the doleful notes spread to involve mankind, particularly those "afflicted" with greatness, and these find corroboration in the indifference of nature. The mood is further amplified through the irremediableness of the human condition, emptied of divine succor and filled with concoctions of reason and science, the negators of whatever is beneficial in illusion. Alongside the path of the sad journey lie strewn many illusions (faith, country, love, beauty) which the poet tries at times to revitalize in vain. He then creates dreams—after *luna* (moon), *sogno* (dream) is perhaps the most frequent word in Leopardi's poetic vocabulary—to offset reality's harshness and sustain fantasies like human brotherhood. Here and there, human beings and animals cross the invariably lovely natural settings, but they are all perceived through tints of sorrow, Leopardi's prismatic optic. One critic tends to make the *Canti* consistent with romantic generalities of sorrow and the so-called secrets of the soul, offering subsequent generations the lexicon with which to express these secrets.[10] Not so; no generation could follow in the footsteps of one so poignantly individual, whose lexicon projected an inimitable poetic personality. Some time ago, an earlier critic, Arturo Graf, said something more cogent about the anguish of the "secrets of the soul," noting the composure, clarity, and sobriety of this poetry, remarking on how such anguish could fit the formal mold with such orderliness, never offset by linguistic artificiality or imagistic devices aimed at dazing the reader in the manner of Hugo. In its secrets, the poetry is "intellective and sentimental," never overflowing into Lamartinian sentimentalism, since feeling is intimately bound to idea, expressing, as the romantic philosopher Friedrich Schelling wanted, the infinite in the particular (an aspect of his *Indentitätsphilosophie*, or philosophy of identity), "and being made in large part of remembrance and dream it results in a whole that is concrete, solid, determined, and evident, that contrasts singularly with, say, the drifting, veiled, flourishing, and shining poetry of Shelley."[11] But this "solid" and "evident" poetry has also the tenderness and serenity of an inner meditation.

Too often it has been said that Leopardi handles concept better than image and that his later poetry, more expressedly philosophical, evidences a reduced use of imagery, hence of metaphor. This view is erroneous. It falsely separates content from form and impairs Leopardi's deft use of the particular to attain the infinite. The difference between the earlier and later poetry comes down to a matter of emphasis, the later, "more philosophical" poems merely reflecting more deeply experienced concerns that always underlay his poetic utterance. But images, however causal they might appear, direct the poems. Like a stylized mimesis, they *are* the stuff of his poetry, emotional guides that merge the form and the content. He does not use them profusely, but, in their subtle infrequency, they function, not entirely like T. S. Eliot's objective correlatives (objects that evoke in the reader an emotional response which the poet does not wish to state directly), but as stokers of the imagination in a mutually suggestive process of object/emotion with which both poet and reader are involved. More often than not, he focuses on a single identification, whether a thrush or young lady or moon or broom plant, in order to make the whole poem be contained in the image. The poem through its guiding image, then, becomes a metaphor of Leopardi's experience which by extension reflects on that of all humanity. Each is a song of solitude, which when intensified turns into loneliness—solitude that gives rise to illusions, designs, and hopes which will later seem vain and bitter but which in the meantime allow man "bit by bit to reconstitute himself, recover himself [from his spiritual fatigue and exhaustion], reclaim his measure of flesh and breath . . ." (*Z, 681*).

In Leopardi, images enjoy a gradation of qualities; they are not just particular or universal, but realities expressed in tonal nuances, more often than not "only lightly sketched" (*Z, 2054*). There are images one might describe through their context as temporal ("Ultimo canto di Saffo"), spatial ("Canto notturno d'un pastore errante dell'Asia"), psychological ("Consalvo"), devotional ("Sopra il ritratto di una bella donna"), apparitional—to use a term of De Sanctis— ("La ginestra"), and so on, all kept on the level of strictest simplicity, lest they impair the lyrical quality of the poem. Leopardi remained as removed as possible from even the slightest semblance of allegory, being diffident of the allegorizing tendencies of commentators who have harmed many an author's work through their reductionism: "Whoever sees allegory in a poem . . . sees total allegory—the character of Francesca da Rimini [in Dante's *Divina commedia*] is made allegorical, so is Ugolino, etc., thereby destroying all our interest in the poem; we may be interested in a person we know to be completely invented by the poet . . ., but not in one we see as allegorical, because then the falseness lies . . . in the author's own intention" (*Z, 4365–66*). Allegory does not transform the normally definite significance we give to words; imagery does. Leopardi either uses images consciously (essential images) or they are engendered fortuitously by what a mere combination of words evokes (accidental images). Sometimes it is even difficult to know whether an image, like the moon—a veritable word-symbol in his poetry—was consciously or unconsciously arrived at, for, in its nocturnal setting, as he makes it brighten ephemerally the darkness of human existence or touch it with melancholy, its likeness springs automatically forward with any mention of night or sadness or serenity or darkness. In even this instinctive manner, the word-symbol almost comes to stand for the poem. "An image is not only not dispersed in Leopardi's poetry, but is its condition, an integral part of the whole; remove it, and his poetry will no longer have meaning. The image fits, and it fits in the modern sense: the poet knows how to pick it from the very bosom of reality."[12]

Furthermore, lest his views on vagueness distort matters, it must be emphasized that Leopardi preferred images of vagueness to vague images, more specifically those that spring "live and true" (*Z,* 184) from memory, that are most delightful when they "don childlike hues" (*Z,* 1987), or derive from "everyday or rustic life" (*Z,* 1777–78). "L'infinito," "Le ricordanze," "Il passero solitario," "Il pensiero dominante," "Il sabato del villaggio," and "Canto notturno di un pastore errante dell'Asia" use such images, which do not depend simply on perception; perception always equals the sum of its parts by comparison with true poetic images, which are always, or should be, greater than the sum of their parts. Hence in discussing Virgil Leopardi shows that the reader must be put in a position of supplying what the restrained poet does not say, "color what the poet hints at, discover those distant relationships that he only alludes to" (*Z,* 2055).

But restraint does not necessarily come easily. Leopardi *worked* at his poetry: "To write without laboring at all and without thinking is perfectly all right, and I commend it, but it doesn't work for me, and I can't do it."[13] Claiming to be unlike "others who write verses," Leopardi wrote to a friend, in greater length:

In my lifetime, I have written only very few and brief poems. In writing them, I have not followed anything except inspiration (or frenzy), so that when I settled down I formed the design and the distribution of the whole composition in just two minutes. Once I do this, I usually wait for another moment [of inner vision] to come, and when it does come (which ordinarily does not happen for a few months), I sit down to compose; but this I do so slowly that is isn't possible for me to finish a poem, though a very short one, in fewer than two or three weeks. This is my method. . . .[14]

Perhaps such difficulty resides in the nature of things if one writes philosophical lyrics, like Leopardi, in order to give Italy "a modern and philosophical literature" (Z, 3195), as he aspired to do and for which ultimately he was recognized (as De Sanctis puts it, Leopardi was "the first who has let poetry spring from philosophy, and who, in conformity with our times, has given prominence to the truth").[15]

Ultimately, of course, everything comes down to a matter of style, or more specifically, language (Z, 2907, 3398). Leopardi's language in the *Canti* represents the hallmark of his artistic greatness and the finest illustration of his poetics. He could not have been more conscious of the function of the word, the nucleus of language, the core of style:

How great a part of style is synonymous with language! . . . Word. . . . And one might even say that every language has its own style, or its styles, which one cannot judge . . . unless one is capable of judging perfectly the language itself. . . . (Z, 2797)

Style so conjoined with language is [characteristic] of Spanish and Italian [Leopardi cannot speak in quite the same way of French, German, English, Russian, Dutch, Scandinavian, but he can, of course, of Greek and Latin]. [Still,] in all languages so much of a part of style belongs to the individual language, that one cannot consider one without the other for any author. Magnificence, strength, nobility, elegance, simplicity, naturalness, grace, and variety—all or almost all qualities of style—are so tied to the corresponding qualities of language that in considering them in any piece of writing it is quite difficult to know, distinguish, and determine exactly how much of each relates only to the style and how much relates only to the language. . . . (Z, 3396)

Language is so much a part of style, being so conjoined with it, that one can consider one of them separately from the other only with difficulty. (Z, 2906–07)

Leopardi's style is magnificent because each word is in place. Charles Augustin de Sainte-Beuve early remarked: "In Leopardi . . ., not a single useless word is conceded either to the necessity of rhythm or to the flow of harmony: primitive Greek simplicity does not differ much from what he has managed to retain and which he observes religiously in his form."[16] His language has both scholarly and quotidian naturalness, consistent with his principle that the vocabulary of poetry should be a combination of classical and everyday expression. It also has the capacity to arouse multiple associations in the reader's mind, "a crowd of concomitant ideas" (*Z,* 1705), as he said, generating an extraordinary richness (that is, rich textures of meaning simply expressed) that makes him hard to translate. Ezra Pound, in translating "Sopra il ritratto di una bella donna," resorted to a series of intensifications to hoist the English language onto an expressive level reasonably compatible with the Italian.[17] Leopardi's words, "simple, sensuous, and impassioned,"[18] acquire a personality; his style moves like a voice that filters through his enthusiasms and melancholies with "precise ambiguities" (not vague images), as it were, leaving behind haunting resonances. Rhymes are sparse, but essential and often internal; alliterations few, assonances many; by and large, he wrote only *canzoni* and blank-verse hendecasyllables (along with seven-syllable lines), which he always believed to be more natural for the interplay of images and more open to variational feelings and intensities. "Rapidity and conciseness" augment the desired simultaneity of a "crowd" of sensations designed to "let the soul float on such an abundance of thoughts, of spiritual images and sensations, that it either cannot embrace them all or does not have time to remain idle and deprived of sensations" (*Z,* 2041): this observation of his also fits his style equally in a longer poem like "Il pensiero dominante" as in a shorter one like "Il tramonto della luna." And at all times the stanzas breathe through their irregular lengths, while the rhythms change with the shift in mood: "With the elimination of a predetermined scheme, Leopardi succeeds instead in giving poetry a construction consistent with the nature of his poetic inspiration, because for him, as for all true poets, liberation from the old bonds is not a simple refusal to be constricted; it is rather the lifting up of a new content onto the realm of poetry, and the concomitant creation of a new rhythm in which that content finds its order and measure."[19]

Style, the key to poetic novelty, as he said, does not come easily, and some of his manuscripts (as published by Francesco Moroncini) show endless reworkings; "one can say that the poet did not let one word rest."[20] Moreover, he did not shun borrowing vocabulary from foreign sources; he cultivated both the flavor of classical elegance and that of everyday simplicity and naturalness; he rejected archaisms as "affected, deliberately sought after, farfetched, and labored, [even if often] clear, expressive, beautiful, and useful. . . . I hate archaisms" (Z, 1098–99), yet he accepted words of ancient literary origin to preserve a sense of purity and primitiveness; he did not welcome dialectical locutions; he extolled what he called propriety—that "bold" quality "capable of deviating in its forms and modes from the order and dialectic reason of discourse" (Z, 2426–27) (Leopardi did not like mathematical precision and conformity to universal grammar in language);[21] and he shied away from synonyms for reasons of simplicity and immediacy, for a language wealthy in synonyms is actually weak and impeded by its own incapacity for subtlety. All this put together means, as he himself suggested, that he wanted to be a poet of the heart, and not, like Monti, of the ear alone (Z, 36). Hence the *Canti* emerge as Leopardi's fundamental aesthetic self-portrait.

Before embarking on the *Canti* proper, one should note that Leopardi left several fragments and a number of other poems, some not included in the famous collection. Several early *canti* sometimes precede modern editions (*primi canti*), and several follow (*canti minori*). Among those not entered with the *Canti*, the most often recognized are the following.

"Frammento XXXIX: Spento il diurno raggio in occidente" ("Fragment 39: Spent is the Diurnal Ray in the West": 1816, 1835 edition, terza rima), is a reduction of "Appressamento della morte" describing a woman going to a tryst in the silent moonlight of a beautiful night when a terrible storm prevents her and leaves her petrified, perhaps dead with fright. "Il primo amore" ("The First Love": 1817, terza rima), was written, like "Memorie del primo amore" ("Memories of My First Love"), following the occasion of Gertrude Cassi's brief visit to the homestead in Recanati and describes the poet's first falling in love, the sleepless night prior to the beloved's departure, the hustle and bustle in the house that morning, and his subsequent melancholy and disinterest in pursuing his studies, asking the heavenly spirits to bear witness to his pure love which is nurtured by recollection. And in "Frammento XXXVIII: Io qui vagando al limitare intorno" ("Fragment 38: As I Wander Here About the Threshhold": 1818, terza rima), also inspired by Gertrude's visit, the poet at night invokes a storm so that she will not be able to leave, and high winds to clear his conscience, but the rain calms down and the sun then rises. Then at the end of the collection, one sometimes finds the minor cantos: "Imitazione" ("Imitation": 1818 or 1828, 1835 edition, hendeca-syllables and seven-syllable lines), paraphrasing "La feuille" ("The Leaf") by the French poet Antoine Vincent Arnault and describing a leaf, fallen from its branch and swept by the wind, becoming not a symbol of the self, as for the Frenchman or in Lamartine's "feuille flétrie," but a symbol—more Leopardian—of the destiny of all creatures. "Scherzo" ("Joke": 1828, 1835 edition, hendecasyllables and seven-syllable lines), recounts the poet's early visit by one of the muses who takes him to tour the poetry factory, among whose tools he detects a missing one: the file, which the muse says had worn out and still had to be replaced. "Dal Greco di Simonide" ("From the Greek of Simonides": 1823–24, published in 1827 [as "La speranza"—"The Hope"], then in the 1835 edition) is in the same free-style stanzas as the previous poems and alludes melan-cholically to the rise and fall of human illusions in a paraphrase of the seventh-century B.C. iambic poet Simonides of Samos. Finally, in "Dello stesso" ("Concerning the Same": also 1823–24, 1835 edition), in the same meter, the poet elaborates, though with a finer "file," on the theme of the preceding poem.

As read today, the *Canti* follow his approved arrangement of the poems in the posthumous Florentine edition of 1845, faithfully executed by Ranieri. Traditionally, they have been grouped in more or less chronological categories: the patriotic canzoni, small idylls, and philosophical canzoni, followed by the great idylls, the Aspasia cycle, sepulchral canzoni, and the final *canti*.

The Patriotic Canzoni

Carducci called the two patriotic canzoni ("All'Italia" and "Sopra il monumento di Dante che si preparava in Firenze") together with the philosophical canzone "Ad Angelo Mai" three sisters in patri-otism, "a chorus of historical threnodies weeping for and imprecating against the abject servitude of Italy."[22] He goes on to comment on how antithesis animates them, the contrast between today and the great yesteryear of the ancients, modern ignorance and old valor. No doubt, part of Leopardi's programmatic desire was to create a viable civic poetry, and had he pursued it, he might well have

succeeded. But the type of patriotism required did not fit the ideological profile of a poet of solitude and moonscapes or the temperament of a "Daedalus" who, not unlike his contemporary
Alessandro Manzoni, stood above the political fray of mice and crabs.
Years later, liberals who expected more utterances in this vein were
disappointed. But in the early years, conversations with Giordani
stoked his youthful and justified nationalistic fervor, before his more
mature, pessimistic view of the human condition preempted all
other concerns. "Sopra il monumento di Dante" ("On the Monument
to Dante": Recanati, 1818, eleven seventeen-line stanzas, one thir-
teen-line) aims to shake Italians from their torpor and spur them,
as the monument in preparation at least promises to do (since a
foreigner would not expect the bard's tomb to be located so far from
Florence and from his birthplace), to celebrate their greatness in
today's misery, which Dante would not recognize, because to the
same extent he did not see Italian women in the arms of occupying
soldiers, Italian artwork removed to France, and Italian men die in
the Russian snows. In its own way, through its disconsolate ex-
hortation—for the monument's promise does not inspire confidence—the poem sings "the death of civic and patriotic illusions
of valor . . . , the antithesis of past-present, grandeur and desti-
tution, the two extreme terms between which the history of the
world flows eternally in single national communities."[23]

"All'Italia" ("To Italy": Recanati, 1818, seven twenty-line stanzas) portrays a prostrate and reviled Italy, once so glorious and today
so subjected to foreign masters; her sons, laments the poet, die
fighting on alien ground, unlike the handful of noble Greeks, victors
over the Persians at Thermopylae, who did so for their own land.
The poet Simonides could sing of that deed to posterity and thereby
commingle his own fame with that of the Hellenic heroes. Leopardi,
obviously, cannot. But he engages in passages of high oratory (see
the many interrogations which seem to elevate the poet to the role
of hero) in this poem which betrays the idealistic background of
Petrarch's "Italia mia" ("My Italy") and of Foscolo's "I sepolcri"
("The Sepulchres"). Yet it has a strong personal quality as well.

> Oh my country, I perceive the walls and arches
> And the columns and the images and the lonesome
> Towers of our ancestors,
> But the glory I see not,

I see not the laurel nor the iron
That our ancient fathers bore. And now unarmed
You show a naked brow and naked chest. . . .

Oh wretched he who in a war is downed,
Not for his native shores and for the consort
Dutiful and children dear,
But by another's enemy
For other people, so that dying he cannot exclaim:
Beloved native soil,
The life you gave me hereby I return to you.

These passages from stanzas 1 and 3 suggest a host of antitheses: the monumental city in its material form and the deeply human soldier-citizen, the meaningfulness of the ancient Greek at Thermopylae (like Foscolo's warrior at Marathon) and the absurdity of the modern Italian losing his life for non Italian causes, the former's sensing his contribution to history and the latter's estrangement from his own heroism. Perhaps the sharpest woe is felt by omission rather than by inclusion, namely, by devoting all the poem after the fourth stanza not to Italy but to Greece, as if the poet would rather forget today's bad thought by indulging in an idealized reconstruction of antiquity. Despite poetic irregularities (the confused final image of stars, the children brought to the tombs to see the noble "footprints," and the poet's intercalation of his own desire for glory), Leopardi at age twenty comes through as a poet already formed in the essential matters of style, manner, and expressiveness.

The Small Idylls

Leopardi called these six compositions simply "idylls." By "idyll," as applied to Leopardi in the strictest sense, it meant a poem that does not fall under the category of the longer "canzone" and that the poet composed generally before 1830. As we know them, there are also the "great" idylls, a distinction made originally by De Sanctis for chronological purposes, the "small idylls" dating from 1819 to 1821, and the "great idylls" from 1828 to 1830. But modern critics are not happy with the separation. In any event, the term is more descriptive than generic, and, in Leopardi's case, the verses are characterized by narrative and meditative (not necessarily pastoral) qualities.

"Alla luna" ("To the Moon": Recanati, 1819 or 1820, blank
verse, hendecasyllables) recalls the unhappy time one year before
when the poet contemplated the moon, though the memory of his
suffering pleases him in that youth always entertains enduring feelings of hope ahead: the "welcome recollection of things past, though
they be sad, and though our pain endure!" So Leopardi begins his
poetics of memory. "Il sogno" ("The Dream": Recanati, 1820–21,
blank verse, hendecasyllables) conjures up the dream of his beloved,
whom he believes incorrectly still alive, and when he discovers the
truth and the harshness for youth to have hope cut off, he asks if
his unhappiness ever moved her to pity; he kisses her hand at her
affirmative reply, and as she leaves he awakens weeping. The compassionate woman is like Petrarch's Laura after death, and the theme
of premature departure "in the flower of my years" adumbrates "A
Silvia." In "La vita solitaria" ("The Solitary Life": Recanati, 1821,
four hendecasyllable stanzas), the early moring rain, rising sun, and
fluttering wings of a hen awaken the poet, then during his noontime
sitting by a quiet lake he recalls a disillusionment of love, and
finally he welcomes the moon as it sees him "wander through the
woods and by the verdant banks, mute and solitary, or sit upon the
grass, content enough, if only heart and breath be left for me to
sigh." The idyll stands out for its suggestiveness, largely—and
symbolically—through its sparse and negative observations (not a
leaf, not a wave, not a cricket, not a butterfly, not a movement),
and through its inner harmonies and selectively poetic vocabulary.
There is something of Parini's "La notte" ("Night") in it, but beyond
that, there is Leopardi's own sense and experience of solitude that
engulfs it, "a tranquillizing invitation to death."[24] The "Frammento
XXXVII: Odi, Melisso, io vo' contarti un sogno" ("Fragment 37:
Hear Me, Melisso, I Want to Tell You of a Dream": Recanati,
1819, blank verse hendecasyllables) recounts a dialogue between
Alceta, who has dreamed that the moon has fallen to earth, extin-
guishing itself like a hot coal in water and leaving a niche in the
sky, and Melisso who advises him that only stars "fall" but that the
moon does so only in a dream. The subject is autobiographical, the
language is a bit artificial, but the meter is precisely conceived.

"L'Infinito" ("The Infinite": Recanati, 1819, hendecasyllables,
blank verse).   The setting could not be simpler. "Recall the vision,"
wrote Leopardi, "of a countryside so sharply slipping that at one

point the eye cannot reach the valley, and a long row of trees, whose
distant boundary is lost to sight, either because of the length of the
row or because it too is dipping. . . . A factory, a tower . . .,
seen in such a way as to appear to rise alone above the horizon,
which is out of sight, produces a most effective and sublime contrast
between the finite and the infinite . . ." (*Z, 1430–31*). The hill
is Monte Tabor, near his home town, almost as far from the Apen-
nines to the West as the Adriatic Sea to the East.

> Sempre caro mi fu questo'ermo colle,
> E questa siepe, che da tanta parte
> Dell'ultimo orizzonte il guardo esclude.
> Ma sedendo e mirando, interminati
> Spazi di là da quella, e sovrumani
> Silenzi, e profondissima quiete
> Io nel pensier mi fingo; ove per poco
> Il cor non si spaura. E come il vento
> Odo stormir tra queste piante, io quello
> Infinito silenzio a questa voce
> Vo comparando: e mi sovvien l'eterno,
> E le morti stagioni, e la presente
> E viva, e il suon di lei. Così tra questa
> Immensità s'annega il pensier mio:
> E il naufragar m'è dolce in questo mare.

With due acknowledgment of the dictum of *traduttore traditore,* a
translation runs something like this:

> This lonely knoll was ever dear to me
> and this hedgerow that hides from view
> so large a part of the remote horizon.
> But as I sit and gaze my thought conceives
> interminable spaces lying beyond
> and supernatural silences
> and profoundest calm, until my heart
> almost becomes dismayed. And as I hear
> the wind come rustling through these leaves,
> I find myself comparing to this voice
> that infinite silence: and I recall eternity
> and all the ages that are dead
> and the living present and its sounds. And so

in this immensity my thought is drowned:
and in this sea is foundering sweet to me.

The fifteen-line meditation presents no concrete details. It replaces the impossibility of sight with the freedom of the imagination, in a setting where vision (space) becomes sound (time), and the idea of infinity being both spatial and temporal comes to mean eternity through the image of the sea. This sea represents the flowing and changing of things, a living and dying that leave echoes in the memory. The poem has a rapidity that highlights the poet's depth of feeling and thought, which become our own as readers, since we must infer to complete Leopardi's vision with our private experience. Such succinctness is attained through what might be called four acts of a drama: act 1, the situation (vv. 1–3); act 2, the development (vv. 4–8); act 3, the climax (vv. 9–13); act 4, the denouement (vv. 14–15).

What the physical eye cannot encompass due to the limitations of the finite (and, as we know, for Leopardi the definite was unaesthetic poetically and deadly philosophically), the imagination contemplates, freely roaming far beyond vision into the invisible, into infinity which quickly modulates into eternity. Leopardi works dialectically on the axes of "interminable spaces" (space) and "supernatural silences" (time)—both, to be noted, in the plural, since even here the singular is too "definite"—the latter being potentially ("almost") more frightening than the former, as contemplation of the eye changes to meditation of the mind, a shift from the uneasy sense of a void to the fearsome sense of quiet.

It is in this blending of space and time, with time made audible through the drifting of the wind "through the leaves" (as if passing from nonbeing to being), that the poet's imagination sees history— its unity ("eternity") and its sequences ("ages")—up to "the living present." The past dead seasons and the current active one combine to suggest not only immensity but passage (of the wind, history, time, thought, feeling, life, and hope). Language provides the tool that combines what one critic calls "sublimity of vision and simplicity of statement,"[25] particularly the repeated and lulling conjunction "and" (eleven times) along with the modest demonstratives "this" (six times) and "that" (two times) and the enjambments (*interminati/Spazi* and *sovrumani/Silenzi*). There are, too, accelerations (maximum nine to ten words between punctuations) and pauses (sixteen punctuations, in a total of four sentences) as a part of the poem's breathing pattern, the flow that abets the mood through its rolling rhythm, allowing the reader to be engulfed like the poet, whose "I" floats like a tiny sail on a vast sea. In fact, it diminishes as time and space blend rhythmically to create an experience of sequence (history): the *Io* of verse 7 becomes *io* (lower case) in verse 9, so that foundering is inevitable. It is like discovering "an unexplored region of the mind."[26]

To some, the drama suggests "breathless agony and lingering anguish"[27]—perhaps an overstatement. Still, the poem moves anywhere from a sense of calm meditation and simplicity to the tragedy of human thought to isolation and wonder to metaphysical sorrow. The conclusion can be terrible, if one thinks that "sweet" is immediately associated with the striking word "foundering," but it also follows it (the adjective does not precede the noun), so that losing one's self in the infinite is a relief. Illusion has a positive effect, though it means drowning. The danger for the reader lies in turning this poem into a philosophical speculation, which it is not; it is an idyll, basically a sensation, a self-possessed "flow" of intellectual feelings. Momigliano sees in it a typical Leopardian double plane construction which figures in many of his poems: "In Leopardi's poetry there are always these two planes: the near one of daily matters and the remote one of the feelings with which the poet always sees it: behind the hedge, the infinite. . . . Always a limit on the first plane, and behind it a limitless, desolate space— and at the same time comforting, as in 'L'infinito.' For in this immensity, the tormented person of the poet withdraws or composes himself in a sepulchral serenity."[28] The poem, perhaps his most famous, strikes us not with its depth but with its brevity, through which universal significance is immediately achieved. It is "paradigmatic," moving from the confidential tones of his lyrical "realism" to the equally lyrical but remote tones of a transcending "reality," the melancholy mystery of the world.[29]

"**La sera del dì di festa**" ("The Evening after the Holiday": Recanati, 1820, blank verse hendecasyllables).   Diction makes this poem one of Leopardi's finest. It sings through its inner sounds, its vocalic and consonantal patterns which, combined, produce an aural hypnotic effect that communicates the message as if with a series of musical murmurs. In other words, "sound and rhythm vitalize the meaning":[30]

> Dolce e chiara è la notte e senza vento,
> E queta sovra i tetti e in mezzo agli orti
> Posa la luna, e di lontan rivela
> Serena ogni montagna. O donna mia. . . .

> Soft and clear is the night and windless,
> and the moon lies still above the roofs
> and over the orchards, from afar disclosing
> every peaceful hill. O lady mine. . . .

For example, if we dissect phonically these first four verses, we note rhythmic stresses in the first on *o* (*Dólce*), *a* (*chiára*), and back to *o* (*nótte*)—however open or closed in the phonetic system—followed by unstressed echoes *sénza vénto*, each following the muting effect of two consecutive *en*s in trochaic pattern. The *a/o* pattern continues in verse 2, unstressed and stressed in the words *queta, sovra, mezzo, agli,* and *orti,* along with the murmuring continuum of the other vocalic sound, *e* (seven times in v. 1, five times in v. 2), before the stresses of this vowel (*quéta, tétti, mézzo*) resolve in the imposing *o* (*órti*). In the third verse, we hear the sonic continuation of the *o* and *a* sounds in words like *Posa* and *lontan,* this time in the liquid context of the consonant *l* (*la, luna, lontan, rivela*), whose effect is enhanced—that is, spread—by the purposeful, "moonlit" sound of the single but long vowel, *u,* of *lúna.* And finally, like a distant recall of the original *o/a* pattern, the sounds repeat in double form (*o-o-a-a: ogni montagna*), indeed to the very end of the verse through *O donna mia,* which, while introducing a new thought, echoes phonically the preceding. It would be hard to maintain that this musical scheme is all due to the natural beauty of the Italian language. On the other hand, Leopardi did not calculate all of this on a chart; it is rather the creative artist in him that has an instinctual sense of his own language and that makes a *genuine* poet.

The dimmed semblance of a loved one—naturally unidentified to heighten the quality of vagueness, the *vago,* which, we should not forget, in Italian also and not coincidentally for Leopardi means beauty—and the insensitivity of "almighty ancient nature which fashioned me to suffer" and which favors others more than the poet, hover in the background. Like her, the poet cannot indulge in pleasant fantasies during the calm evening after a holiday. Nature allows his "eyes not to shine except with tears." But the woman, too, is cold; her beauty obscured in this night of tender clarities and peaceful quiet, she lies sleeping in her still room,

> e non ti morde
> Cura nessuna; e già non sai nè pensi
> Quanta piaga m'apristi in mezzo al petto.

> and there no single care
> consumes your rest: and so you neither know nor think
> how sad a wound you opened in my breast.

After an interplay of *n*'s and *m*'s, the thrice sounding heavy labial *p* in a single verse is particularly appropriate to express the poet's distress over things he never enjoyed: love, youth, life.

Leopardi develops an antithesis between the condition of the lady and that of the poet, orienting it in two directions: the progression moves from his agitated waking contrasted with her peaceful slumber to her happy dreams contrasted with his despair. The key verses come in the middle:

> Questo dì fu solenne; or da' trastulli
> Prendi riposo; e forse ti rimembra
> In sogno a quanti oggi piacesti, e quanti
> Piacquero a te: non io, non già ch'io speri,
> Al pensier ti ricorro. Intanto io chieggo
> Quanto a viver mi resti, e qui per terra
> Mi getto, e grido, e fremo. Oh giorni orrendi
> In così verde etate!

> This was a solemn day: now from amusements
> you seek repose: and in a dream perhaps
> You will recall how many hearts you pleased today,
> how many, too, pleased you: I find no place,
> nor can I hope to now, among your thoughts.
> Meanwhile I ask how long a life is left to me,
> and at this point I fling myself aground and groan, and rage.
> O horrid days in years so green!

The poet's mind then rises above his own present sorrow by drawing it into the infinite flux of events. The voice of a returning workman triggers the thought:

> Ahi, per la via
> Odo non lunge il solitario canto
> Dell'artigian, che riede a tarda notte,
> Dopo i sollazzi, al suo povero ostello;
> E fieramente mi stringe il core,
> A pensar come tutto al mondo passa,
> E quasi orma non lascia.

> Alas, not far
> along the road I hear the solitary song
> of the workman returning late at night,
> after recreation, to his poor abode;
> and my heart aches acutely,
> as I think how all in life passes away
> and hardly leaves a trace.

So we enter the second part of the poem, but both parts refer to the holiday, now a reminder of universal caducity. "Even my despair amounts to nothing [*un niente*]," he had just written to Giordani:[31]

> Ecco è fuggito
> Il dì festivo, ed al festivo il giorno
> Volgar succede, e se ne porta il tempo
> Ogni umano accidente.

> And lo, this festal day
> has fled, and ordinary day
> follows the feast, and time carries away
> with it each human deed.

Fleetingness suggests dream; the idyll finds its shape in the feeling of a dream that gradually pulls away and vanishes. At first there is the tangible portrait of the sleeping lady and the violence of the poet's sadness; then comes the more distant image of a workman and a melancholy historical recollection; and finally an even more melancholy boyhood memory, appropriately sinking in the distance, in which the syllables seem to fade and the thought process itself is eclipsed:

> Or dov'è il suono
> Di que' popoli antichi? or dov'è il grido
> De' nostri avi famosi, e il grande impero

Di quella Roma, e l'armi, e il fragorio
Che n'andò per la terra e l'oceano?
Tutto è pace e silenzio, e tutto posa
Il mondo, e più di lor non si ragiona.
Nella mia prima età, quando s'aspetta
Bramosamente il dì festivo, or poscia
Ch'egli era spento, io doloroso, in veglia
Premea le piume; ed alla tarda notte
Un canto che s'udia per li sentieri
Lontanando morire a poco a poco,
Già similmente mi stringeva il core.

              Where is the sound now
of those ancient nations? Now where is the fame
of our glorious ancestors, and that great empire
that was Rome, its arms and all the clamor
it circumfused about the land and sea?
All is peace and stillness, all the world
is rest, and speaks of them no more.
In my boyhood I would await
with anxious breath the holiday, and then
when I found it passed, in woeful mood
I would wake upon my bed; and late at night
a song that crossed the field paths
dying slowly as it dwindled in the distance,
even as this one now, would choke my heart.

One appreciates particularly the effect produced by the long, floating and "departing" present participle "lontanando" ("dwindled in the distance": the Italian is especially effective through its double "an-án") followed by the six short syllables (five with elision), with again a repetition of sounds, "a poco a poco" ("slowly," or "little by little").

Not only do the sections of this poem create their own rhythm—one that progressively fades in the distance—but each section has inner rhythms created by pauses that are occasioned by words like *O, Intanto, Ahi,* and *Ecco,* by profuse punctuation (many colons and semicolons), and by short phrases like *O donna mia, Tu dormi* (repeated twice), *mi disse, non io, e grido, e fremo,* and *io doloroso, in veglia.*

Such a nocturne of sad and enchanting recollection Edward Young would have admired. With "groan and rage," it becomes auto-

contemplation, but since others resemble the poet, his holding up
his own soul for auscultation is like holding up that of a simple
laborer or that of a grand empire as well and bespeaks the bitterness
of the human condition, its melancholy sadness as measured on the
level of modest accomplishment or signal achievement. Hence the
"choking heart." De Robertis finds the poetic line interrupted by
thoughts that mar the "lyrical discourse," whose sorrow "disguises
but does not deepen the lyric sentiment."[32] His comment has all
the right ingredients without hitting the mark, because what he
misses is the psychological truth of the event; more than in the
clarity of daytime occupations, it is in the intimacy of the nocturne
that the philosophical-lyrical mind wanders off in various directions,
set into motion by the impetus of a single incident. A nocturne
proposes its own manner of discourse.

The Philosophical Canzoni

These number seven in all, although two more are usually added
because of thematic similarity. In "Nelle nozze della sorella Paolina"
("For My Sister Paolina's Marriage": Recanati, 1821, seven symmetrical stanzas, hendecasyllables and seven-syllable lines except in
stanza 4), the poet advises his sister and the future mother on the
education of her children, on the centrality of woman in a nation,
on their need to despise corruption and bring up strong offspring,
and uses Virginia who inspired the Romans to rebel against tyranny
as an example of "feminine fate." "A un vincitore nel pallone" ("To
a Victor in a Football Game": Recanati, 1821, five stanzas in a
similar scheme) describes popular acclaim following a football (*pallone*)[33] triumph, hopefully rekindling ancient valor which, though
illusory, is a "happy deceit" and might avert total decadence for
Italy; at another time, the winner would have become famous, but
may he even today look high ("but for yourself lift straight your
mind unto the goal"): our life acquires value only when we expose
it to danger. After all, "all is game on earth, and what we think
as true is not less vain than fiction."[34] "Alla primavera, o delle
favole antiche" ("To Spring, or On Ancient Fables": Recanati, 1822,
five stanzas in a similar scheme) finds the poet, though young, old
with illusions destroyed by truth—illusions of a natural Arcadian
past when nature pulsed with human feelings; but man's laments,
echoed to the gods by Echo, found their way even into the night-

ingale's song, and now that ancient imagination has run dry, may nature give the poet his original flame of hope, if on earth today there exists "not a merciful soul but at least a spectator." Leopardi defends thus the classical beauty of fantasy against modern European romanticism that rebelled against old myths. "Inno ai patriarchi, o de' principii del genere umano" ("Hymn to the Patriarchs, or On the Beginnings of the Human Species": Recanati, 1822, blank verse hendecasyllables, six stanzas) sings of our patriarchal forefathers who, closer to God, did not suffer as much as their descendants, and these, far guiltier, made life hateful: Adam the generator of misadventures, Cain the creator of cities and slavery, Noah a fine man though his progeny transmitted sadness across the waters, Abraham and the joyous announcement regarding Isaac, Jacob and his service to Laban for Rachel's hand—life was content not through fables but through illusions, like today in California, adds the poet, where our desire to know has not yet violated nature and alienated the human species from happiness.[35] Leopardi points to man's corruption extremely far back in history (cf. *Z, 2939–41*), indeed in biblical history,[36] to the origin of the development of reason and knowledge of the world.

One of the two *canti* added to the core of philosophical canzoni is "Alla sua donna" ("To His Lady": Recanati, 1823, five stanzas of hendecasyllables and seven-syllable lines with the final two verses of each rhymed) which addresses the idea of feminine beauty—did she once or will she once live? She will never be a real woman, for our imagination outshines reality; if she did live, the poet would then follow fame and lead a divine life, and though illusions fall her image would awaken his senses, if only he could preserve that image, be it purely mental or otherworldly. This woman, in Leopardi's 1825 footnote, is "celestial and ineffable . . ., *the woman we do not find* . . ., [sought] among Plato's ideas . . . or in the stellar systems. If this canzone should be called amorous, it will still be true that such love can neither cause nor suffer jealousy, because, besides the author, no terrestrial lover will want to make love to a telescope." Thus Leopardi's Platonic *Ewig-Weibliche* or Eternal Feminine, as in the "Dialogo di Torquato Tasso e del suo Genio familiare," exists as a creature of our imagination, impossible—alas—to find as envisioned. There is something stylistically Petrarchan here about Leopardi's manner of idealization. The other *canto* added to the philosophical canzoni, "Al conte Carlo Pepoli"

("To Count Carlo Pepoli": Bologna, 1826, blank verse, hendecasyllables, six stanzas), likens human life to an anguished dream:
"This troubled and travailed sleep we call life . . ." (the opening
lines), sluggish like that of all persons not conscious of pursuing
material need; nature had provided for unhappiness to be forgotten,
and brutish creatures intent only on basic living are less unhappy
than others. Man, who knowing it or not is oppressed by tedium,
must anticipate his death, however he seek distractions through his
activities. Pepoli[37] seeks poetry; may he always safeguard his "dear
imaginings," something the poet feels diminishing in himself (and
for this he will seek [surprisingly for Leopardi] more philosophical
speculation which "though sad has its pleasures") as the desire for
fame has died in him. The *canto* exudes something academically
intellectual, perhaps proper for an epistolary piece written for a
public session of the Accademia dei Felsinei, to which Leopardi had
been invited.

In "Ad Angelo Mai" ("To Angelo Mai": Recanati, 1820, twelve
fifteen-verse stanzas, hendecasyllables, and seven-syllable lines), Leopardi takes his Italian contemporaries to task because of their neglect
of their illustrious past. To his "dead century" he opposes the philological discoveries of Mai: perhaps, he would wish to think, the
gods are still merciful to Italy. But in fact he despairs, harboring
no faith in Italy's future, yet he invokes those "heroes" who lived
and produced before nature lifted the veil of comforting illusions
from reality, before too much knowledge of the truth diminished
man's imagination, before the sole certainty of existence—sorrow—
had not yet been fully disclosed, and before common opinion's
notion of the social and hard sciences had not pushed poetry into
the background: Dante, Petrarch, Columbus, Ariosto, Tasso, and
Alfieri—all (except Alfieri) experienced deep sorrow, notes Leopardi. "Oh famed discoverer," he urges Mai, "go onward, wake the
dead, since the living sleep; arm the extinguished tongues of ancient
heroes, so that in the end this century of mud will either yearn for
life and rise to deed illustrious, or will be shamed."

Perhaps a tone-setter for Leopardi's pessimism, this poem to Mai[38]
presents a happy blend of inspiration and eloquence which Momigliano, however, finds not as fluid as other poems like "Bruto
minore" or "All'Italia" that engage Leopardi more personally and
give him a "clearer voice."[39] Yet the poem has excitement, especially
in the way philology, according to one critic, is transfigured in

order to become an activity for civic regeneration.[40] In this, too, one may find a contradiction: why seek out the great of the past to spark present glory when all is illusion? The answer to such lack of logic was given by De Sanctis some time ago: "Art does not obey abstract logic, just as life does not, and often what is most marvelous in history and art moves farther away from logic. Art has its own logic which derives its criteria not from intellect alone but from the whole soul, as it is at a given moment; therefore art is life and not a concept. Contradiction, which repels the intellect, is the most interesting phenomenon of the human heart, the most poetic part of the story of human passions and imagination. Here there is the same contradiction that existed in the poet's mind, and if there were no contradiction, we would have a piece of cold rhetoric in conventional form, foreign to the soul."[41]

"Bruto minore" ("The Younger Brutus": Recanati, 1821, eight fifteen-verse stanzas, hendecasyllables, and seven-syllable lines) recalls the Roman hero after the battle of Philippi as he ridicules the concept of virtue. The gods, he opines, are not moved by the fate of humans, who accept death with resignation. Leopardi makes the hero claim some victory over such destiny through suicide, which the gods are incapable of understanding. Typically, Leopardi conjectures how nature once had man happy and free, and how reason introduced unhappiness. He asks why the divine injunction against suicide, noticing that animals are not ruled by it, only the sons of Prometheus. Beasts and birds are ignorant of the world's destinies, and the stars indifferent. On the threshold of death, Leopardi's Brutus will not invoke the gods or the stars or posterity; his greatness will not enjoy understanding among men, so let his name and memory, the poem concludes, be dispersed.

Leopardi has the moon rise above waters still stained with the red of fratricidal blood while the hero stands alone in the open countryside littered with cadavers, all suggesting that the poem is less a welcoming of suicide than a lament of isolation. Critics have debated the emphasis, but it would seem, knowing the author's eventual view of suicide, that the stress should fall on disconsolate solitude: "There is nothing more despairing than seeing yourself totally alone, as if cursed by heaven and not loved on earth."[42] Emerging from the battlefield, the protagonist would seem to give the poem a patriotic hue, but in point of fact the underlying lyrical emotion of the individual rising in absolute solitude, locked into his illusion of valor, dominates it. Originally denounced, valor and virtue (*virtù*) are exalted through Brutus's act, in which yielding is less a protest than an overcoming, among other things an overcoming of the oblivion into which the human species has been cast: "Oh fate! Oh foolish race! an abject part of things we are; nor have the blood-stained glebes, nor have the groan-filled caverns paid heed to our woe, nor have the stars through human plight grown pale." Leopardi's "agonism," as it has been called, consists in an active, if finally resigned, acceptance of fate, together with an eloquent protest against the laws of nature.

The last of the philosophical canzoni, "Ultimo canto di Saffo" ("Sappho's Last Song": Recanati, 1822, four sixteen-verse stanzas, hendecasyllables, and seven-syllable lines), portrays the serene night and setting moon that disclose the natural spectacle which once had brought Sappho comfort, but now, because of an adverse destiny, brings only misery. After asking why, and suggesting that no one can understand our lot, that even nature shows hostility, Leopardi has Sappho ask herself what she did before she was born, or what she did as a child, to deserve such unhappiness. All is suffering, externality, she concludes; the virile deeds, music, and poetry of the deformed do not impress anyone. She will die, and with illusions and youth gone, she will descend into the infernal, black night: "Jove did not sprinkle me with honied nectar from his niggard urn."

Leopardi's is a legendary rather than a historical Sappho, as has been pointed out,[43] demonstrating, in his own words, the unhappiness of a delicate, tender, sensitive, noble, and warm soul located in an ugly and young body. "The person with imagination, feeling, and enthusiasm, deprived of physical beauty, is to nature about what a very ardent and sincere lover is to his beloved when his love is not returned . . .; [when he notes that] the thing he admires and loves and feels does not belong to him . . ., his folding into himself is always painful" (Z, 718–19). Like Brutus, Sappho is near suicide, but the tone of the Roman soldier is dramatic, while that of the Greek poetess is elegiac. She dissolves, as it were, into the contemplation of night, a setting in which Leopardi mixes with great lyrical fantasy some of his favorite themes, like nature and the beauty of the world, infelicity and the impossibility of love. "Disease creeps in, old age, the shadow of icy death. Behold, of all she hoped-for palms and sweet delusions, Tartarus remains; and my gallant mind is held by sable night, by the infernal queen, and by the silent shore."

The Great Idylls

As already suggested, the term "idylls" can be debated in this group of seven that includes poems like "A Silvia" and "Canto notturno di un pastore errante dell'Asia." Whatever the importance of the generic or chronological debate, here we separate the "small" from the "great" for purposes of convenience, and also because the later "idylls" show more thematic variety, richness, and complexity. They mark Leopardi's return to writing poetry after a dry period, thanks largely to his Pisan "resurgence." A fitting example is "Il risorgimento" ("The Revival": Pisa, 1828, twenty eight-line stanzas, seven-syllable lines): The poet had all but given up hope of feeling and loving any more, but suddenly ancient images speak to him with renewed freshness—surprising, since nature is deaf to man's desire for felicity, and the unhappy person finds no succor in a generation that does not appreciate noble studies or in women who cannot comfort through love. "The shore, the wood, the hill return with life to me, the spring speaks to my heart, with me the sea converses." Leopardi's renewal, outgrowing his recent aridity ("Who will restore my tears after so much oblivion?"), takes on an unusual meter (for him), the unvarying seven-syllable line he used as a youth, as if in a symbolic attempt, in the new Tyrrhenian climate, to recapture a pristine energy.

"A Silvia" ("To Sylvia": Pisa, 1828, six stanzas, free-style hendecasyllables, and seven-syllable lines). In this famous poem, Leopardi recalls, at a distance of ten years, the death of Teresa Fattorini, the teen-aged daughter of the family coachman (she had died at age twenty-one in 1818). Through her, he has occasion to lament his shattered illusions of youth. The evocation is not circumstantial, however, but lyrical, thus enabling him to proceed from the particular to the universal. The piece blends narration, portrait, and meditation in a special tonality: that of poignant melancholy, which draws from both the serenity and the heartache of his inspiration. The theme is presented in the first stanza:

> Silvia, rimembri ancora
> Quel tempo della tua vita mortale,

Quando beltà splendea
Negli occhi tuoi ridenti e fuggitivi,
E tu, lieta e pensosa, il limitare
Di gioventù salivi?

Sylvia, do you still remember
that period in your mortal life
when beauty shone
through your happy and elusive eyes,
and when, both gay and thoughtful,
you neared the threshold crossing into youth?

Sylvia died as she approached adulthood, concurrently with Leopardi's sharp premonition of his own declining energies and abilities,
he too in the prime of youth. In this sense, Sylvia stands as a symbol
of tragic caducity and loss. Such a theme is not uncommon among
Western poets, especially since Petrarch (cf. his poem "Che debb'io
far" ["What Am I to Do"]), but Leopardi not only endows it with
personal grief but also shapes it architecturally to make the poem's
very structure a conveyer of meaning.

The second stanza portrays Sylvia at her daily chores during "il
maggio odoroso" (fragrant May), enlivening the environment with
her "perpetuo canto" (constant song), and feeling "assai contenta
Di quel vago avvenir che in mente avevi" (happy enough with what
vague future occupied your mind). Thus all elements converge in
a setting of serenity: the blooming Spring, her song, and her reasonably carefree happiness. And in the third stanza, Leopardi shifts
the attention to himself, reacting delectably to her voice "and to
the nimble hand which sped about the patient [laborious] weave,"
thereby creating a spiritual equation, analogous to their youthful
enjoyments, with how he worked in his study on his "sudate carte"
(labored pages). Sylvia's *vago avenir* balances psychologically the
poet's:

Mirava il ciel sereno,
Le vie dorate e gli orti,
E quinci il mar da lungi, e quindi il monte.

I looked at serene skies,
and golden ways and gardens,
and here the distant sea, and there the mountains.

The fourth stanza then becomes pivotal (if the first serves as the introduction, then the fourth is the middle stanza of the subsequent five) in a structural sense, since, of the twelve verses, the first four summarize the preceding stanzas, the central four express the spiritual essence of the poem, and the last four anticipate the last two stanzas:

> Che pensieri soavi,
> Che speranze, che cori, o Silvia mia!
> Quale allor ci apparia
> La vita umana e il fato!
> Quando sovviemmi di cotanta speme,
> Un affetto mi preme
> Acerbo e sconsolato,
> E tornami a doler di mia sventura.
> O natura, o natura,
> Perchè non rendi poi
> Quel che prometti allor? perchè di tanto
> Inganni i figli tuoi?

> What fair thoughts,
> what hopes, what harmonies, my Sylvia!
> How human life and destiny
> appeared to us then!
> When I recall the teeming dreams,
> a passion grips me
> bitter, disconsolate,
> and I again return to mourn my fate.
> Nature, Oh nature,
> why do you never yield
> the things of promise past? why so betray
> your very children?

Appropriately, the first group of verses, looking back, is characterized by exclamation; the middle group, stating the present, is declarative; and the final group, looking ahead, becomes interrogative.

After this point, as the poem progresses, so do Leopardi's lyrical tones: they wax under the increasing emotion of memory, the loss of youth and hope, of love and illusion, and death, reaching a chilling climax in the final verses:

Tu pria che l'erbe inaridisse il verno,
Da chiuso morbo combattuta e vinta,
Perivi, o tenerella. E non vedevi
Il fior degli anni tuoi;
Non ti molceva il core
La dolce lode or delle negre chiome,
Or degli sguardi innamorati e schivi;
Nè teco le compagne ai dì festivi
Ragionavan d'amore.

Anche peria fra poco
La speranza mia dolce: agli anni miei
Anche negaro i fati
La giovanezza. Ahi come,
Come passata sei,
Cara compagna dell'età mia nova,
Mia lacrimata speme!
Questo è il mondo? questi
I diletti, l'amor, l'opre, gli eventi
Onde cotanto ragionammo insieme?
Questa la sorte dell'umane genti?
All'apparir del vero
Tu, misera, cadesti: e con la mano
La fredda morte ed una tomba ignuda
Mostravi di lontano.

Before the winter frosted cold the grass,
besieged and beaten by a strange disease,
you breathed your last, Oh feeble child. You never knew
your years of gentlest flower;
nor did your heart grow soft
at sweet praise of your ebon hair,
or your shy enamoured glances;
nor did your companion girls at holidays
ever talk with you of love.

Even so and soon with me
my sweet hope lay dead: the fates
also denied my years
their youth. Alas, how,
Oh how you have left,
dear companion of my younger life,
my tear-mourned hope!
Is this the world? these

the joys, the love, the deeds, the happenings
which together and so often we discussed?
Is this the lot of humankind?
With truth disclosed,
you sank away, poor girl; and with your hand
you pointed from afar at chilling death
and at a naked tomb.

The poem thrives on its felicitous and suggestive choice of words. [*Tua vita*] *mortale* in verse 2 sets the tone of caducity (except to serve this purpose, Leopardi could have said simply "your life"), followed by eyes that were [*ridenti e*] *fuggitivi*, the latter adjective describing her glances but also containing a meaning of ephemeralness. Similarly, [*lieta e*] *pensosa*, in the first stanza, is full of premonition. Hence the *chiuso morbo* of the penultimate stanza, by now exuding a meaning greater than itself, and its effect on someone *tenerella*, an effective diminutive expressing frailty and innocence, and preparing the cold "truth" of *Tu, misera, cadesti* which follows dramatically a series of questions.

In his poetic remembrance, which commingles with his own sentiments for Sylvia and their many shared hopes and "teeming dreams," Leopardi feels a similar destiny: "the feeling of a common fate, unconscious in her, more powerful and cosmically wide but still inexpressible also in him."[44] A sense of identity binds them, both denied youth and illusion, both children of nature, both deceived, as if dispersed like dead leaves; the history of humanity reflects itself in them.[45] Petronio calls this poem Leopardi's "purest page of poetry."[46] Perhaps, as Croce (who called it his "masterpiece") surmised, the fascination lies in its vagueness—which the critic prefers to call abstractness[47]—the vagueness of a profound melancholy experienced suddenly in sentimental retrospect and penned "in its stanzaic divisions and subdivisions, not with architectural regularity but with the regularity of a song."[48] It is the work of a poet, neither romantic nor classical, who saw in Art not an observation or a reproduction, "not a confession or a venting but a consecration of life."[49] His deep regret does not lead to despair in that it is alleviated by the word, by the transmutation of and escape into Art. He claimed to have found his "heart of yesteryear."[50] But it is a yesteryear of accumulated and chilling meditations: "Coldness, emptiness, and nothingness invade the picture. This is, after all, the reality that constitutes the depth from which the lyrical vision emerged and into which it plunges in the end. And it is this very coldness that helps make the images of life more fascinating and the words of hope and despair richer with chiaroscuro. In this negative limit, those images and words are tempered in a calm light full of sweetness and melancholy."[51]

In "Il passero solitario" ("The Solitary Thrush": Recanati or Florence, 1829–30 or 1830–31, three stanzas, blank verse, hendecasyllables, and seven-syllable lines), Leopardi observes that, throughout the spring day, the solitary thrush sings while other birds frolic in the air, and that, like the thrush, he walks away from the celebrants in the village, leaving behind the joys of love and youth, in the direction of the sunset. At the end of its life, continues the poet, the thrush will not lament its ways, while he, on the contrary, if old age beset him, will "many times look back at them, but quite disconsolate."

Thus the instinct-guided thrush, or sparrow, and the reason-guided poet are companions in solitude and isolation from the hustle and bustle of living. But more than a simple comparison between two living beings, like Petrarch's sonnet to the nightingale (*Canzoniere,* 226), the poem suggests man's universal inclination toward what is apart and alone, in a way—autobiographically—Leopardi's inability to communicate with people, and by extension to cope with life. "Solitude," he wrote, "is the natural state of [most] animals, and probably still of man" (Z, 679). The potential bitterness of the poem is transcended by calm, indeed mellifluous contemplation, the product of a mature artist who may have conceived it around 1819, as some commentators argue, but who shaped it a decade or so later. The lonely bird is a topos in literature, but Leopardi makes it a soulful alter ego in a melancholy elegy that bears all the marks of maturity: "As for me, if I cannot avoid by any means the hateful gate of age, when these eyes before all other hearts shall stand by mute, and the whole world for them seem void, and each day darker and more tedious than the last, what shall I think of this desire? and of these years of mine? and of myself?"

"Le ricordanze" ("Remembrances": Recanati, 1829, seven stanzas in free style [unequal lengths], blank verse hendecasyllables) sees Leopardi returning to Recanati, at which point he remembers how the "bright stars of the Bear" used to kindle dreams at night, and how by day the mountains suggested happiness beyond them. He ignored then, he recalls, how often he would invoke death as deliverance from affectionless suffering, or how he did not expect the malevolent crassness of his townsmen, not to mention a life without love. The pealing of the bell on the city hall used to comfort his midnight fears, even as the "old halls" and the "frescoed walls" had stirred his imagination then when life held some promise. There was, too, the fountain in whose waters he had "thought of ending . . . [his] dreams." Leopardi remembers all of this with tenderness and regret, all these "dulcet illusions," now that he has seen life in its squalid self, and given those recollections, he meditates, even death will not be as sweet. Then he suddenly evokes another image of the past: no one can ever forget the lovely illusions of youth, like those associated with young Nerina (a fictitious name), who was stripped of life when it seemed most promising. She has remained for Leopardi the lamented vision of all that has departed.

Leopardi blends the "then" and the "now" contrapuntally as in a braid. "The farther off remembrance is . . ., the more it elevates, constricts, saddens sweetly . . ." (Z, 1860). A sense of what is old, of another era, permeates the poem, giving memory the cast of eternity. Again in solitude, the past mounts as a spectacle that fills the soul with delectable vagueness and infinity. The Arcadian idylls of Salomon Gessner lend their background of fascination, what Sapegno likens to "pages of a diary"[52]—meaning, among other things, that the present provides them with the living force of life: "Indeed, more than once, we do not know if they proceed from the present or if the present proceeds from them."[53] The introspection concludes with "a vain desire for a still unhappy past," for which remembering is bitter and not remembering impossible. The words "I have been" ring with all the possible finality of the past tense, the consequence of "my mortal state." And with the thought of death, of youth and death interlocked, rises the image of Nerina, an invocation that looms as an apparition that draws the spotlight to her silent infelicity until the conclusion of the poem. More than a vision, however, she is a feeling, evanescent like the poet's desire, yet a tenacious illusion of his "lovely imaginings" that leave his "remembrance" with a sour taste. "Oh Nerina! . . . That time has been. Your days are bygone, my sweet beloved. You have passed . . . and your life was like a dream . . ., and of my every lovely dream and tenderest feeling, of my heart's emotions sad and dear, companion will be bitter memory."

"La quiete dopo la tempesta" ("Quiet After the Storm": Recanati, 1829, three stanzas, blank verse, hendecasyllables, and seven-syllable lines) recounts the town's rhythm that resumes after the storm: the song of birds and "the refrain" of the hen, the artisan's tune, the women bustling after rainwater, and the screeching cart on the highway. Life truly seems welcome, muses the poet, as when one has escaped death: "When else is life as now so welcome and so sweet? When else with so much love does man tend to his work? or resume his tasks? or undertake new plans? when is he less aware of his misfortunes?" Then Leopardi intones pessimistically: this is "bounteous nature's sole gift: the avoidance of sorrow," and pleasure is "relief from pain"; the human race is "blest only when death relieves you from all sorrow."

Not untypically for Leopardi, the poem, idyllic at the outset, becomes an ironic meditation. "The convulsion of the elements and other things that cause the travail and evil of fear in natural or civilized man . . . are in a way necessary for the happiness of the living" (Z, 2601). So before we know it, the idyll yields to a negative philosophical inquiry (note the question marks) that develops ironically as it progresses and ends in bitterness. Lyricism, description, meditation, pessimism—the course is typically Leopardian, a skyscape whose patches of sunlight quickly cloud over. The process creates a myth, "with its volontarily dissimulated organization and style, simple and familiar, so much that it seems impossible that a modern poet created it without a shade of effort, and in the long run with hardly the reflection of a superior smile."[54] Not the least virtue of the poem is its suggestive rhythmic variety. The initial dancelike gait of joy, says Flora, is followed by a much livelier tempo of concerned, emotional excitement.[55] The quiet after the storm produces in its bosom its own storm, the anxiety of living, "seeing lightning, clouds, and winds move to threaten us. Oh beauteous nature, these are then your gifts, and these the pleasures you extend to mortals. For to us relief from pain is pleasure."

In "Il sabato del villaggio" ("Saturday in the Village": Recanati, 1829, three stanzas, blank verse, hendecasyllables, and seven-syllable lines), Leopardi presents a series of images, all of villagers eager to complete their chores before the next day's holiday, a day of rest: the young lady with a bouquet of roses and violets, the old lady spinning at the wheel and recalling her youth, the children playing in the square, the farmer returning from the fields, the carpenter working until dawn. Yet, he considers, the festive expectation will yield only tedium and the sad thought of the continuing "drudgery" of tomorrow, for youth is like Saturday; therefore, let us not be so eager to leave it behind.

Echoes of Virgil and Tasso give this poem an archaic flavor, as do the moralizing hints at the end. While the idea is clear (happiness exists only in our imagination, in our imaginative expectations) and is worked out as in "Quiete dopo la tempesta" (the lyrical moment is superseded by meditation), the subtlety comes in the poem's tone, the gentleness with which it treats a potentially sermonic subject matter, which has made more than one critic view it as a myth: "If it is true that the serene light of the first stanzas reverbrates to light up the last ones, it is also true that the meditative melancholy of the last ones reverberates in turn onto the first ones, giving them depth, elevating the humble peasant idyll almost to the height of a myth or a symbol."[56] And again: "the language [of this poem as of 'Quiete dopo la tempesta'] is pulled back in time in order to create more amenably the atmosphere of a myth."[57] Hence the debated images "maiden" and "frolicsome little boy," along with "the old woman" and "the carpenter," which in the mythical context and with the desired Leopardian vagueness are in no way troublesome, or, for that matter, the "bunch of violets and roses" which, some have observed not without a bit of pedantry, were out of season (for some reason) in May. The details are as "clear" as "the twilight hues . . . beneath the whiteness of the rising moon," as clear for poetic purposes as what Flora calls the poet's "sorrowful tenderness."[58] The poem is, again, a dialectic of clarity and vagueness.

"Canto notturno di un pastore errante dell'Asia" ("Night Song of a Wandering Asian Shepherd": Recanati, 1829–30, blank verse, six long stanzas [143 vv.], hendecasyllables, and seven-syllable lines). The shepherd watches the moon, the "eternal pilgrim," cross the sky as it in turn watches the earth, and asks the sense of the eternal movement and a host of questions related to it: being born, struggling, misery—questions, to be sure, remaining unanswered, of no concern to the sheep. The inspiration for the poem came from an item in the *Journal des Savants* of September 1826 concerning the Khirghiz, a North-Central Asian nomadic tribe,

some of whom "spend the night seated on a rock and looking at
the moon, and improvising rather sad words on equally sad airs"
(Z, 4399). The idea, however, had occupied Leopardi's mind for
some time before 1826; in fact, the poem has been variously referred
to as a lyrical compendium of the poet's anguished thoughts concerning existence, once involving only himself and his fellow creatures, now involving the whole cosmos. His wonder at the universe,
dialogue with the stars, dream of the infinite, unhappiness with
beautiful but indifferent nature, concern with time and eternity,
envy of the unconscious animal state, despair over solitude, over
physical and moral suffering, over transitoriness and insignificance
and precocious death, and over the profound need to find a worthy
goal for life[59]—all these themes blend in one culminating—and
distant—poem in which existence wears a "color of death."[60] The
distant setting provided a way for Leopardi to get out of Recanati
and its immediate memories, that is, to get out of the experienced
present itself, and to travel topographically and geographically far
away into remote open lands where philosophical thought can roam
without any danger of stumbling over known and familiar objects.

Through the stars and the moon, the first stanza stresses visible
eternity, emphasized in the second by the theme of the ephemeralness of all human endeavors. It is the key to Leopardi's speculative
mysticism, hovering between the uncertainty of human existence
and any outward negation of it.

> Che fai tu, luna, in ciel? dimmi, che fai,
> Silenziosa luna?
> Sorgi la sera, e vai,
> Contemplando i deserti; indi ti posi.
> Ancor non sei tu paga
> Di riandare i sempiterni calli?
> Ancor non prendi a schivo, ancor sei vaga
> Di mirar queste valli?
> Somiglia alla tua vita
> La vita del pastore.
>
> Sorge in sul primo albore,
> Move la greggia oltre pel campo, e vede
> Greggi, fontane ed erbe;
> Poi stanco si riposa in su la sera:
> Altro mai non ispera.

Dimmi, o luna: a che vale
Al pastor la sua vita,
La vostra vita a voi? dimmi: ove tende
Questo vagar mio breve,
Il tuo corso immortale?

Vecchierel bianco, infermo,
Mezzo vestitio e scalzo,
Con gravissimo fascio in su le spalle,
Per montagna e per valle,
Per sassi acuti, ed alta rena, e fratte,
Al vento, alla tempesta, e quando avvampa
L'ora, e quando poi gela,
Corre via, corre, anela,
Varca torrenti e stagni,
Cade, risorge, e più s'affretta,
Senza posa o ristoro,
Lacero, sanguinoso; infin ch'arriva
Colà dove la via
E dove il tanto affaticar fu volto:
Abisso orrido, immenso,
Ov'ei precipitando, il tutto obblia.
Vergine luna, tale
È la vita mortale.

What do you do in the sky, Oh moon, tell me
what do you do, Oh silent moon?
You rise in the evenings, and wander,
scanning the wastes; and then you set.
Are you not weary yet
to roam the same eternal ways?
Are you not sated yet, do you yet wish
to gaze upon these vales?
Your life is so much like
the shepherd's life.

He rises in the early dawn,
he moves his flock across the plain, and sees
but flocks and springs and verdant fields;
then tired he rests when evening falls;
he hopes for nothing more.
Tell me, Oh moon: what worth
has life for the shepherd,
your life for you? tell me: what purpose

has my brief drifting,
or your immortal course?

An old man, white-haired infirm,
bare-footed and half-clad,
an aching burden on his shoulders,
over mountains and through valleys,
over sharp rocks, deep sand, and thickets,
through wind and storm, through scorching day
and then through icy cold,
runs on, and runs, and pants,
crosses torrents and marshes,
falls, rises again, and hurries ever faster,
without pause or rest,
mangled, bleeding; when he finally arrives
where his journey
and his heavy toil tended:
a ghastly abyss, immense,
in which he plunges headlong, all forgetting.
O maiden moon, such
is the life of man.

The thought is echoed seventeen verses later, in the third stanza,
with the verses

Se la vita è sventura,
Perchè da noi si dura?
Intatta luna, tale
È lo stato mortale.

If life be misery,
why do we endure it?
Oh virgin moon, such
is our mortal state.

A surrogate for the poet, indeed for any man at any time in
history before the mystery of the universe, the shepherd in his
primitive state knows as little about existence as the poet in his
advanced modern age. Man has always asked himself the ultimate
question, long before he started organizing his thoughts in writing;
he always sensed that life is but an arduous journey toward death,
producing "the sense of a self existing in time and being borne by

time to the . . . immense abyss—nothingness. . . ."[61] As an image, the abyss (death) owes its power through the effect it makes, as an unshaped poetic vision, on the human mind; it offers no comment, of course, on the essence of the phenomenon of death. All whys remain unanswered, and the moon, "giovinetta immortal" (immortal damsel), like the one seen by Brutus, shines on, cold. It is frighteningly silent, though the initial queries are directed at it: *Che fai tu, luna, in ciel?* And beneath it symbolically "an old man, white-haired, infirm, . . . runs on, . . ." The vastness of the contemplation develops in the fourth stanza, divided into two scenes: the spectacle of life seen from the stars, and the spectacle of the stars seen from the earth—an immensity, in other words, pinpointed down here in the remote solitude of Asia, where the dwarfed condition of man is most easily discerned. Russo calls this a "surrealistic transfiguration necessary for a poetic myth,"[62] though we must hasten to add how firmly anchored in reality the whole sense of the poem is. Through a process of interweaving, stanza 1 relates to 4, the stanza where visible eternity (the asters) is fully developed, which in turn prefigures the last. Such interweavings are common in the poem:

> Pur tu, solinga, eterna peregrina,
> Che sì pensosa sei, tu forse intendi
> Questo viver terreno,
> Il patir nostro, il sospirar, che sia;
> Che sia questo morir, questo supremo
> Scolorar del sembiante,
> E perir della terra, e venir meno
> Ad ogni usata, amante compagnia.
> E tu certo comprendi
> Il perchè delle cose, e vedi il frutto
> Del mattin, della sera,
> Del tacito, infinito andar del tempo.
> . . . .
> Mille cose sai tu, mille discopri,
> Che son celate al semplice pastore.
> Spesso quand'io ti miro
> Star così muta in sul deserto piano,
> Che, in suo giro lontano, al ciel confina;
> Ovver con la mia greggia
> Seguirmi viaggiando a mano a mano;

E quando miro in ciel arder le stelle;
Dico fra me pensando:
A che tante facelle?
Che fa l'aria infinita, e quel profondo
Infinito seren? che vuol dir questa
Solitudine immensa? ed io che sono?

And yet, lone, eternal pilgrim,
you who are so pensive understand perhaps,
what is this earthly living,
our sufferings and sighs;
what is this dying,
final paling of the face,
and perishing from earth, fading away
from every old, beloved fellowship.
You must surely be aware
of the why of things, and see the fruit
of morning and of eve,
of the everlasting, silent flow of time,
. . . .
You know and you lay bare a thousand things,
which are still hid from the simple shepherd.
Often when I look to you
resting mute above the desert plain,
whose far horizon borders with the sky;
or when I see you traveling step by step
and following my flock and me;
and when I see the stars flame in the sky
I say within me musing:
why all those glowing torches?
wherefore the boundless air, and that profound
calm infinite? what means
this immense solitude? and what am I?

And nine verses later, a brief echo: "Ma tu per certo,/ Giovinetta immortal, conosci il tutto" (But you, immortal damsel,/ surely have knowledge of the whole). *Io che sono?* marks a sudden return to the self, from the cosmic distance the poet has fixed between himself and the earth, indicating that the individual and totality act correspondingly, as counterparts, joined only superficially by contrast, for it is in the universe primarily that man seeks the mystery of the self. This is the kind of seeming contrast, which turns out to be comparison, that motivates the poem internally. Another is Leopardi's invocation of the moon, supposedly conscious of what goes on, followed by his turning to address the flock of sheep, unconscious of it.

Hence the important words in the poem's long title: *notturno* and *errante,* referring to the moon and the shepherd respectively. Both stress simplicity, through setting and station. We note the simplicity of language, befitting that of a shepherd, or a fable with the overtones of a psalm—more an elegy than an idyll. But more than that, it is the simplicity of the psyche or of the mind that the language registers, stripped of all qualifiers and modifiers, querying, with total genuineness and purposely avoiding the artifice of elegance, the ultimate and baffling problem of being: "What do you do in the sky, Oh moon, tell me . . .," "if life be misery, why do we endure it?," "as for me, my life is pain." The changing rhythms— or changing harmonies—of style produce the haunting musical impression "of an ancient and primitive dirge."[63] The rhythms help underscore the emotional depth of the poet's experience, like a kind of heavy breathing; they intone his painful understanding in the sight of the silently transient and disappearing moon. In K. Kroeber's words, "This process of achieving painfully intensified understanding is the very substance and system of the Leopardian lyric."[64]

In the last stanzas, the poet turns again to the moon and the flock:

> O greggia mia che posi, oh te beata,
> Che la miseria tua, credo, non sai!
> Quanta invidia ti porto!
> Non sol perchè d'affanno
> Quasi libera vai;
> Ch'ogni stento, ogni danno,
> Ogni estremo timor subito scordi;
> Ma più perchè giammai tedio non provi.
> . . . .
> Se tu parlar sapessi, io chiederei:
> Dimmi: perchè giacendo
> A bell'agio, ozioso,
> S'appaga ogni animale;
> Me, s'io giaccio in riposo, il tedio assale?
>
> Forse s'avess'io l'ale
> Da volar su le nubi,

E noverar le stelle ad una ad una,
O come il tuono errar di giogo in giogo,
Più felice sarei, candida luna.
O forse erra dal vero,
Mirando all'altrui sorte, il mio pensiero:
Forse in qual forma, in quale
Stato che sia, dentro covile o cuna,
È funesto a chi nasce il dì natale.

Oh flock of mine at rest, how happy
that you do not know, I think, your misery!
How much I envy you!
Not only that from sorrow
you are almost free;
that you forget at once
each harm, privation, and great fear;
but too that you never experience weariness.
. . . .
If you could answer, I should ask you:
Tell me: why is it
that lying at sweet ease, and idle,
every beast is well contented;
I, if I rest, am seized with spleen?

If I, perhaps, had wings
to soar above the clouds,
and one by one compute the stars,
or like the thunder roam from peak to peak,
I might be happier, my gentle flock,
I might be happier, Oh candid moon.
Or perhaps my thought
strays from the truth, when it observes another's fate:
perhaps whatever form, whatever state
is ours, in cradle or in lair,
the day of birth is black to anything that's born.

This last stanza serves as the *commiato,* or envoy. In retrospect, its ending on *natale* brings together in a single phonic unity all previous stanzas, each of which ends with the same rhyme, *-ale,* just as the poem itself is held together by the word-symbol *luna,* which either shines directly over everything or hides temporarily behind passing clouds. It acts like a magnet, enticing the poet's thoughtful imagination to transcend the limits of its own nature, in terms of a sway of conscience (*noverar le stelle*) and a pull of power (*tuono errar*). This, too, becomes a feature of "intensified understanding."

The Aspasia Cycle

This group of five poems derives its name from Pericles's beautiful and cultured courtesan. Biographically, she is Fanny Targioni-Tozzetti, the Florentine lady Leopardi loved deeply and in whose love he felt deceived. The underlying theme of the cycle, then, is love. "Amore e morte" ("Love and Death": Florence, 1832 or 1833, four stanzas, blank verse, hendecasyllables, and seven-syllable lines) opposes death to the pleasures of love, whose first effect is a languorous wish for death, though we need love's "furious desire" to avert the aridity of life. In the heat of passion, death is often invoked, and many humble people kill themselves for it or are killed by it. But may death not delay in taking the life of him, the poet, who has fought serenely against destiny. Thus Leopardi takes the favorite romantic dyadic theme and turns love into death, both a single reality. Croce identified this love as a ravaging power of the senses, a "sweet and tremendous, elementary force of nature."[65] The reciprocity furnishes an arcane explanation of existence. In "Consalvo" (Florence, 1831–33, seven stanzas, blank verse, hendecasyllables), the protagonist, abandoned on his deathbed, has only Elvira at his side, to whom he had never revealed his love; he does so in this extreme hour and asks for a kiss which, moved, she bestows several times. Consalvo admits to happiness, now that he knows two things: love and early death, and wishing his lady a blissful life, he dies before daybreak. This kind of sentimental, dramatic narrative, on which Leopardi's own poetics looked down, and in which the poet transfers himself into an objectified character, was not Leopardi's forte. Elvira herself appears most beautiful but rather impassive, and her kisses reflect the simple emotion of regret at being in the presence of someone whom she will never see again. But Consalvo's dying words are full of passion, however on the melodramatic side and stylistically unLeopardian: "Oh Elvira, Elvira, Oh happy he, Oh blessed above the mortals, to whom you disclose your smile of love. . . . But my breath and life now fail these words of love; the time is gone, nor is it given me to recollect this day: farewell, Elvira. . . ."

"Il pensiero dominante" ("The Sovereign Thought": Florence,
1831–32 or 1833, fourteen stanzas, blank verse, hendecasyllables,
and seven-syllable lines) refers to the effects of the love passion, to
how the poet's mind is dominated by the thought "like a tower
gigantic and alone in a solitary field." To him it seems impossible
that he had tolerated unhappiness without turning to love, which
thwarts the notion of death and therefore appears noble and disin-
terested. It gives life, he goes on to say, a bearable meaning; like
a dream, it withdraws us from reality and resists death, and the
poet then feels the delight of fantasy pervading his mind. At this
point he asks: what more can he wish but to look into her eyes?
Indeed, "What may I ever ask . . . or ever have more sweet than
thought of you?"

Here Leopardi makes love not death but a "powerful, most kind
sovereign of my innermost mind, a terrible, yet precious gift of
heaven . . ., a source of every other grace, the sole true beauty."
The Platonic ideal of "Alla sua donna" here modulates to moving
passion, sustained from beginning to end not with "sweet and
dreamy" tones[66] but with energetic emphasis. This time Leopardi
throws himself willingly into the arms of illusion without concern
about "the infinite vanity of all things," allowing his imagination
to flow in the tender rhythms of love. It is not directed by an outer
vision—a Sylvia or a Nerina, a moonlit prairie or a volcano—but
by purely inner impulses; hence it communicates not as a dialogue
but as a soliloquy. Nerinas and moonlight, after all, are external
objects of joy, fashioned by fantasy; but an inner sensation, nourished
independently of the external object (like Fanny), enjoys an enduring
splendor because it is an "experience of oneself, revealing oneself to
oneself . . . [so that] in one's eyes life takes on a new aspect . . .
and one feels in its midst, perhaps not happier but . . . stronger
than before. . . ."[67] Hence, along with "Il risorgimento," Leopardi's happiest poem.

"A se stesso" ("To Himself": Florence, 1833 or 1835, sixteen
verses, hendecasyllables, and seven-syllable lines) is his most desperate composition. He urges that the poet's heart be allowed to
rest forever now, after the latest deception of love, all of whose
desires now lie dead: "Bitter and dull is life, nothing more ever;
and the world is mire." The only certainty, Leopardi agonizes, is
death; for himself he has scorn, as for nature, "and the infinite
vanity of all things."

This represents Leopardi at his lowest ebb in the throes of the delusion of love. The poem explodes through the power of condensation into a handful of verses. The style is as tense in its terse imperatives and rapid rhythms as the message, full of aesthetic silences that conjure up a wasteland of emotions, yet vibrant with the energy of angry disillusion. Two or three word sentences, jagged gait, starkly pushing ahead without images, and basically angry exhaustion: this is the personality of the poem. The "poetic corpus is dry, scabrous, robust, beating internally with tight pulsations"[68]— fitting for a poem that finds the poet addressing provokingly his own heart. What emerges from the acid despair is an affirmation of conscience and an autonomous dignity over the "mire" and "vanity" of everything.[69]

Comforting, at least in Leopardian terms, is "Aspasia" (Naples, 1834 or 1835, three stanzas, blank verse, hendecasyllables), a poem alluding to the image of a woman, a domestic mother of incomparable beauty, elegance, and maternal femininity, a "ray divine" that stimulates the feminine ideal in a man in love, a fantasy that exceeds reality. When the man discovers this, Leopardi comments, he blames her unjustly, but she in turn cannot see the noble feelings that feed his delusion. So Aspasia does not know the emotions she has inspired, and now she is dead because his former vision of her is dead, his former divine idea. The enchantment broken, the poet thinks of her in his tedium; "for a life bereft of sweet illusions and of love is like a starless night," but he finds comfort in lying on the grass to smile at "mortal destiny."

At moments sounding like "a polemic against the unununderstanding feminine sex,"[70] the poem confesses Leopardi's mortification at having been a slave to the siren of love, then it rises to reinstate his wounded dignity, and beyond that his philosophy of superiority that smiles at the vanity of things. For reasons such as these, some critics have not acclaimed the poem for its sincerity beyond the tempting beauty of woman and the poet's sense of humiliation. There is something "too logical" about it "to be lyrical."[71] But this is Leopardi's declaration of freedom from the vanity of love as of all other things. Its tenor needs to be intellectual. Aspasia is the symbol—not a living Nerina or Elvira—of a loved woman; she is a thought associating this poem's Platonic love theory with the last two stanzas of "Il pensiero dominante." In this context, there can be no feeling of immediacy or proximity for the sake of "sincerity."

The idea promotes not an emotion of the heart but an emotion of the mind. "For I loved not you but that goddess who lived and now lies buried in my heart." Leopardi can, therefore, view his "shame and scorn" less acridly than in "A se stesso," though the wound is still open as he lies "timid and trembling . . . of my own self deprived" in his sentimental suffering. But the poet-philosopher reasserts his moral dignity: "And though they teem with tedium, after servitude and long infatuation I embrace with joy my judgment and my freedom." The intellect regains its solitude and pride has reason to smile. "And comfort I find, that upon this grass, indolently lying motionless, at sea and land and sky I gaze and smile."

The Sepulchral Canzoni

The last major period of Leopardi's poetic production includes these canzoni and the final *canti,* poems that eschew particular effects in favor of altruistic meditations on his deep-seated concerns over man's destiny, especially over death, which inspire him to compassion and to a benign acceptance of suffering. "Sopra il ritratto di una bella donna, scolpito nel monumento sepolcrale della medesima" ("On the Portrait of a Beautiful Lady, Sculpted on Her Tomb": Naples, 1834–35, four stanzas, blank verse, hendecasyllables, and seven-syllable lines) speaks of how the beauty of human beings is reduced to dust and bones after seemingly promising hope and happy futures. Music gives rise in our soul's infinite emotional imaginings, but a single misplaced note destroys the ecstasy. How, in our frailty, asks Leopardi, do we experience such noble feelings? If there is something noble involved, he continues, why are the finest sentiments destroyed so ignobly by matter and death? Reminiscent of the intellectualizing of "Aspasia," though less lyrically worked out, this poem focuses on life's frailty and caducity, contrasting, one might say, the evanescence of beauty with the permanence of the sepulchral stone: "the semblance of vanished loveliness. . . . Now you are mud and bone—the ignominious wretched sight a stone conceals."

In "Sopra un bassorilievo antico sepolcrale, dove una giovane donna è rappresentata in atto di partire, accommiatandosi dai suoi" ("On an Ancient Sepulchral Bas-Relief, Where a Young Woman Is Represented in the Act of Leaving, Saying Farewell": Naples, 1834–

35, seven stanzas, blank verse, hendecasyllables, and seven-syllable lines), Leopardi hesitates to call the young lady fortunate or unfortunate. Perhaps, he can only surmise, she is happy, but her destiny inspires pity, since she passed away in the flower of her beauty. He asks how nature could bring this upon an innocent person. Yet if death, "a most beautiful young maiden," is a good, why lament it? The queries continue. Nature engenders our illusions and struggles, so why should death appear frightening? If life is tantamount to misfortune, could we still wish a loved one's death, knowing we still suffer from the loss, unless we reunite in the hereafter? The painful fact is that, if nature cared about us, she would not "tear a friend from friendly arms . . ., and killing that one, the other keep alive."

"We weep for the dead," wrote Leopardi in his notebook, "not as dead but as live beings: we lament that person who was alive and dear to us. . . . This misfortune *having befallen* him—this is the cause and subject of our compassion and weeping. As for the present, we lament his memory, not him" (Z, 4278). Again Leopardi meditates sadly on the finality of things human; the common lot of man leaves not even death as the final comforter. A number of the *Operette morali* come to mind, such as the "Dialogo della Natura e di un'anima," "Dialogo della Natura e di un Islandese," and especially "Dialogo di Tristano e di un Amico," as well as other poems like "Il pensiero dominante," "Le ricordanze," "Amore e morte," "Ad Arimane," "Ultimo canto di Saffo," "Il tramonto della luna," "Risorgimento," and especially "La ginestra"—all of which is to suggest the compendious nature of Leopardi's later poetry, however insistent his whole production is on his favorite themes. One hears the concern with human solidarity and the affection for "one's dear ones" with stronger voice, in a counteracting posture to nature's cruelty and human misery: "friend [for] friend, brother [for] brother, child [for] parent, beloved [for] lover."

The Final Canti

This last category, even more arbitrary as a category than the previous ones, betrays disparate moods, ranging from the intellectually philosophical to the lyrically social and the sentimentally meditative. "Palinodia al marchese Gino Capponi" ("Retraction to Marquis Gino Capponi": Naples, 1835, eight stanzas, blank verse, hendecasyllables) ironically presents the poet rectifying his error of having believed life miserable and the present age stupid, for now he has read the newspapers and knows of the coming golden age of machines, business, and progress. But wars, epidemics, political and economic vice, and despotism will continue, regardless of science. Material luxury, rapid travel, and street lighting will increase, enough to make those happy who will partake of the benefits of statistics and gazettes (the sole sources of modern learning). Yet nature will always destroy the works of man, who will still have pain, sickness, old age, and death, despite those who believe that the roads to happiness have been charted. New generations like to destroy yesterday's idols. A friend of Capponi's urged the poet to forget these ills and sing the new age (if he wanted to achieve fame)— at which the poet laughed, but he knows better now. Markets and factories and beards—these help the fatherland, these are the purveyors of felicity. The old and the young will see it all, "and beards wave two spans in length." In this parody of Virgil's "Messianic Eclogue," Leopardi makes a composite portrait (the Greek *palinodia* relates to portraiture) of his pessimistic beliefs in the garb of his contemporaries' optimistic creeds. It is a versification, as it were, of the "Dialogo di Tristano e di un amico." As a poem, it has less merit than it would as a prose dialogue, but its ironic touches often save it from intellectual flatness. The polemic against scientific inventions, machines, progress, newspapers, the activities of the secret republican society of the bearded Carbonari (which recalls the *Paralipomeni della Batrocomiomachia*), and the pretensions of the social sciences—suggesting to today's reader that the world has not changed much—remain noteworthy. The implied characters—not his friend Capponi[72] whom he esteems—are those of hs satire, *I nuovi credenti* (*The New Believers*), who in effect represent society as a whole from which Leopardi feels both excluded and liberated. He can, then, in the best manner of Machiavelli and Alfieri, mock the human intellect which takes itself seriously in inverse proportion to its ignorance.

In "Il tramonto della luna" ("The Setting of the Moon": Torre del Greco, 1836, the last six verses supposedly dictated to Ranieri two hours before dying on 14 June 1837, four stanzas, blank verse, hendecasyllables, and seven-syllable lines), Leopardi sees youth abandoning life and its deceptions the way the moon sets and leaves the world in the dark. On this planet, the philosopher-poet cogitates, man is a stranger, stripped of youth by the gods who granted more time for maturity and old age, in the latter of which all desires remain unsatisfied while troubles multiply. The land, he observes, will not stay long in the dark, for the sun will rise, but man, once his youth has set, will receive no more light, "and for the night which blights our other years, as goal the gods have given us the tomb."

Imaginative suggestions and mythical feelings, images of youth and crepuscular illusions, moonlight and ineluctable destiny—Leopardi's elegy is complete. The cherished principle of vagueness is used most effectively: "As in a lonely night, above the silvered countryside and waters . . ., and distant shadows weave a thousand shifting forms and deceiving objects among the tranquil waves and trees and hills. . . . So youth vanishes. . . . Too mild the law that sentences each living thing to death." As if to mark man's inevitable fate—and if the German historian H. Wilhelm Schulz's testimony is correct about Leopardi's dictation two hours before his death[73]—Leopardi's last poetic word, "tomb" or "burial" (*sepoltura*), rings oppressively, but at the same time that final act of dictation confirms a reverse, positive attitude toward the only true consolation he ever knew: Art.

"La ginestra, o il fiore del deserto" ("The Genista, or The Desert Flower": Torre del Greco, 1836, seven long, uneven stanzas, blank verse, hendecasyllables, and seven-syllable lines; the caption comes from John 3: 19: "And men loved darkness more than light"). Even after appreciating Leopardi's famous *canto,* the English reader will never be able to respond to a translator's "broom" or "broom-plant" the way an Italian responds to the original "*ginestra.*" Perhaps it would be best to forget the word "broom" for this poem and adopt its botanical name "genista," though it smacks of cultural snobism and betrays the imagistic simplicity of the humble plant. However, whatever we call it, the poem it inspired remains one of Leopardi's tragic lyrical masterpieces, an arresting phrasing of the conflict between life and death. When genistas bloom, one can from a distance discern a sea of gold, but up close— Leopardi's optic—they can grow so far apart as to seem solitary. And Leopardi's genista *is* solitary, like a gentle and sweet spirit not only accepting its fate, but while doing so never ceasing to spread

its fragrance about, as far as nature and breezes decree, or as far as
the area where that of a sister plant takes over.

In its broadest outlines, the poem says the following:

> Qui su l'arida schiena
> Del formidabil monte
> Sterminator Vesevo,
> La qual null'altro allegra arbor nè fiore,
> Tuoi cespi solitari intorno spargi,
> Odorata ginestra,
> Contenta dei deserti.

> Here on the arid ridge
> of this exterminator mountain,
> dread Vesuvius,
> gladdened by no other tree or flower,
> you spread around your solitary shrubs,
> sweet-scented genista,
> in desert wastes content.

Under the lava once flourished famous cities, like Pompeii; now
there is only the plant's consoling scent. Leopardi stresses nature's
destructive powers and man's impotence before her; intellectuals
keep praising man's supposed accomplishments, but the poet knows
better. Who are we, he would ask, the products of a rationalistic
Enlightenment, to stand up to the modest grandeur of the humble
flower, and dare invoke the word "progress"? (Manzoni, too, had
derided what Leopardi calls the "magnificent progressive destinies";[74] any really thinking person will always question a social
scientist's optimistic "analysis.")

> Dipinte in queste rive
> Son dell'umana gente
> *Le magnifiche sorti e progressive.*

> Qui mira e qui ti specchia,
> Secol superbo e sciocco,
> Che il calle insino allora
> Dal risorto pensier segnato innanti
> Abbandonasti, e volto addietro i passi,
> Del ritornar ti vanti,
> E procedere chiami.

Depicted on these banks
are humankind's
magnificent progressive destinies.

Gaze here and mirror your image,
Oh proud and mindless age
that did forsake the path
till then marked out by thought revived,
and now with your steps retrograde
you boast of your return
proclaiming it progress.

Nature is *the* enemy, and the poet urges self-defensive brotherhood
and the renunciation of wars. Only he who admits his frailty is
noble:

Uom di povero stato e membra inferme
Che sia dell'alma generoso ed alto,
Non chiama sè nè stima
Ricco d'or nè gagliardo,
E di splendida vita e di tesor mendìco
Lascia parer senza vergogna, e noma
Parlando, apertamente, e di sue cose
Fa stima al vero uguale.
Magnanimo animale
Non credo io già, ma stolto,
Quel che nato a perir, nutrito in pene,
Dice, a goder son fatto,
E di fetido orgoglio
Empie le carte, eccelsi fati e nove
Felicità, quali in ciel tutti ignora,
Non pur quest'orbe, promettendo in terra
A popoli che un'onda
Di mar commosso, un fiato
D'aura maligna, un sotterraneo crollo
Distrugge sì che avanza
A gran pena di lor la rimembranza.
Nobil natura è quella
Che a sollevar s'ardisce
Gli occhi mortali incontra
Al comun fato, e che con franca lingua,
Nulla al ver detraendo,
Confessa il mal che ci fu dato in sorte,

E il basso stato e frale;
Quella che grande e forte
Mostra sè nel soffrir, nè gli odii e l'ire
Fraterne, ancor più gravi
D'ogni altro danno, accresce
Alle miserie sue, l'uomo incolpando
Del suo dolor, ma dà la colpa a quella
Che veramente è rea, che de' mortali
Madre è di parto, e di voler matrigna.

A man of poor estate and feeble body
being of generous and noble soul
supposes not or claims himself
a man of wealth and health,
nor makes among the crowd
a risible display
of splendid life or figure brave;
but beggared of strength and treasure
avows unfeigned and blameless,
rates himself with candor, while he judges
his affairs by giving truth its due.
Great-minded creature
I deem him not, but a fool,
who, born to perish, in sorrow bred,
says: I was made for joy,
and with offensive pride fills many a page
promising grand worldly destinies and new
felicities, in heaven unknown,
much less on earth,
to those who by one wave
of surging sea, one breath
of tainted air, one subterranean shock
so outright are destroyed
as scarse to be by memory recalled.
He is of noble nature
who dares lift up against
our common fate
his mortal eyes, and who with fearless tongue,
while mincing naught of truth,
admits the ills decreed on us
by fate, our frail and wretched state;
who brave and strong
reveals himself in suffering; who will not add

fraternal hate and wrath,
the worst of all things evil,
to his other miseries by pointing blame
for his own grief at man,
but charges it on her alone
so truly guilty, she who is of mortals
mother in birth, step-mother in will.

Nature treats man, who thinks he is so much, like a puny creature—
a disparity that makes Leopardi both laugh and weep:

Sovente in queste rive
Che, desolate, a bruno
Veste il flutto indurato, e par che ondeggi,
Seggo la notte; e su la mesta landa
In purissimo azzurro
Veggo dall'alto fiammeggiar le stelle,
Cui di lontan fa specchio
Il mare, e tutto di scintille in giro
Per lo vòto seren brillare il mondo.
E poi che gli occhi a quelle luci appunto,
Ch'a lor sembrano un punto,
E sono immense, in guisa
Che un punto a petto a lor son terra e mare
Veracemente. . . .
Non so se il riso o la pietà prevale.

Often by night
upon these desolate slopes,
cloaked in mourning hues by the rock-hardened flow
which seems to surge, I sit, and wide over the saddened plain
I see stars
high up above in purest blue effulgent,
mirrored by the ocean
from afar, and all the world
revolve through space serene with brilliant sparks arrayed.
And when I fix my eyes upon those lights
that seem to them a speck,
yet are so vast,
that earth and sea compared with them
are indeed a mere dot. . . .
Laughter or pity, I know not which prevails.

Like an apple which crushes an ant colony, nature's cataclysms destroy in a matter of seconds, and the husbandman is always alert.

Come d'arbor cadendo un picciol pomo,
Cui là nel tardo autunno
Maturità senz'altra forza atterra,
D'un popol di formiche i dolci alberghi,
Cavati in molle gleba
Con gran lavoro, e l'opre
E le ricchezze che adunate a prova
Con lungo affaticar l'assidua gente
Avea provvidamente al tempo estivo,
Schiaccia, diserta e copre
In un punto; così d'alto piombando,
Dall'utero tonante
Scagliata al ciel profondo,
Di ceneri e di pomici e di sassi
Notte e ruina, infusa
Di bollenti ruscelli,
O pel montano fianco
Furiosa tra l'erba
Di liquefatti massi
E di metalli e d'infocata arena
Scendendo immensa piena,
Le cittadi che il mar là su l'estremo
Lido aspergea, confuse
E infranse e ricoperse
In pochi istanti. . . .
E il villanello intento
Ai vigneti, che a stento in questi campi
Nutre la morta zolla e incenerita,
Ancor leva lo sguardo
Sospettoso alla vetta
Fatal, che nulla mai fatta più mite
Ancor siede tremenda, ancor minaccia
A lui strage ed ai figli ed agli averi
Lor poverelli.

As a small apple dropping from a tree,
which in lingering autumn
falls only by its ripeness' force,
crushes, devastates and buries
in an instant all the snug abodes

of a hive of ants, scooped in soft loam
with careful labor, along with the works
and wealth which that industrious tribe
with long travail had garnered
providently through the summer months;
even so, plummeting from on high,
from that thundering womb,
hurled deep against the sky,
a night-black devastation
of cinders, stones and pumice
mixed with boiling streams,
or down the mountain's flank
raging across the grass
the molten mass
the liquid metal and the burning sand
immensely swarming mighty,
overwhelmed and shattered and interred
in just few moments those cities
on yon shore, once washed
by waves of sea. . . .
And still the husbandman,
tending his vineyards that the dead
incinerated clods around those fields can hardly feed,
does raise mistrustful eyes
up to that fatal summit,
which in no wise less ruthless than before
still stands tremendous, threatens still
disaster for himself, his children
and his starveling home.

Tourists visit the unearthed Pompeii while the volcano keeps smoking; nature, obviously, does not heed human affairs. And the genista, too, will succumb to the lava, but it remains far wiser than we, concludes Leopardi, who boast eternity.

> E tu lenta ginestra,
> Che di selve ordorate
> Queste campagne dispogliate adorni,
> Anche tu presto alla crudel possanza
> Soccomberai del sotterraneo foco,
> Che ritornando al loco
> Già noto, stenderà l'avaro lembo
> Su tue molli foreste. E piegherai

Sotto il fascio mortal non renitente
Il tuo capo innocente:
Ma non piegato insino allora indarno
Codardamente supplicando innanzi
Al futuro oppressor; ma non eretto
Con forsennato orgoglio inver le stelle,
Nè sul deserto, dove
E la sede e i natali
Non per voler ma per fortuna avesti;
Ma più saggia, ma tanto
Meno inferma dell'uom, quanto le frali
Tue stirpi non credesti
O dal fato o da te fatte immortali.

And you, pliant genista,
who with your fragrant brushwood
lend adornment to these desolated plains,
you too must soon succumb
to the cruel force of the subjacent fire
which to its wonted haunts
returning will extend its greedy hem
over your tender boscage. And you then will bend
your innocent head
beneath the fatal weight without resistance;
but until then you will not bow
in vain and cowardly beseechingness
before the future oppressor, nor point erect
with overweening pride against the stars,
nor lord above the waste
where birthplace both and home
you found allotted you by chance, not by your will;
but wiser far and so much
less infirm in this than man, you did not think
your fragile stock endowed
by fate or by yourself with immortality.

Leopardi observed the plant from fairly close quarters from the
Villa Ferrigni. He sees Vesuvius as the smoking, destructive power
of nature—not the gentle nature of a genista, but the cruelly indifferent nature of unlimited force against which man is like a
solitary, hapless and hopeless plant. In a universe without God, is
there anything socially to counteract natural adversity except through
the solidarity produced by common suffering? Seeing mankind as

nothing more than a colony of ants in an anthill, easily smashed by a falling apple, Leopardi urges at the very least antiwar behavior and brotherhood against natural disasters; this is his final, humanistic position. His view of Pompeii reminds us spiritually of Foscolo's "I sepolcri." Man's misery lies in himself, in his psychic drives, in his shaping of social civilization, but let us not forget, Leopardi reminds us, that it lies, too, and significantly, in nature, in the eruption of lava rather than in the profusion of blossoms. If we really *think,* this is the only conclusion attainable. Hence those who claim to "think" betray the cause of thinking when expounding optimistic philosophies. To look ahead, real thinking, Leopardi might have said with more confidence later in 1860/1870, led to the Italian "arousal" (Risorgimento) against predatory and murdering foreigners, an arising-uprising that meant freedom from the bonds of domination, no different than from those of thought—for freedom of thought means civic liberty.[75] And this in turn, for Leopardi, spells solidarity. Thus the doomed genista may be beheld in an ennobling and inspiring perspective.

It could be argued that Leopardi's stress on human brotherhood, so unlike the cynicism of the *Pensieri,* appears abruptly in the final phase of his poetic life, but such is not the case; it developed out of his long-felt love for life that his pessimism betrays as well as out of his opposition to the ways of nature, and it stands not as an observation but as an appeal. It is erroneous, however, to see moments of germination in, say, the *Pensieri,* which, according to one critic, contains a concrete social program through his notion of universal human nature.[76] Leopardi, the counter argument goes, is a skeptic who sees the perversity of society as well as the human being who recognizes its potential beauty. Before Freud, Nietzsche, and Michel Foucault, it has been pointed out, Leopardi spoke of a purely horizontal progress of mankind, without ignoring "the generous ones" destined to be "more than men."[77] His affection for man, however, comes through his admiration of simplicity and honesty in all its manifestations (the concept is as much a part of his philosophy of nature as it is of his poetics). The genista stands for faithfulness to one's destiny, counteracting in its solitary humility the violence of the volcano's eruption. If mankind takes note of this, it might then unite in brotherhood.

These are implications of the poem, assessed through its imagery and "clarity of vagueness." Its meanings gurgle, like the waters the

peasant observes in his well. They reflect, in their alternation between the philosophical and the lyrical, the plight of the presump-
tuous intellect, scourged by nature and rationalism and fearsome of
self-disparagement and nullity, yet despite it all capable of grandeur
and willing to unmask the truth of the human condition. There is
an immense distance between our own inner poles. Gaston Bachelard[78]
says that immensity is *within* ourselves, and, as quoted by another
scholar, "in our daydreaming or meditation on immensity, even if
we are made acutely conscious of our puny selves by way of a
relentless dialectics, we experience grandeur."[79] This conjoins Leopardi with Pascal. But Leopardi goes beyond self-disparagement and
nullity, and unmasks human truth leading to salubrious attitudes:
to distinguish "limitations from capabilities, creative illusions from
destructive ones, wishes from realities, friends from foes."[80]

Because of this conceptual richness, the poem's philosophical and
polemical parts have always injured the purists, who have liked to
pose the problem: is this didactic poetry, or is this a most beautiful
lyrical expression? Vossler is correct in resolving the issue (though
not for everyone) by saying that this is a meditation. Those who
would have it an imperfectly realized meditative poem—and there
are those critical intellects, as if finer than the poet's, who would—
still admire it, fascinated by what they deem its incompleteness, à
la Michelangelo Buonarroti: rational force and emotive passion coun-
terbalancing—but not balancing—each other, leaving much cre-
atively between the spaces, call them interstellar spaces. Yet this is
the flower, unconquerable in the heart of a true poet, that reminds
us of self-sacrifice (far more convincingly—because modestly and
unmystically—than the protagonist in T. S. Eliot's *Cocktail Party*),
that is, Love—a spirit Leopardi found in the simple genista[81] which
seems to know its own insignificance and is humble, like Wordsworth's "lowly wise."

It is easy to see how a religiously oriented author, like Manzoni,
would have converted the plant into a Christian symbol. Not so
Leopardi, who preferred more sense-directed ways of looking at life.
"Against a reborn Catholic spiritualism and the idealistic currents
. . ., Leopardi places his unchanged faith in materialistic and sen-
sationalistic doctrines . . .; he regrets that this body of thought
which, after originating in Renaissance philosophy and developing
during seventeenth century rationalism, freed us from superstition
and error, should be abandoned by the intellectuals of his day . . .

in favor of new spiritualistic positions"[82] (which included Catholic
liberalism). The *genista* is not a figure of Christ. Such is not the
intellectual background of the poem. In that background, however,
lay the accusation of misanthropy leveled at Leopardi for holding
to his antiprogressivism, as well as the distoring comments that his
pessimism flowed from his unfortunate physical condition. As a
symbol of man's unhappiness, the *genista* encouraged the poet in
his message of fraternity which, after all, he saw as dating back to
the origins of human life on earth, and as bespeaking an instinctive
moral sense in man. Leopardi appeals to man's reason, or better
put, his common sense; he wanted to end the *Canti,* one would say,
in this vein. So one critic comments: "The composition can be named
after the humble plant of the *genista,* letting it become not just a
pretext but an intimate lyrical motif, and then from this image the
poem develops along definite 'agonsitic' lines, later in vast cosmic
contemplations, finally closing in an affectionate dialogue once again
with the living thing that initiated the *canto.*"[83] The lyrical and the
philosophical remain intertwined in this poetic discourse, though
as the composition unfolds, each manner moves separately of the
other, thus giving the reader a better perspective of the shifting
moods of language and emotion, rhythm and meaning.

In "La ginestra" are found the most accomplished descriptions
ever fashioned by Leopardi.[84] In their fashioning was injected a
distinctive musicality. "[In the poem] it is hard to trace a regular
order in which poetry, rather than blending totally with discourse,
appears to be a kind of accompanying music which now and then
stresses the more agitated passages."[85] The images are internal to
the poem, or the message, not external or ornamental—thus mer-
iting intrinsically the designation of musicality, not in a linear but
in an inherently symphonic sense.[86] This means, too, that the prosaic
danger of philosophical exposition is invariably superseded by the
poetic element. Hence Leopardi's poetic testament, his most significant legacy, reversing his own biblical caption: his "light" rather
than his "darkness."

As a compendium of the *Canti,* "La ginestra" offers most of the
best in Leopardi, although it does not achieve the melodic magic
of "A Silvia," "L'infinito," or "Canto notturno di un pastore errante
dell'Asia." In the course of the collection, Leopardi establishes himself with marked individuality in the poetic traditions of Love,

Chapter Six
Conclusion: In a Comparative Context

Leopardi's ubiquitous word-symbol, the moon, became unfixed in the heavens, according to Alceta's dream in the "Frammento XXXVII," growing ever larger as it approached the earth in its fall, where it gave off a cloud of sparks. By way of a metaphor, we are tempted to suggest that, in the Western heavens, Leopardi's star should not have fallen as his relative lack of recognition outside Italy leads us to believe, for the closer we get to him the greater he becomes and the brighter his illuminations. Understandably, he has appealed less to readers culturally used to regular doses of optimistic interpretations of life, or at least to more words of encouragement. Not all can muster the enthusiasm for his writings of a James Thomson, an affectionate editor, a John Heath-Stubbs, an admiring translator, or an Unamuno, an erudite reader. Or a Sainte-Beuve, who liked the learnedness and the art, a Santayana who appreciated the prayerful quality of the poetry, a Nietzsche who as the author of *Also Sprach Zarathustra (Thus Spake Zarathustra)* savored the poetic prose and welcomed the notion of the suffering elite, or a Schopenhauer who relished the outright pessimism. Even in his own country, for that matter, whose many scholars place him among the glories of Italian poetry, Leopardi far from satisfied libertarian idealists like Giuseppe Mazzini, who could not stomach the depressing messages, not to mention conservative critics like Niccolò Tommaseo, who arrogantly saw in Leopardi nothing more than a little count who croaked like a frog, or a scholar like Croce, whose pronounced philosophical bent often made him impervious to the subtleties of Leopardi's lyrical intellect. There are, however, various Marxist critics, like Timpanaro and Cesare Luporini, who have contributed substantially to Leopardian scholarship, however wary of formalist contexts. Even some contemporaries who praised him were uneasy: Manzoni, for example, who like William Gladstone was too Christian a reader to appreciate fully the godless, existential wasteland. These were not unlike Matthew Arnold, who loved Leopardi as a modern poet but felt he missed in him something a bit more positive, or a host of lesser known literary figures who did not feel excessive sympathy for the gloom and the nihilism.[1] The search for forerunners of post—World War II existentialism (most often mentioned have been Pascal, Sören Kierkegaard, Nikolai Gogol, and Luigi Pirandello, among others) occasionally brought forth the name of Leopardi, but nothing much developed. Perhaps it all comes down to a question of cultural relativism.

At this point of our study, a few summarizing and concluding remarks are required, in order to place Leopardi in the international context in which he belongs. After all is said and done, we must look at *the man and his art,* and less at the various aesthetico-theoretical schools that may quote him, or the various disciplinary definitions that he may fit, or the various socio-political ideologies that may dictate the moods of reception of his work. Solidly in a tradition cultivated by many Italian critics, yet with the best objectivity of an "outsider," Whitfield correctly sees in him the humanist.[2] We should add to this an encompassing designation: That of *poeta universalis,* because his poetic personality, subdued in many ways as it is, is very far-reaching, like the illuminations of the moon, establishing a kinship with most major authors we might be discussing at any given time.

Leopardi's life, creative and otherwise, was shaped by a constant drama between reason and illusion.[3] It can be explained with Henri-Frédéric Amiel's words to the effect that the more a man loves the more he suffers, and that the sum of his possible grief exists in proportion to his degree of perfection. In Leopardi's poems, the pervasive theme of unhappiness is punctuated at every opportunity by recurring notes of consoling force: at least youth, love, dream, and the sweet deceptions of nature and beauty may be approached this way. To speak of idealism in a Platonic sense is inaccurate, for Leopardi admired physical more than ideal beauty, regardless of Kant's concern over its ephemeralness. This does not mean that Leopardi confined his notion of beauty to the flesh and bones of the feminine body and that he did not place it in loftier focus. In fact, he perceived beauty as an emanation rather than as a contained quality, or as a "ray divine" which was nonetheless the creation of the mind, rather than as the Greek philosopher's divine reflection whose source lay in an absolute realm very removed from this world.

Were it not in his mind, it would no longer be an illusion. The realities that delude man into believing in a fruitful, prosperous, and peaceful outcome of his many painful occupations are ultimately useless because of the very nature of that outcome, while the illusions usually characterized as useless by pragmatic calculations emerge as useful. Hartmann's attitude comes close to Leopardi's: beauty's power of consolation for life's ubiquitous misfortune, a temporary therapy that strengthens us at sporadic moments.

Pessimism becomes, therefore, a fallacious term if it is used to label Leopardi's thought in any absolute sense. As the years passed, he lamented his declining capacity for illusion—his lost youth, in other words—and the happiness that proceeds from its untried and unsoiled fantasies. The illusions he associated with his youth and caressed so fondly suggest archetypes which he sought yearningly but never attained. Hence his pessimism, a metaphysical anguish which, if one may judge from the usual disparity between his physical torments and the elevated tone of his poetry, was unrelated to bodily concerns. Beauty, as Georg Hegel and Schopenhauer had argued it and Keats had illustrated it, was for Leopardi, too, the portrayal of an idea or feeling in a work of art. As such, Art provided the release and emancipation that made his pessimism only relative. The juxtaposition of "foundering" and "sweet" in the last verse of "L'infinito" is both acrid in its reality and uplifting in its illusion. Schiller and Herbert Spencer may have regarded Art as deception divorced from the real; Leopardi preferred to value it for its very deception, for raising fiction to the level of a metareality, and for providing man with a purpose. This was his subjective idealism. He did, then, promote an aesthetic optimism for lack of which the life of Werther suffered and through which Goethe survived the malaise of his own hero (before he rejected him). Leopardi's pessimistic themes, however sharp the stings of despair and scorn, are orchestrated lyrically in serene, consoling tonalities ("A se stesso" notwithstanding), and are never gratingly discorded by the acrimony and psychosis of a Baudelaire.

In this context, it would seem logical that Nature, which occupies a medial position between man and destiny, should command less regard than Art. If Nature is beautiful, Art is sublime. But Nature, the dispenser of illusion, is the very life-source of Art, and Leopardi loved it with all the solitary passion of a Werther or a René, albeit usually in its gentler and simpler forms, like the flowers and rain and grass of Wergeland. We might recall his letter to Giordani in 1820, when he sighs for spring, almost medically, after hearing at night distant dogs bark and seeing moonbeams—all of which made him go mad with rapture and freeze with fear at any prospect of having to tolerate life without illusions and live affections.

Yet, attached as he is to Nature's physical exhilarations, he is not a colorist or a pictorial poet in any grand sense. Unlike someone like Hugo or Nicolaus Lenau, or certainly Wergeland with his intense astral symbols, his brushstrokes are light; the pigments are those of water colors rather than of oils. His scenes are rapid, accurate enough, indeed visual, in scattered details, but more often indeterminate, like pale backdrops that give relief to the central ideas. He achieves his "pictorial" clarity through vagueness. Biographically speaking, Leopardi's geographical horizons were limited, during his brief lifetime, to a few Italian cities. He knew he was too frail of body to sustain the efforts required to reach the Alpine panoramas dear to Rousseau, or the more exotic vistas described by travelers like Byron, Shelley, and Chateaubriand, let alone those who wandered off to the climes of Asia and California. Although highly suggestive through his indefiniteness, he is not a poet of colorful plasticity in the Parnassian manner of Charles Leconte de Lisle and Théophile Gautier, or in the uniquely descriptive manner of Coleridge. Vigny's account of the dying wolf and Charles Swinburne's impression of the swallow betray a far stronger desire to interpret animal nature plastically with words, in this instance, than Leopardi ever displayed, despite his numerous allusions to animals in his poetry and notebook.

The depth of his emotional response to Nature, however, cannot be fathomed by surface comparisons with his European contemporaries. He transcended the Alps, the desert sands, the Spanish towns, and the forests of the New World with his imagination, akin in its sheer breadth to Balzac's and to some extent Wordsworth's, aimed directly at achieving a cosmic view of existence and propelled by that same sense of wonder that had motivated Pascal's trembling before "the eternal silence of the infinite spaces." Hence the leitmotivs of the sun and especially the moon, the former with its awakening clarity and compulsion to pursue life's labors, the latter with its preferable invitation to meditation and dream. But behind them both, indeed everything, extends the Asian shepherd's nothingness, that abyss (*gouffre*) that Baudelaire said Pascal took everywhere with him. However, this interstellar fright finds no mystical resolution in Leopardi, whose despair can be more existential than anyone in the twentieth century has yet managed to express. If absence provides a measuring stick, Leopardi's universe, then, is vaster than Pascal's, stretching in today's cognizance beyond the galaxies (hence the implication of the modern theory of relativity in "Il Copernico-Dialogo"), as Isaac Newton's universe—it has been suggested—expanded into that of the Marquis de Laplace for whom God was an unnecessary hypothesis.[4] Friedrich Schleiermacher could not have acceded to such a dearth of religious spirituality.

Rather than look up at the spectral or diabolical or grotesque moon of the English poets or of Poe or Lenau or Musset, Leopardi, while lifting the shepherd's eyes to its silent indifference or so often his own eyes to its friendliness, seems to gaze downward from it upon the world of men, whose size hardly exceeds that of an anthill. This downward direction that characterizes his mode of contemplation obviates the possibility of mysticism, to which he was temperamentally averse. In this he differed from the praying Lamartine and the hymning Novalis. And when he turns his sight away from the sky to appreciate Nature from the common vantage point of other men, there is still no mystique involved, but rather a restrained admiration for its many wonders. Leopardi sketches them accordingly, with a feeling of elegiac simplicity which contrasts with the impetuousness of Byron, the lushness of Chateaubriand, the pomp of Hugo, or the challenging fervor of Walt Whitman. Under the spacious heavens, a sunny field or a hazy mountain, a flowery shore which lines a stretch of sea, a genista on a wasteland, a border of trees around a lake, a wandering hen or a thrush or a flock of sheep, seem to attract the poet at regular intervals as if for his approval, which he gives most willingly. He must have exclaimed many times with Faust: "Stay, Oh moment: thou art so fair!" Simple love and simple beauty make intimate allies.

Intellectual experiences later dampened the warmth of his affection, as happened with Vigny, as opposed to Wordsworth, Henry Wadsworth Longfellow, and "Jean Paul" Richter who sang mainly of Nature's joys; he was disillusioned in discovering that his love remained unreciprocated. Washington Irving and Ralph Waldo Emerson might not have understood this. Leopardi's moral sensibilities were aroused at the injustice of Nature when he declared her not only an indifferent but indeed a malevolent "stepmother" or "harsh nurse," referring of course to her cataclysmic manner. Disillusionment with an object of admiration leads to alienation, a distinctively Leopardian trait. Thereupon the poet constructs his own mythology, focusing on his personal symbols and seeing the world through them from an intimately consistent vantage point. With Byron and Wergeland, this produced self-dramatization, with Wordsworth a silent (meaning private) communication with Nature, with Keats a confidential contemplation of sensuous beauty. With Novalis's union of reality and imagination, the real world became a fairy tale, and with Mikhail Lermontov, a sense of gloominess and emptiness and a distrust in his generation gave him, as he said, a secret coldness in the blood. The responses are noticeably varied and disparate, but they stem from an individualistic posture à la Vigny in the face of the rest of the world, more often than not characterized by injured pride. None of these postures, including Lermontov's, comprehends Leopardi's, which is more profoundly speculative philosophically, more keenly penetrating psychologically, and more mellifluously accomplished aesthetically. Of course, having the *Zibaldone* assisting us in determining this helps.

Vigny sides proudly with the majesty of human suffering, and in so doing gives vent to a deep-seated hatred of Nature; Leopardi, with broader or more indulgent vision, could not reject her categorically. Illusion cannot submit totally to the eventual dictates of reason. The value of Beauty to offset Truth, not to corroborate it in Keats's terms, was too necessary to warrant its entire repudiation on realistic grounds. When Hölderlin had confessed that Nature had died for him with the disappearance of his dreams of youth, Leopardi, even in his very last poem, continued to be captivated by Nature's other presence, the "silvered countryside and waters," and the "dawning rise of morn." The goddess is implacable, yet, in the light of her countless beauties, some ill-defined hope sets the poet's heart astir. Hope lives, to paraphrase Coleridge, because it has an object.

Death completes the trinity of Love and Beauty—perhaps the only inalienable Truth. The triple association, from which Solomon had derived such frequent inspiration, gives Leopardi a marked individuality in the poetic tradition of Death. For the authors of ancient Greece and Rome, whether portrayed in the eerie and ugly terms of Euripides or Horace or Seneca or simply in its relationship to Sleep and Night as in Cicero or Sophocles, Death was an integral part of the natural order. Christianity and the Middle Ages converted it from a law into a punishment (analogously the Middle Ages and courtly fashion converted Love from a natural phenomenon into an occurrence comprising suffering and death), and Milton did not exaggerate this view when he made it a monster. In between, Dante's and Petrarch's ennobling experiences after the passing away of Beatrice and Laura, had led them to hail Death as gentle and desired and sweet. Novalis's experience with Sophia was no different, unlike Nerval's in search of Aurélia. But Leopardi, who had put aside early the hopeful faith or the lugubriousness of the other poets, saw Death with finality, as the inelucable "abyss" in which the personal drama of reason and illusion ends forever. Death and its variation, imprisonment, push Lermontov to yearn for faraway places; not so Leopardi, who sees it as "the sole goal of being," and therefore beautiful and eliciting our love. What Baudelaire will fear and hate, Leopardi adorns and deifies. What de Lisle salutes as divine, the author of "Sopra un bassorilievo antico sepolcrale" depicts as a "most beautiful young maiden." And Consalvo exclaims: "Two things of beauty has the world: love and death."

Death must be understood in a more universal sense than in the petty meaning given to it by suicide. While sympathizing with the nature of Brutus's and Sappho's decisions, Leopardi concluded that suicide stems from love of life rather than from a negation of living. Schopenhauer had asserted that the act is not directed against existence itself, and Leopardi's purpose is to affirm a negative totality of existence, in which suicide is not an issue. Debunking life gives man no right to feel superior in Pascal's sense, which stressed the nobility of knowing what is crushing him and that he is dying; on the contrary, to know and yet to have to stand by helplessly makes for an abject, groveling condition to which not even plants and animals are subjected.

Suicide resolves nothing. If there is one feeling that grows, or should grow, spontaneously from universal unhappiness, it is reciprocal compassion, each man's love for all men, occasioned by an awareness of a common and inalienable destiny. Compassion and mutual assistance he calls supreme duties, caring little about the juxtaposition of this attitude with his belief in "the infinite vanity of all things." Perhaps a sense of responsibility is an illusion, but it is a beneficial one. The poet speaks out of a candid sense of goodness, and prefers to be conciliatory rather than dogmatic, humane rather than dialectic, where mankind is concerned. He stands above the politics that made Wergeland a supreme poet of political freedom. A profound, moral exigency or concern with ethical philosophy prompted the author of "La ginestra" to appeal to a heroic humanity to band together in stoic opposition to the vicious forces of Nature, notwithstanding the ultimate decrees of destiny. Besides, action has the power to divert our concentration from gloomy meditation. For Leopardi, irresolution was worse than desperation. "To what avail our life?" he questions in "A un vincitore nel pallone": "only to condemn it; blessed then when fraught with perils, it forgets itself, and does not count the harm of slow and sordid hours, or listen to their gliding by." The *Zibaldone* often speaks of giving life a goal in the totality of things—which could be a career; Leopardi cannot understand how the jobless and carefree can be happy who go from pleasure to pleasure, without ever asking of what use their lives will be to them (*Z,* 4063, 4228, 4518). The Leopardian ethic is composed of the theory of Action and the rule of Love: to act out of Love of one's neighbor, to succor him in bearing the pain of existence, and to confine one's deeds to those that are consistent with goodness. Leopardi's pessimism, developing into a metaphilosophy, seeks heroically and finally achieves its own redemption.

The contest between Truth and Dream never caused paroxysms of extreme unhappiness, because the absence of abject, contemptible despair permitted Leopardi to clothe his pessimism in serenity. There is something of Montaigne's calm wisdom in this serenity, thanks to its cosmic viewpoint and conscious understanding of the mind's every movement. There is never the indignation of an Aleksandr Pushkin who rears a monument unto himself. The optics of distance, which allows him to withdraw from the tyrannical cares of daily life into the "infinite spaces," mitigates the optics of closeness, which telescopes his vision and focuses it onto a few modest town or countryside items, whereby he notices the most transitory of motions with the myopic pleasure one detects at times in more scientific poets like Lucretius, Dante, or Goethe. Illusion and reality are, after all, as much a question of optics as of metaphysics. Not a small part of Leopardi's greatness lies in his ability to fuse optics and metaphysics, or, as Schelling would have it, to mirror the macrocosm in the microcosm. *Wehmuth* and *Sehnsucht* are misleading terms which may be applied with greater security to Lamartine and Shelley; they cannot describe Leopardi's philosophical-idyllic poetic structures which reflect, rather than attitudes or dispositions, deeply studied—and painful—beliefs that resist labels when lyricized, because, like Whitman's self-description, they contain multitudes. In comparison with his genuinely profound experience of suffering, the blatant songs of others tend to pale, though they are perhaps no less appropriate for what their authors were attempting to convey in their own contexts: the derisory bitterness of Heinrich Heine, the ostentatious tragedy of Byron, the melodramatic disemboweling of Musset through his pelican, the sword swinging shepherd of Johann Ludwig Uhland, or the delirious black banner driven through a skull of Baudelaire. As it is sober, it is not egoistic; the fanatical and pathological concentration on the ego that has carried into many poets' idioms of the current century neither dominates nor appears. His cosmic view objectifies the self and precludes the morbidly subjective.

Leopardi never actively sought themes or moods for his poetry: they came to him without foreplanning. And when they did, they were invariably themes of sorrow, unlike those of Goethe which embraced the experiences of both sorrow and pleasure. Shelley sighed that our sweetest songs are those that tell of saddest thought—and so with these famous lines he might well have described Leopardi. Whether an impression, a remembrance, or an image, the point of departure was brief: a bird, a flower, a shepherd, the moon, a girl, a hedge, a tomb. As Giuseppe Ungaretti has written: "Memory for Leopardi is not so much a process of the intellect, a pure activity of the spirit, as a physical pain, a conscious awareness present not only in the history of individuals, but in that of civilizations and even of the universe. . . . A work of art is convincing when, enriched by our memories, it moves our imagination so completely as to give back to us the gaze of innocence. Memory and innocence are the two inseparable poles of Leopardi's poetry."[5] These poles blend, mingling like themes in—some critics have insisted on saying—a Ludwig van Beethoven symphony, developing into expanded statements of lament over a solitary existence, of appeal for man's solidarity, of grief over a hostile destiny, of desire for the unpossessable, of fright at the insignificance of the intellect, of despair over irreparable losses and ruins and unlived lives. In the singleness of a fleeting note, Leopardi can capture the cosmic harmonies of man's history and nature's infinity, and prove, in the words of Novalis, that poetry is a universal metaphor of the spirit.

In this "musical" presentation, illusion had to supplant reason by forging its own *raison d'être,* its own reality—a superreality. The resulting voice is eternal, even with the demolition of every other value in life. Art as form cannot be abstracted from its content, but rather is made tangible by it. Leopardi devalues and achieves, in his metaphilosophy, a superior revaluation—in Nietzschean fashion—which endows Art with ultimate significance. Transfiguration becomes transubstantiation. Through such aesthetic optimism, Art, even in pessimistic garb, affirms and exalts life. Leopardi knew this, and, like every great thinker, must have cherished his notion while reason and illusion were surfacing in his mind in almost capricious alternation. If, on the one hand, the alternation appears as a drama, especially if one confronts his life with his prose and poetry, on the other it seems, less pretentiously, an interplay. Not that as an interplay it has no afflictive ramifications. It has, but the culminating experience, Art, eventually endows it with a halo of accomplishment and satisfaction. When Leopardi passed from speculative analysis to lyrical creation, or from the raw and momentary image to the luminous world of visions, he attained spheres of poetic loftiness of which he himself may not have been conscious, along with an undoubtedly profound and cathartical self-realization. The philosophy he molded for himself out of a background of such sorrow was absorbed with consummate lyricism into the godly superreality of Art, the result of unrequited questioning, but, more important, the product—like all great art—of personal dignity.

Notes and References

Chapter One

1. Letter to his father Count Monaldo, 24 December 1827. All quotations from Leopardi's correspondence are taken from *Tutte le opere di Giacomo Leopardi: Le lettere,* ed. Francesco Flora, 2d ed. (Milan, 1955).
2. To Antonietta Tommasini, 5 July 1828.
3. Karl Vossler, *Leopardi.* Translated by T. Gnoli (Naples: Ricciardi, 1925), 52–53.
4. To Giulio Perticari, 30 March 1821.
5. Iris Origo and John Heath-Stubbs, *G. Leopardi: Selected Prose and Poetry* (New York, 1966), 20.
6. To Giampietro Vieusseux, 4 March 1826.
7. To Giulio Perticari, 30 March 1821.
8. To Pietro Giordani, 26 March 1819.
9. To Carlo, 22 March 1823.
10. To Giordani, 4 June 1819.
11. To Leonardo Trissino, 27 September 1819.
12. To Giordani, 20 March 1820.
13. To Carlo, 30 April 1817.
14. To Giordani, 5 May 1828.
15. To Giordani, 13 July 1821.
16. We might say that he also loved—but in a less personal and more spiritual way—the fifteen-year-old (near sixteen) sister-in-law of his Florentine landlord in 1828, Teresa Lucignani, like a Beatrice of innocence, "this very first flower of life," as he says of her in the *Zibaldone* (entry 4310).
17. To Carlo, 30 May 1826.
18. To Carlo, 25 November 1822.
19. To Antonietta Tommasini, 5 July 1828.
20. To Giannantonio Roverella, 8 December 1820.
21. To Pietro Brighenti, 2 June 1821.
22. To Vieusseux, 16 November 1827.
23. See Mario Sansone, *Leopardi e la filosofia del Settecento* (Florence: Olschki, 1964), 142.
24. To Giuseppe Grassi, 8 February 1819.
25. To Giordani, 21 June 1819.
26. To Brighenti, 28 April 1820.
27. To Carlo, late July 1819.

28. To Giacomo Tommasini, 30 January 1829.
29. To Giordani, 6 March 1820.
30. To Brighenti, 7 April 1820.
31. To Giordani, 17 December 1819.
32. See *Tutte le opere di Giacomo Leopardi: Poesie e Prose,* ed. F. Flora, 7th ed., vol. 2 (Milan, 1962), 685.
33. To Count Monaldo, 29 November 1822.
34. To Count Monaldo, 28 May 1832.
35. *Zibaldone,* entry 216. All quotations from the *Zibaldone* are taken from the *Tutte le opere di Giacomo Leopardi: Zibaldone di Pensieri,* ed. Francesco Flora, 2 vols., 3d ed. (Milan, 1949). The reader may also consult the ample, two-volume selection prepared by A. M. Moroni for the Oscar Paperback series (Milan: Mondadori, 1972).
36. *Zibaldone,* entries 1981–82.
37. *Zibaldone,* entries 393–394.
38. To Carlo, 25 November 1822.
39. To Carlo, 6 December 1822.
40. To Giordani, 26 April 1823.
41. To Giordani, 28 April 1823.
42. To Carlo, 22 January 1823.
43. To Carlo, 20 February 1823.
44. To Giuseppe Melchiorri, 19 December 1823.
45. To Melchiorri, 2 January 1824.
46. To A. Jacopssen, 23 June 1823.
47. To Paolina, 19 April 1823.
48. To Perticari, 9 April 1821.
49. To Giordani, 18 June 1821.
50. To Antonio Fortunato Stella, 13 March 1825.
51. A "little cape" worn by members of the Papal Court. To Carlo, 22 March 1823.
52. To Karl Bunsen, 16 November 1825.
53. To Bunsen, 1 February 1826.
54. To Paolina, 18 May 1830.
55. To Luca Mazzanti, 15 May 1826.
56. To Francesco Puccinotti, 17 October 1825.
57. To Carlo, 7 September 1825.
58. To Antonio Papadopoli, 3 July 1827.
59. To Giordani, 24 July 1828.
60. He also disagreed with them on the question of the abolition of slavery, whose existence he condoned as an institution of classical antiquity (cf. *Zibaldone,* 912–923 and 1172–74 especially). He did, however, disavow any unhumanitarian implications of this stance since they contradicted his notion of moral philosophy.

61. To Paolina, 12 November 1827.
62. To Paolina, 25 February 1828.
63. To Paolina, 12 November 1827.
64. To Count Monaldo, 24 July 1827.
65. Letters to De Sinner, 3 October 1835 and 22 December 1836.
66. To De Sinner, 24 May 1832.
67. To Gioberti, 17 April 1829.
68. To Puccinotti, undated, except 1826.
69. To G. Tommasini, 30 January 1829; Luigi De Sinner, 24 December 1831; and Giovanni Rosini, 15 January 1829 respectively.
70. To Stella, 23 November 1827, 27 November 1826, 19 September 1826, and 22 November 1826 respectively.
71. See letter to Stella, 19 August 1828.
72. To Vieusseux, 3 March 1830.
73. It is possible that Nerina was one of the two young daughters (the other being Lauretta) of Lady Mountcashell, whom Leopardi had met and been attracted to (cf. *Zibaldone,* where he alludes to the attractiveness of young ladies aged 16 to 18, entry 4310). Lady Mountcashell, the first daughter of Viscount Kingsborough, earl of Kingston, was a pupil of Mary Wollstonecraft Shelley, a theoretical Republican, and the author of a work on the physical education of children. She died in Leghorn in 1835.
74. To Vieusseux, 8 January 1830.
75. To Pietro Colletta, 26 April 1829. Leopardi claimed that the first of the *Operette morali,* "La storia del genere umano" ("The History of the Human Race"), was what had kept him from winning the prize, because of its irreligious sentiments and fantastic tone.
76. To Antonietta Tommasini, 19 June 1830.
77. The offer, a remarkable tribute, stands as one of the most generous gestures in literary history. Colletta wrote: "I will hand over to you, every month, the . . . sum in advance, but I shall have no other responsibility besides that one. Nothing will come out of my purse. The donors do not know to whom the gift is destined—and you, the receiver, do not know from whom it comes. . . . You have no obligation. May it be Italy's good fortune that, as your health improves, you will be able to write works worthy of your genius. But this hope of mine places you under no obligation" (*Epistolario di Giacomo Leopardi,* ed. F. Moroncini, G. Ferretti, and A. Duro, 7 vols. [Florence, 1934–49], vol. 5, 23 March 1830). The subsidy ceased when Leopardi left Florence, however.
78. To Fanny Targioni-Tozzetti, 5 December 1831.
79. Befuddled, some critics have hinted at homosexuality, ignoring Leopardi's view of pederasty as "infamous," a form of "human barbarism" and "shameful unnaturalness" (*Zibaldone,* items 1841 and 4047), as well

as Ranieri's propensity to chase after women (including Fanny, who probably preferred the Neopolitan to the poet from Recanati).

80. To Carlo, 15 October 1831.

81. See Italo De Feo, *Leopardi: l'uomo e l'opera* (Milan, 1972), 480.

82. In point of fact, the work had been "signed": "1150," which, translated into Roman numerals, gives Monaldo's initials: "MCL."

83. To Melchiorri, 15 May 1832.

84. To Giordani, 30 June 1820.

85. To Brighenti, 14 August 1820.

86. "Ad Arimane" (1833), in *Carte Napoletane,* no. 66. See *Leopardi: Opere,* ed. Riccardo Bacchelli and Gino Scarpa (Milan, 1935), 1244.

87. To Count Monaldo, 1 September 1833.

88. Quoted from De Feo, *Leopardi,* 525.

89. To Count Monaldo, 27 November 1834 and 3 February 1835.

90. To De Sinner, 20 March 1834.

91. To Giordani, 19 November 1819.

92. To Brighenti, 28 April 1820.

93. To Giordani, 30 June 1820.

94. Quoted from De Feo, *Leopardi,* 554–55.

95. To Leonardo Trissino, 27 September 1819.

96. To Vieusseux, 4 March 1826.

97. To Count Monaldo, 11 December 1836.

98. To Count Monaldo, 27 May 1837.

99. To Bunsen, 5 September 1829.

100. The cause of death was primarily "the increasing constriction caused by the pressure of his deformed thorax on both his lungs and heart" (Origo and Heath-Stubbs, *G. Leopardi,* 177).

101. Some believe that Ranieri did not succeed in proving that his death had not been due to the cholera epidemic, and that as a result Leopardi's body was thrown into one of the common ditches for all those who died of the disease, the burial in San Vitale having been merely staged by Ranieri to grant his friend due honor. (See, for example, Gian Carlo D'Adamo, *Giacomo Leopardi* [Florence: Le Monnier, 1976], 5.) This was probably not the case. In 1939, the casket was transferred to the side of the great cliff of Margellina, above "Virgil's tomb," overlooking the bay and Mt. Vesuvius.

102. Quoted from De Feo, *Leopardi,* 584.

103. Ibid.

Chapter Two

1. See J-P. Barricelli, "Leopardi," in *The Encyclopedia of Philosophy,* ed. P. Edwards, 8 vols. (New York: Macmillan Co., 1967), 4:437–38. In the section "On the Vanity and Suffering of Life," Schopenhauer in-

dicates his admiration of Leopardi's pessimism. He wished he had met him. For this, see Giovanni Mestica, *Studi leopardiani* (Florence: Le Monnier, 1901), 415. Unamuno sees the parallel with his own view regarding the conflict between the rational mathematical and volitive/theological sense of the universe and Leopardi's conflict between aspiration and reason.

2. The term is used by C. Luporini (see below), who, however, does not see Leopardi as a philosopher. It must be noted, in passing, that Leopardi's use of the word *sistema* is not to be interpreted as strictly as those critics who deny him a formally conceived philosophy would have it. But as a thinker, he still viewed his thoughts in a systematic fashion. "Whoever does not think by himself and seek the truth with his own faculties may perhaps believe in one thing or another without bringing them together, without considering how they could be true in relation to each other; this person remains without a system, happy with individual truths that are detached and independent from each other. To be sure, this is most difficult, because fact and reason demonstrate that even these persons always formulate some kind of system, though they may be ready to change it at times in accordance with new knowledge or new opinions that come their way. But the thinker is not so. He naturally and necessarily seeks a connecting thread in considering things. It is impossible that he be satisfied with isolated notions and truths. And if he were, his philosophy would be most trivial, most petty, and would not obtain any results" (*Zibaldone*, 946–47).

3. Vincenzo Gioberti, *Del primato morale e civile degli Italiani,* vol. 3 (Turin: Unione tip., 1927), 248.

4. G. De Sanctis, "Leopardi," in *La letteratura italiana nel secolo XIX,* ed. Walter Binni, vol. 3 (Bari: Laterza, 1953), 199.

5. C. Luporini, "Leopardi progressivo," in *Filosofi vecchi e nuovi* (Florence, 1947), 185.

6. B. Croce, *Poesia e non poesia* (Bari: Laterza, 1964), 102.

7. B. Croce, "Leopardi," *La Critica,* 20 July 1922.

8. Letter to Karl Bunsen, 1 February 1826.

9. Alberto Frattini, *Critica e fortuna dei "Canti" di G. Leopardi* (Brescia: La Scuola, 1965), 152, quoting Carmelo Nifosì, *La filosofia di Giacomo Leopardi* (Modica, 1949).

10. F. Schlegel, *Athenaeum,* fragment 171, among others.

11. Antonio Prete, *Il pensiero poetante* (Milan, 1980), 9.

12. Origo and Stubbs, *G. Leopardi,* 76–77.

13. Giuseppe De Robertis, *Saggio sul Leopardi* (Florence: Vallecchi, 1944), 63.

14. Letter to De Sinner, 2 March 1827.

15. D'Adamo, *Giacomo Leopardi,* 288. There are those who have tried to rehabilitate the *Pensieri.* In 1915, Manfredi Porena ("I centoundici

Pensieri," in *Scritti leopardiani* [Bologna, Zanichelli, 1959], 255–79) showed the origin of Leopardi's thought underlying seventy of them, calling him an *"antropofobo,"* or an anthropophobe—hence the discredit acquired by the collection. In 1970, Alessandra Diamantini ("Sui centoundici pensieri di G. Leopardi," in *Rassegna della letteratura italiana*, [Florence: Sansoni], 32) attempted to show the "fusion of objective universality of thought and communication, and the impassioned presence of the person who thinks and communicates." This hardly means that through his angry passion Leopardi had a social program in mind, as some critics have it, even making him Hobbesian in this respect: see Cesare Galimberti, "Fanciulli più che uomini," *Giacomo Leopardi, Pensieri* (Milan: Rizzoli, 1982), n. 78, p. 151, pensiero C, p. 168, and L, p. 130.

    16. See Prete, *Il pensiero poetante*, 10.

    17. See Geoffrey L. Bickersteth, *Leopardi and Wordsworth* (London: Oxford University Press, 1927), 22. Bickersteth, however, does not give Leopardi "speculative" credit.

    18. As earlier, *Zibaldone* references are identified by the page of the entry in the original manuscript, but, for the sake of space, the references are entered directly in the text (Z standing for *Zibaldone*). In the Francesco Flora edition (*Tutte le opere di Giacomo Leopardi*, 3d ed.), the *Zibaldone* is in two volumes and contains bracketed indications of the original manuscript pages.

    19. The same idea is expressed elsewhere this way: "Whoever does not have or has never had imagination, feeling, a capacity for enthusiasm, heroism, live and great illusions, strong and varied passions, whoever does not know the immense system of the beautiful, whoever does not read or does not feel, or has never read or felt the poets, absolutely cannot be a great, true, and perfect [accomplished] philosopher . . ." (Z, 1833).

    20. Henceforth, all quotations from the *Pensieri* will be cited in the text as *P*.

    21. See B. Biral, "Il significato di 'Natura' nel pensiero di Leopardi," *Il Ponte* 15, no. 10 (1959):1270–74. (See also B. B., *La posizione storica di G. Leopardi* [Turin: Einaudi, 1974].)

    22. Salvatore Battaglia, *L'ideologia letteraria di Giacomo Leopardi* (Naples, 1968), 29.

    23. Biral, "Il significato di 'Natura' . . . ," 1274.

    24. One critic, Ugo Dotti, puts Leopardi's *"noi collettivo"* ("collective we") several years prior to "La ginestra" (*Storia di un'anima* [Milan, 1982], 7). The *Epistolario* might suggest this modestly, but the poem is still its strongest literary expression.

    25. See, for example, Friedrich's "Cloister Graveyard in the Snow" (1810), Runge's "Rest on the Flight into Egypt" (ca. 1805), and Chateaubriand's *Le Génie du Christianisme* (*The Genius of Christianity*, 1802).

Lamartine's *Méditations poétiques (Poetic Meditations)* are of 1820. Pellico's *Le mie prigioni (My Prisons)* came later, in 1832, and it too is suffused with a sense of antirationalistic abandonment to the gentle folds of religious faith. Ivanov's famous painting *The Appearance of Christ before the People* took twenty years to execute and also came later: 1837–57. One should not overlook, also, the work of the Russian Pietists in the early nineteenth century.

26. See J. H. Whitfield, *Giacomo Leopardi* (Oxford, 1954), 161.

27. Ibid., 175.

28. M. Vinciguerra, "Leopardi antinaturista," in *Leopardi e l'ottocento: Atti del II Convegno internazionale di studi leopardiani* (Florence: Leo S. Olschki, 1970), 629.

29. See also subsequent pages, to *Z,* 1201.

30. Leopardi noted how judgment regarding the beauty of Addison's *Cato* varied radically, from England, where it was not praised, to Italy, where it was criticized (*Z,* 1410).

31. There is no indication that Leopardi was acquainted with the works of Hutcheson, however.

32. Jerome Stolnitz, "Beauty," in *The Encyclopedia of Philosophy,* 1:265.

33. Carmelo Nifosì, quoted in Frattini, *Critica e fortuna,* 149–50.

34. See F. De Sanctis, *Studio su Giacomo Leopardi* (Naples: A. Morano, 1921), 157.

35. Adriano Tilgher (*La filosofia di Leopardi* [Bologna, 1979]), who takes Leopardi entirely too literally, finds an immediate contradiction between this statement and the statement concerning self-love and hate, by which man, having made self-love natural to him has made hatred of others equally natural (51). The supposed contradiction is unclear; rigid literalism blurs.

36. Ibid., 43.

37. Prete, *Il pensiero poetante,* 23.

38. Tilgher, *La filosofia di Leopardi,* 17–21.

39. Luigi Tundo, "Leopardi/Istinto e progetti di morte," *Prospetti,* nos. 30–31 (June–September 1973):24.

40. Frattini, *Critica e fortuna,* 151.

41. Prete, *Il pensiero poetante,* 113.

42. Ibid., 115.

43. Ibid.

44. Ibid., 118. See Hobbes's second law of motion. Hobbes, however, arrives at the notion of the "utility" of the social contract. Leopardi's notion remains more negative and antisocial.

45. Ottavio Mark Casale, *A Leopardi Reader* (Urbana, 1981), 22. Pasquale Getti, in his *Esposizione del sistema filosofico di Giacomo Leopardi,*

2 vols. (Florence: Le Monnier, 1908), shows how Leopardi anticipated pragmatists like William James.

46. F. De Sanctis, "Schopenhauer e Leopardi," *Rivista contemporanea,* vol. 15 (Turin: Unione tipografico-editrice, 1858), 369–408.

47. As a "poetic" word, however, *pietà* appears frequently in the *Canti.*

48. Casale, *A Leopardi Reader,* 22.

49. In *Del sentimiento trágico de la vida,* Leopardi often serves as a point of reference.

50. Casale, *A Leopardi Reader,* 14.

51. Norbert Jonard, "Leopardi et le sentiment de l'ennui au XVIIIᵉ siècle," in *Leopardi e il settecento: Atti del I Convegno Internazionale di studi leopardiani* (Florence: Olschki, 1964), 381.

52. See J-P. Barricelli, *Encyclopedia of Philosophy,* 4:438.

53. Quoted from Ferdinando Giannessi, "Leopardi," in *Letteratura Italiana: I Maggiori* (Milan: Marzorati, 1956), 2:1142.

54. De Feo, *Leopardi,* 9.

Chapter Three

1. Whitfield, *Giacomo Leopardi,* 251.

2. Others are a "Dialogo tra due bestie p.e un cavallo e un toro" ("Dialogue between Two Animals, e.g., a Horse and a Bull"), a "Dialogo di un cavallo e un bue" ("Dialogue between a Horse and an Ox"), and "Murco, Senatore romano, filosofo greco . . ." ("Murco, Roman Senator, Greek Philosopher . . ."). They were written between 1819 and 1822.

3. Letter to Stella, 31 May 1826.

4. De Sanctis, *La letteratura italiana nel secolo XIX,* vol. 3, chaps. 26–32.

5. G. Gentile, *L'unità del pensiero leopardiano nelle "Operette morali"* (Pisa: Mariotti, 1917).

6. See Luigi Blasucci, "La posizione ideologica delle 'Operette morali,' " *Critica e storia letteraria: Studi offerti a Mario Fubini,* vol. 1 (Padua: Liviana Editrice, 1970), 622–24. The author identifies primarily Giuseppe De Robertis, M. Fubini, Riccardo Bacchelli, K. Vossler, Angelandrea Zottoli, Attilio Momigliano, and Giovanni Getto as important contributors to an interpretation of the *Operette morali* in the wake of Gentile's study.

7. Among others, see Francesco Flora, *Poetica e poesia di Leopardi* (Milan: Malfasi, 1949), 158, and Mario Fubini, introduction (dated 1933) to the *Operette morali,* 3d ed. (Turin, 1966), 30ff.

8. Letter to Count Monaldo, 8 July [1831?].

9. Giovanni Cecchetti, introduction to *Operette Morali: Essays and Dialogues* (Berkeley, 1982), 4.

10. L. Blasucci, "La posizione ideologica," 627.

11. Ibid., 637.

12. Letter to Paolina, 28 January 1823.

13. Respectively, Cesare Galimberti, ed., introduction to *Operette morali* (Naples: Liguori, 1977), xx, and Paolo Ruffilli, ed., introduction to *Operette morali* (Milan: Garzanti, 1982), xxvii.

14. The notions of the poetical and the mythical have been put forth variously with reference to the *Operette morali;* they have been successfully combined recently by G. Cecchetti, ed., *Operette morali,* 3.

15. Maristella Mazzocca, review of P. Ruffilli's edition, in *Lettere italiane* 35, no. 2 (April–June 1983):279.

16. Letter to Stella, 26 April 1826.

17. De Feo, *Leopardi,* 250.

18. Letter to Stella, 16 June 1826.

19. Letter to Stella, 12 March 1826.

20. Origo and Heath-Stubbs, *G. Leopardi,* 101.

21. E. Bigi, "Tono e tecnica delle *Operette morali,*" in *Dal Petrarca al Leopardi* (Milan: Ricciardi, 1954), 116.

22. *Zibaldone,* 2171–72. The passage is also quoted in D'Adamo, *Giacomo Leopardi,* 72–73.

23. Glauco Cambon, introduction to Casale, *A Leopardi Reader,* x.

24. Goffredo Bellonci's preface, echoing Montani and Bacchelli, referred to in De Feo, *Leopardi,* 258. The statements by Cambon and Bellonci reveal a questionable knowledge of musical-literary terminology and methodology.

25. Mario Sansone, "Il carattere delle *Operette morali,*" *Nuova Antologia* 91 (1956):36–37.

26. Letter to Stella, 16 June 1826.

27. *Zibaldone,* 1393.

28. See L. Russo, *Ritratti e disegni storici* (Bari: Laterza, 1946).

29. Great Flood survivors in a Greek creation myth.

30. The title is Leopardi's invention, the profession meaning possibly "label writers," though some of ancient Greece's satirists were known as "syllographs."

31. A brief allusion to Goethe's *Faust,* to its "novelty and boldness," appears in *Zibaldone,* 4479.

32. Another Leopardian invention; the name of the city means "beyond the clouds."

33. Casale, *A Leopardi Reader,* 106, suggests an analogy with *Candide.*

34. *Operette morali,* ed. Fubini, 126.

35. Leopardi subscribes to the legend that Tasso was persecuted and jailed for loving Duke Alfonso II's sister, Eleonora d'Este.

36. Casale, *A Leopardi Reader,* 113.

37. Peter the Great was so taken by Ruysch's mummies that he purchased them and transferred the whole museum to St. Petersburg.

38. Riccardo Bacchelli, *Leopardi: commenti letterari* (Milan: Mondadori, 1962), 313.

39. Ottonieri was an imaginary Socratic philosopher who is said to have lived most of his life in Nubiana (Cloudville), in the province of Valdivento (Wind Valley). Leopardi's *operetta* reflects Xenophon's *Socrates' Memorable Sayings,* Lucian's *Lives of Enchantment,* and Foscolo's *Notizia intorno a Didimo Chierico (Notice Concerning Didimo Chierico).*

40. Giuseppe De Robertis, *Saggio sul Leopardi,* 125.

41. Some of the particulars, particularly in Columbus's last speech, seem to have been drawn from William Robertson's *History of America,* published in London in 1777.

42. M. Mazzocca, review in *Lettere italiane,* 281 (see n. 15 above).

43. Copernicus did in fact dedicate his treatise, *Nicolai Copernici thorunensis de revolutionibus orbium caelestium libri VI* (1543, though written much before), to Pope Paul III (Alessandro Farnese) in order not to be accused of avoiding the opinion of competent and illustrious personalities, and to benefit from papal protection.

44. Letter to De Sinner, 21 June 1832.

45. *Zibaldone,* 4284.

46. See Andrea Gustarelli, *Giacomo Leopardi* (Milan: Vallardi, 1938), 83–85.

47. G. Getto, *Saggi leopardiani* (Florence, 1966), 190–92.

Chapter Four

1. Ghan Singh, *Leopardi and the Theory of Poetry* (Lexington, 1964). This is a discerning and seminal work to which I am much indebted in the preparation of this chapter. Another excellent study is that of Nicholas J. Perella, *Night and the Sublime in Giacomo Leopardi* (Berkeley, 1970). See, too, René Wellek, *A History of Modern Criticism, 1750–1950,* 3 vols. (New Haven: Yale University Press, 1965), 3:272–78.

2. Singh, *Leopardi,* x.

3. "Il Parini, ovver della gloria," in *Tutte le Opere di Giacomo Leopardi,* ed. F. Flora, 1:898. Singh singles out the three principles of Leopardi's poetic theory, Memory, Imagination, and Imitation (*Leopardi,* 94).

4. Perella, *Night and the Sublime,* 69–70.

5. The matter of Leopardi's romanticism or classicism relates to both an aesthetic and a philosophy. Since the latter has been treated in chapter 2, this chapter will stress the matter of his aesthetic, though attention is called to its conclusion, where the two are briefly linked. See

the informative presentations by Riccardo Massano, " 'Werther,' 'Ortis,' e 'Corinne' in Leopardi: (filigrana dei 'Canti')," in *Leopardi e il settecento: Atti del I Convegno internazionale di studi leopardiani* (Florence: Olschki, 1964), 415–35, followed by Ettore Mazzali, "Osservazioni sul 'Discorso di un italiano,' " in ibid., 437–46. Also pertinent: Fernando Figurelli, "Leopardi e il classicismo," in *Leopardi e l'ottocento: Atti del II Convegno internazionale di studi leopardiani* (Florence: Olschki, 1970), 277–310; Luigi Malagoli, "La transformazione degli impulsi romantici nel primo Leopardi," in ibid., 409–14; and Pietro Mazzamuto, "Il giudizio critico del Leopardi sulla letteratura romantica," in ibid., 427–53.

6. See "Leopardi" in Hugh Lloyd-Jones, *Blood for the Ghosts* (London: Duckworth & Co., Ltd., 1982), 108.

7. Ferdinando Giannessi, "Giacomo Leopardi," in *Letteratura Italiana: I Maggiori* (Milan: Marzorati, 1956), 2:1137.

8. *Leopardi: Opere,* ed. Bacchelli and Scarpa, 841.

9. Natalino Sapegno, "Noterella leopardiana," in *Rinascita*, 5:1948.

10. Perella, *Night and the Sublime,* 71.

11. Singh, *Leopardi,* 10.

12. Prete, *Il pensiero poetante,* 21.

13. See David Hume, *Treatise on Human Nature,* ed. L. A. Selby-Bigge (Oxford: Clarendon Press, 1967 [1888]), bk. 1, pt. 4, sec. 7.

14. The comparison with Coleridge is made by Singh, *Leopardi,* 218–19.

15. Ibid., 69–70. The Leopardi quotation is from *Zibaldone*, 3310–11.

16. *Discorso di un italiano, ecc.,* in *Poesie e Prose,* 2:508.

17. Singh, *Leopardi,* 291–92. The Empson quotation is found in *Seven Types of Ambiguity,* 2d ed. (London: Chatto & Windus, 1947), 21.

18. *Poesie e Prose,* 2:541.

19. Dedication, *Canti,* 1830 edition (Florence).

20. Letter to Giordani, 30 June 1820.

21. Letter to De Sinner, 24 May 1832.

22. He saw Ariosto's *Orlando furioso* as a series of poems, given its various arguments, and he probably would have looked at Tasso's *Gerusalemme liberata* similarly.

23. Singh, *Leopardi,* 85.

24. Wellek, *A History of Modern Criticism,* 2:275. The first quotation is from a letter to Melchiorri, 5 March 1824, the second from *Zibaldone,* 4356. A number of anticipations are attributable to Leopardi, such as impressionism, pure poetry, psycho-aesthetics, and creative criticism. Not unlike Coleridge, he believed criticism to be less an evaluating than a creative act undertaken by practitioners and not just observers of the art ("it is not enough to be used to writing oneself, but one must be able to

do so almost as perfectly as the writer himself whom one is going to judge
. . . as if to transfer that excellence into oneself"). Every text must be
capable of explication, at face value, to deserve good standing, but the
critic must also evaluate the reaction of the audience for which the text
is intended. In other words, he must know what the work truly is,
intrinsically or intextually (to use today's terms and adumbrate New Criticism) and analyze its effect on the reader, on how it is received (to
adumbrate Reception Studies). The critic must be mature, but free from
the baggage of ideological constraints, which means—typical of Leopardi—that he must judge with the emotion of youth (see *Poesie e Prose*,
1:894–95). To the list of "adumbrations," one might also add the syn-
aesthesia of the symbolists ("The theory of sounds and voices, and of music,
is greatly related to that of tastes and smells, and also of colors . . ." [Z,
1738]). And something of Victor Hugo's division of literary ages into
lyric-epic-dramatic, already suggested by Vico in the eighteenth century,
is anticipated by Leopardi.

    25. Wellek, *A History of Modern Criticsm*, 2:274.

    26. Nerval achieves it through his magic verbal formulas (cf. "Les
Chimères"), Brentano through the sound of words (cf. "Abendständchen"
or "Wiegenlied"), and Bécquer through fantasizing (cf. "Leyendas").

    27. Wellek, *A History of Modern Criticism*, 2:275.

    28. See Mario Andrea Rigoni, *Saggio sul pensiero leopardiano* (Padua:
CLEUP, 1982).

    29. Prete, *Il pensiero poetante*, 160.

    30. See Perella, *Night and the Sublime*, 112–13.

    31. Perella goes on to deny any Platonic sense to these words in
terms of "a metaphysical or transcendental reality that we grasp for or to
which we are transported by means of objects or combinations of circumstances of this life. Leopardi very early rejected the Platonic realm of ideas
as chimerical, and it would be the grossest sort of misreading to attribute
to him the cloudy poetic principle of a poet . . . (followed in this by
Baudelaire). . . ," 113.

    32. *Discorso*, in *Leopardi: Opere*, ed. Bacchelli and Scarpa, 846.
The reader might wish to consult a more recent edition: *Discorso, ecc., con
una antologia di testimonianze sul romanticismo e un saggio introduttivo di Francesco Flora*, ed. Ettore Mazzali (Bologna: Cappelli, 1957).

    33. L. Peer, "*Mimesis* in Manzoni's Literary Theory," paper read at
the Manzoni Symposium, Brigham Young University, Provo, Utah, 5
November 1984; to be published shortly in the proceedings of that symposium.

    34. Singh, *Leopardi*, 31. The Leopardi quotation is found in *Poesie
e Prose*, 2:514.

    35. Ibid., 96.

Chapter Five

1. Ernesto G. Caserta, introduction to *The War of the Mice and the Crabs* (Chapel Hill, 1976), 19.
2. *Pensieri,* 1–2, 24, 26, 73, 76, 99, 105.
3. I owe the translations of these bizarre names to E. G. Caserta's fine introduction to his translation of Leopardi's work (cf. n. 1 above).
4. See E. Donadoni, "I *Paralipomeni della Batracomiomachia,*" in *Scritti e discorsi letterari* (Florence: Sansoni, 1921); Riccardo Bacchelli, "Digressione sui Paralipomeni" and "I *Paralipomeni della Batracomiomachia,*" in *Leopardi* (Milan: Mondadori, 1962); M. Capucci, "I *Paralipomeni e la poetica leopardiana*" and "La poesia dei *Paralipomeni* leopardiani," *Convivium* 22 (1954):581–94 and 695–711; Walter Binni, *La nuova poetica leopardiana,* 2d ed. (Florence, 1971); A. Brilli, *Satire e mito nei "Paralipomeni" leopardiani* (Urbino: Argalia, 1967); Gennaro Savarese, *Saggio sui "Paralipomeni" di G. Leopardi* (Florence: La Nuova Italia, 1967).
5. Vincenzo Gioberti, *Il gesuita moderno,* vol. 3 (Lausanne: Bonamici, 1846–47), 484.
6. Caserta, introduction to *The War of the Mice and the Crabs,* 25.
7. D'Adamo, *Giacomo Leopardi,* 225.
8. Binni, *La nuova poetica leopardiana,* 126–27.
9. Quoted from Singh, *Leopardi,* 251.
10. Mazzocca, in *Lettere italiane* 35, no. 2 (1983):282.
11. Arturo Graf, *Foscolo, Manzoni, Leopardi* (Turin: Chiantore, 1898), 354–55.
12. F. De Sanctis, *Saggi Critici,* ed. L. Russo, vol. 1 (Bari: Laterza, 1953), 172.
13. Letter to Papadopoli, 25 February 1828.
14. Letter to Melchiorri, 5 March 1824.
15. De Sanctis, *La Critica,* vol. 14 (Bari: Laterza, 1916), 23.
16. A. de Sainte-Beuve, "Leopardi," in *Portraits contemporains,* vol. 4 (Paris: Calmann Lévy, 1876), 397.
17. See Gian Piero Barricelli, "A Poet of a Poet: Comments on Ezra Pound's Translation of Leopardi's 'Sopra Il Ritratto Di Una Bella Donna,' " *Italian Quarterly* 16 (1964):68–75.
18. Singh, *Leopardi,* 207.
19. Fubini, *Introduzione ai Canti,* xxix.
20. See De Feo, *Leopardi,* 520.
21. Emilio Bertana has written: "In spite of his classical education and his protestations of his deference to tradition, in spite of the times, the friendships and the environment, and the idea that without an ancient tongue there cannot be elegant literature, Leopardi was, in point of language . . . a convinced liberal and modernist" ("La mente di G. Leopardi," *Giornale storico della letteratura italiana* 41 [1903]:214; quoted by Singh,

Leopardi, 224). Leopardi also objected, in his liberalism, to the idea of restricting a nation's language to one province alone—in Italy's case, to Tuscany, or to the Florentine language, as his compatriot Manzoni was urging.

22. Giosuè Carducci, *Poesia e storia* (Bologna: Zanichelli, 1905), 256.

23. F. Figurelli, "Le 2 canzoni pattriottiche del Leopardi e il suo programma di letteratura nazionale e civile," *Belfagor* 6 (1951):35.

24. Perella, *Night and the Sublime,* 55.

25. Renato Poggioli, in *The Poem Itself,* by Stanley Burnshaw (New York: Holt, Reinhart & Winston, 1960), 277.

26. *Canti,* ed. Fubini, 115.

27. Poggioli, in *The Poem Itself,* by Burnshaw, 277.

28. Attilio Momigliano, *Introduzione ai poeti* (Milan: Tumminelli, 1946), 173.

29. See Salvatore Battaglia, *L'ideologia letteraria di Giacomo Leopardi* (Naples: Liguori, 1968), 316.

30. John Frederick Nims, in *The Poem Itself,* by Burnshaw, 271.

31. Letter to Giordani, 19 November 1819.

32. G. De Robertis, *Canti di G. Leopardi* (Florence: Le Monnier, 1944), 125.

33. An Italian game played with a large ball struck with a wooden guard worn over the hand and wrist (consult Barbara Reynolds in *The Cambridge Italian Dictionary* [Cambridge: Cambridge University Press, 1962]).

34. Umberto Bosco, *Titanismo e pietà in Giacomo Leopardi* (Florence: Le Monnier, 1957), 4.

35. For Leopardi, Californian meant man in a primitive state. "We need not remind ourselves that California is on the extreme end of the continent. The nation of Californians, as travelers recount, lives in far greater naturalness than we might think, if not believable, at least possible for the human species. Certain parties that are working to reduce these people to a social state will, I have no doubt, in time succeed in their endeavor; but we can recognize that no other nation shows sign of wanting to succeed so little in the European school" (quoted from *Giacomo Leopardi: Canti,* ed. G. A. Levi [Florence: La Nuova Italia, 1937], 92–93). For other references to Californians, see *Zibaldone,* 3179–80, 3304, 3660, 3801–2.

36. This poem was to be the first in a series of *Inni cristiani,* which never got beyond this first composition.

37. A generous and helpful friend, Pepoli was vice president of the Felsinei Academy. He was a cultured man, a liberal involved in the 1831

movements, because of which he became an exile in London until his return to Italy in 1859.

38. Angelo Mai, an erudite philologist, had resurrected many significant texts as head librarian of the Ambrosiana and the Vatican Library.

39. Attilio Momigliano, *Antologia della letteratura italiana,* 9th ed., vol. 3 (Milan: Principato, 1947), 115.

40. L. Russo, *Canti di G. Leopardi,* 107.

41. F. De Sanctis, *Giacomo Leopardi,* ed. W. Binni (Bari: Laterza, 1953), 152. He continues perceptively: "Logic as commonly understood means coherence with ideas, the correspondence of means and ends; the logic of art means coherence of language and of conduct in the combined play of all vital forces, of how and when ideas, imagination, feelings, passion, also physical, moral, and intellectual states operate at a given moment of existence. This is the logic of Dante and Shakespeare, the most illogical of poets because the truest, the most penetrating into the secrets of nature and of history. I say this because often judging art we introduce intellectual and moral criteria that are foreign to it."

42. Quoted by Angelandrea Zottoli, who subscribes to the emphasis on isolation: *Leopardi, storia di un'anima* (Bari: Laterza, 1927), 111. See also Russo, *Canti di G. Leopardi,* 169.

43. C. Calcaterra, *G. Leopardi: Canti* (Turin: S. E. I., 1947), 83.

44. Vossler, *Leopardi,* 145.

45. See G. De Robertis, *Saggio sul Leopardi* (Florence: Vallecchi, 1936), 198–99.

46. Giuseppe Petronio, "Introduzione al Leopardi," *La Nuova Italia* 7, nos. 10–11 (1937):299.

47. B. Croce, "Leopardi," *La Critica,* 20 July 1922.

48. *Canti,* ed. Fubini, xxxi.

49. A. Momigliano, *Introduzione ai poeti,* 174.

50. Letter to Paolina, 2 May 1828.

51. Giovanni Getto, *Saggi leopardiani* (Florence: Vallecchi, 1966), 221. The passage is quoted in D'Adamo, *Giacomo Leopardi,* 177.

52. N. Sapegno, *Compendio di storia della letteratura italiana,* 3:253.

53. Gustarelli, *Giacomo Leopardi,* 42.

54. De Robertis, *Saggio sul Leopardi,* 200.

55. F. Flora, *Storia della letteratura italiana,* vol. 4 (Milan: Mondadori, 1940), 180.

56. Petronio, "Introduzione al Leopardi," 299.

57. Russo, *Canti di G. Leopardi,* 56.

58. Flora, *I Canti e Prose scelte* (Milan: Mondadori, 1937), 282.

59. See Giulio Augusto Levi, *Giacomo Leopardi* (Messina: Principato, 1931), 318–19.

60. De Robertis, *Saggio sul Leopardi,* 201.

61. Perella, *Night and the Sublime,* 59. "What is life?" asks Leopardi in his *Zibaldone* (4162–63): "The voyage of a cripple and sick person with a very heavy load on his shoulders, who walks over very steep mountains and highly bitter, laborious, and difficult places, through snow, ice, rain, wind, the heat of the sun, and who does so without ever resting, day and night for many days to get to such a precipice or ditch and inevitably tumble into it."

62. Russo, *Canti di G. Leopardi,* 57.

63. *Canti,* ed. Fubini, 181.

64. Karl Kroeber, *The Artifice of Reality: Poetic Style in Wordsworth, Foscolo, Keats, and Leopardi* (Madison, 1964), 102.

65. B. Croce, *Poesia antica e moderna* (Bari: Laterza, 1940), 374.

66. W. Binni, *Scrittori d'Italia,* 10th ed., vol. 3 (Florence: La Nuova Italia, 1960), 269.

67. *Pensieri,* 82.

68. D. Consoli, ed. *G. Leopardi: Canti* (Turin: S. E. I. 1967), 357.

69. The draft of a hymn, "Ad Arimane" (in ancient Iranian religion, the personification of evil), has been associated with "A se stesso," since the works appear to be contemporary and speak of desperation.

70. D'Adamo, *Giacomo Leopardi,* 202.

71. Gustarelli, *Giacomo Leopardi,* 51.

72. Gino Capponi was a Florentine friend from 1827, an educationalist and historian, author of a *Storia della repubblica di Firenze,* who with Vieusseux founded the *Antologia* and the *Archivio Storico Italiano.*

73. Schulz reported the event in *Allgemeine Zeitung Beilage,* 1840, and in his "Giacomo Leopardi" piece in *Italia,* vol. 2 (Berlin: Reumont, 1840).

74. These words Leopardi took with acknowledgment from Terenzio Mamiani, who, in his dedication to his *Inni sacri,* had made allusion to the "magnificent and progressive lots of mankind." Mamiani was a cousin of Leopardi's, and in no way held Leopardi's quoting him against him.

75. See De Feo, *Leopardi,* 561.

76. See Elisabetta Burchi, "I 'Pensieri' e lo 'Zibaldone': analisi di un rapporto," *Rassegna della letteratura italiana,* 1977, 332. Mazzocca correctly wonders about the correctness of Burchi's position, pointing to Pensieri 89, 99, 105, and 16, among others (*Lettere italiane* 35, no. 2, [1983]:285).

77. See Cesare Galimberti, ed., *Operette morali,* p. 102, n. 2, where he claims that the *Pensieri* were psychologically ahead of their time, prefiguring Freud, the assimilation of paternal and state authority, the subordination to economic culture in a nascent industrial civilization, the phenomenon of celebrity that captures social sympathies instead of merit,

the question of group dynamics in society, and the political inconsistency of isms.

78. Gaston Bachelard, *La poétique de l'espace* (Paris: Presses univer-sitaires de France, 1957), 179.

79. Perella (quoting Bachelard), *Night and the Sublime,* 136.

80. Casale, *A Leopardi Reader,* 16.

81. See Bickersteth, *Leopardi and Wordsworth,* 29–30.

82. D'Adamo, *Giacomo Leopardi,* 213.

83. *Canti,* ed. Fubini, 243–44.

84. A. Graf, *Foscolo, Manzoni, Leopardi,* 354ff.

85. *Canti,* ed. Fubini, see from xxix on.

86. See Binni, *La nuova poetica leopardiana,* 137.

Chapter Six

1. H. C. Merivale, a recent critic, is one. Consult James Thomson, *Essays, Dialogues and Thoughts of Giacomo Leopardi* (London, 1905), and Giovanni Carsaniga, *Giacomo Leopardi: The Unheeded Voice* (Edinburgh, 1977).

2. See Whitfield, *Giacomo Leopardi.*

3. See Jean-Pierre Barricelli, "Leopardi's Drama of Reason and Illusion," in *Giacomo Leopardi: Poems* (New York, 1963), 11–32. The volume is out of print; these final remarks are taken in good part from the conclusion of this essay, modified and expanded, 25–32.

4. See Origo, *Leopardi,* 13.

5. Giuseppe Ungaretti, preface to the translation into French of Leopardi's complete works; quoted from Origo, *Leopardi,* 26. See Franco Di Carlo, *Ungaretti e Leopardi, ecc.* (Rome: Balzoni, 1979).

Selected Bibliography

PRIMARY SOURCES

1. Italian Editions

Canti. Edited by F. Moroncini. Bologna: Cappelli, 1929.

Canti. Edited by G. A. Levi. 3d ed. Florence: La Nuova Italia, 1937.

Canti. Edited by L. Russo. Florence: Sansoni, 1945.

Canti. Edited by M. Fubini and E. Bigi. Turin: Loescher, 1964.

Canti. Edited by D. Consoli. Turin: S. E. I., 1967.

Canti. Edited by G. De Robertis. Florence: Oscar Studio, 1978.

Crestomazie: La Prosa, La Poesia. Edited by G. Bollati and G. Savoca. 2 vols. Turin: Einaudi, 1968.

Epistolario di G. Leopardi. Edited by F. Moroncini, G. Ferretti, and A. Duro. 7 vols. Florence: Le Monnier, 1934–41.

I Paralipomeni della Batracomiomachia. Edited by E. Allodoli. Turin: Unione tipografico-editrice torinese, 1927.

Leopardi: Opere, Saggi Giovanili, Carte Napoletane. Edited by Riccardo Bacchelli and Gino Scarpa. Milan: Officina Tipografica Gregoriana, 1935.

Opere. Edited by Walter Binni and E. Ghidetti. 2 vols. Florence, Sansoni, 1969.

Opere minori approvate. Edited by F. Moroncini. Bologna: Cappelli, 1931.

Operette morali. Edited by G. Gentile. Bologna: Zanichelli, 1918.

Operette morali. Edited by F. Moroncini. Bologna: Cappelli, 1929.

Operette morali. Edited by M. Fubini, 3d ed. Turin: Loescher, 1966.

Tutte le opere di G. Leopardi (Le Poesie e le Prose, Zibaldone di Pensieri, & Le Lettere). Edited by Francesco Flora. 5 vols. Milan: Mondadori, 1937–40.

2. English Translations

Barricelli, Jean-Pierre. *Giacomo Leopardi: Poems.* New York: Las Americas Publishing Co., 1963. Includes an essay: "Leopardi's Drama of Reason and Illusion."

Bickersteth, Geoffrey L. *The Poetry of Leopardi.* Cambridge: Cambridge University Press, 1923.

Casale, Ottavio Mark. *A Leopardi Reader.* Urbana: University of Illinois Press, 1981.

Caserta, Ernesto. *Giacomo Leopardi: The War of the Mice and the Crabs.* Chapel Hill: University of North Carolina, Department of Romance Languages, 1976.

Cecchetti, Giovanni. *Operette morali: Essays and Dialogues*. Berkeley: University of California Press, 1982.

Cliffe, Francis H. *The Poems of Leopardi*. London: Remington, 1893.

Creagh, Patrick. *Moral Tales*. Manchester: Carcanet New Press, 1983.

De Luca, A. Michael, and Giuliano, William. *Selections from Italian Poetry*. New York: Harvey House, Inc., 1966. Leopardi translations by J-P. Barricelli.

Di Piero, W. S. *Pensieri: Giacomo Leopardi*. New York: Oxford University Press, 1984.

Edwardes, Charles. *Essays and Dialogues of Giacomo Leopardi*. London: Trübner, 1882.

Flores, Angel, ed. *Leopardi: Poems and Prose*. Bloomington: Indiana University Press, 1966. Translations by R. Yorck, K. Elmslie, T. Bergin, D. Durling, M. Kittel, K. Flores, E. Morgan, J-P. Barricelli, G. Rizzo, M. Miller, J. Wilhelm, N. Shapiro, W. Davis, J. H. Whitfield, and D. Donno.

Heath-Stubbs, John. *Poems from Giacomo Leopardi*. London: J. Lehmann, 1946.

Kay, George R., ed. *The Penguin Book of Italian Verse*. Baltimore: Penguin Books, Inc., 1960. Prose translations unidentified.

Maxwell, Patrick. *Essays, Dialogues and Thoughts of Count Giacomo Leopardi*. London: W. Scott, 1893.

Morrison, J. M. *The Poems ("Canti") of Giacomo Leopardi*. London: Gay & Bird, 1900.

Origo, Iris, and Heath-Stubbs, John. *Giacomo Leopardi: Selected Prose and Poetry*. Oxford: Oxford University Press, 1966.

Thomson, James. *Essays, Dialogues and Thoughts of Giacomo Leopardi*. London: Routledge, 1905.

Townsend, Frederick. *Poems of Giacomo Leopardi*. New York: Putnam's Sons, 1887.

Whitfield, John H. *Leopardi's Canti Translated into English Verse*. Naples: G. Scalabrini, 1962.

SECONDARY SOURCES

Battaglia, Salvatore. *L'ideologia letteraria di Giacomo Leopardi*. Naples: Liguori, 1968. A sensible presentation of various elements of Leopardi's philosophy (Rousseau, linguistics, nature, illusion, memory), including the conceptual function of poetry through such themes as sentiment and youth.

Binni, Walter. *La nuova poetica leopardiana*. 2d ed. Florence: Sansoni, 1971. A reevaluation of Leopardi's poetics, ideology, and poetry subsequent to the "great idylls," maintaining how the poet implemented his existential views more directly and less elegiacally.

Biral, Bruno. *La posizione storica di Leopardi.* Turin: Einaudi, 1974. A tempering of the strict Marxist point of view, stressing the nonsociopolitical aspects of Leopardi's pessimism.

Carsaniga, Giovanni. *Giacomo Leopardi: The Unheeded Voice.* Edinburgh: Edinburgh University Press, 1977. A brief but broadly conceived overview of Leopardi's work, including biographical and political considerations and analyzing various Leopardian modes, especially helpful in the areas of philosophical antinomy, irony, and love-death.

De Feo, Italo. *Leopardi: l'uomo e l'opera.* Milan: Mondadori, 1972. An easy and sympathetic introduction to Leopardi, biographically organized.

Dotti, Ugo. *Storia di un'anima.* Milan: Rizzoli, 1982. An annotated selection from the *Epistolario,* ending with letters expressing fatigue and "absence," not without self-irony, that gives everything a sense of vanity.

Frattini, Alberto. *Il problema dell'esistenza in Leopardi.* Milan: Gastaldi, 1950. A philosophical view, taking into account the Enlightenment and romanticism in an existential context, quite opposed to that of stricter, Marxist orientation.

Galimberti, Cesare. *Linguaggio del vero in Leopardi.* Florence: Sansoni, 1959. The notion of truth, coming under the heading not of realism but of Enlightenment thought, as expressed by the poetic word in the context of various literary problems.

Getto, Giovanni. *Saggi leopardiani.* Florence: Vallecchi, 1966. A refreshing attempt to leave aside the much discussed questions of Leopardi's ideology and philosophy by concentrating on Leopardi the poet and writer of human sensibilities and the universal values of poetry qua poetry.

Kroeber, Karl. *The Artifice of Reality: Poetic Style in Wordsworth, Foscolo, Keats, and Leopardi.* Madison: University of Wisconsin Press, 1964. Useful for comparative purposes, dealing especially well in topics like poetic humanism, myth, and the treatment of space, and containing good discussions of various poems.

Luporini, Cesare. "Leopardi progressivo." In *Filosofi vecchi e nuovi.* Florence: Sansoni, 1947. Leopardi as moralist rather than philosopher, working in the direction of antibourgeois revolutionary democracy (hence progressive), seen from a strict Marxist perspective and aware of Leopardi's uncertain materialism that had much to do with his "primitive vitalism."

Nifosì, Carmelo. *La filosofia di Giacomo Leopardi.* Modica: Soc. Tip. Scapellato & Cafiso, 1949. An attempt to reconstruct Leopardi's philosophy not by the juxtaposition of texts from the *Zibaldone* but by analytical penetration of the essence of his thought in relation to historical forces.

Origo, Iris. *Leopardi: A Study of Solitude.* 2d ed. London: Hamish Hamilton, 1953. A classic, introductory work in English: a sensitive analysis of all aspects of the man and his work.

Perella, Nicholas J. *Night and the Sublime in Giacomo Leopardi.* Berkeley: University of California Press, 1970. A penetrating look into the nature of inspiration in Leopardi, sustained by a solid display of scholarship.

Prete, Antonio. *Il pensiero poetante: saggio su Leopardi.* Milan: Feltrinelli, 1980. A difficult but rewarding conceptual "essay," with a sociological bent, successfully blending aesthetics with modern philosophical concerns.

Singh, Ghan Shyam. *Leopardi and the Theory of Poetry.* Lexington: University of Kentucky Press, 1964. The best and broadest treatment of Leopardi's poetics, with useful comparisons with the English romantic poets and their romantic philosophies of aesthetics.

Tilgher, Adriano. *La filosofia di Leopardi.* Bologna: Massimiliano Boni, 1979. Brief but provocative insights rather than a logically developed analysis of the most important philosophical issues in Leopardi.

Timpanaro, Sebastiano. "Il Leopardi e i filosofi antichi." In *Classicismo e illuminismo nell'ottocento italiano.* 2d ed. Pisa: Nistri-Lischi, 1969. A valuable study that includes Leopardi's political noninvolvement and the sensualistic materialism that shaped his view of the human condition.

Whitfield, John H. *Giacomo Leopardi.* Oxford: Basil Blackwell, 1954. A useful introduction to Leopardi, somewhat rambling but insightful, covering his poetry, prose, and the *Zibaldone.*

Index

Addison, Joseph, 44
Aesop, 130
Africanus, Julius, 3
Alexander (the Great), 100
Alfieri, Vittorio, 3, 10, 12, 88, 113, 156, 180
Alfonso II, Duke, 211
Alighieri, Dante, 10, 23, 74, 92, 126, 128, 133, 138, 144, 156, 199, 200, 217
allegory, 138–39
Amiel, Henri-Frédéric, 194
Anacreon, 3
animals, 66, 91–92, 92–93, 157, 164, 173–74, 196
antiquity/ancients, 63, 107, *112–15,* 121, 145
Apuleius, 81
Aquinas, St. Thomas, 33
Ariosto, Ludovico, 84, 156, 213
Aristotle, 33, 38, 103, 120, 122, 123
Arnault, Antoine Vincent, 143
Arnold, Matthew, 125, 194
art, 33, 67–69, 70, 95, 122, 125, 157, 163, 181, 195, 202
Ascoli, Graziadio Isaia, 128
Augustine, St., 120, 122

Bacchelli, Riccardo, 89, 133, 206, 210, 211
Bacchylides, 57
Bachelard, Gaston, 190
Bacon, Francis, 10
Balzac, Honoré de, 38, 105, 196
Barricelli, J-P., 67, 141, 194, 206
Battaglia, Salvatore, 39, 149
Baudelaire, Charles, 67, 102, 122, 124, 195, 196, 197, 201, 214
Bayle, Pierre, 38, 69
beauty, 17, 27, *43–45,* 49, 61, 68, 79, 90, 111, 124, 125, 137, 178, 179, 189, 192, 194, 195, 198
Bécquer, Gustavo, 120, 214
Beethoven, Ludwig van, 77, 201
Bellonci, Goffredo, 77
Bembo, Pietro Cardinal, 126
Bertana, Emilio, 215
Bianchi, Marshal, 134

Bickersteth, Geoffrey, 36, 190
Bigi, E., 76
Binni, Walter, 133, 136, 176, 191, 207
Biral, Bruno, 39, 40
Blake, William, 106, 107
Blasucci, Luigi, 71, 73
Boccaccio, Giovanni, 71, 76
Boileau, Nicolas, 68, 103, 123
Bosco, Umberto, 46, 154, 201
Bossuet, Jacques Bénigne, 90
Botta, Carlo, 23
Breme, Ludovico di, 104, 107
Brentano, Clemens, 120, 214
Brighenti, Pietro, 18
Brilli, A., 133
brotherhood, 20, 22, 24, 28, 29, 41, 63, 67, 137, 179, 183, 189, 191, 199, 200, 201
Browne, Sir Thomas, 56
Brutus, 11, 14, 15, 20, 199
Buffon, 57, 60, 89, 92, 117
Bunsen, Karl, 18, 22
Buonarroti, Michelangelo, 190
Burchi, Elisabetta, 189
Byron, George Gordon, Lord, 41, 67, 104, 106, 114, 117, 130, 197, 198

Cabanis, Pierre-Jean, 61
Caesar, Gaius Julius, 15, 82, 100
Calcaterra, C., 158
Calmeta, Vincenzo Collo, 125
Cambon, Glauco, 77
Camões, Luis de, 83
Camus, Albert, 33
Canosa, Prince of, 134
Capponi, Gino, 133, 134, 177, 180
Capucci, M., 133
Carafa, Enrichetta, 28
Carducci, Giosuè, 78, 143
Carlyle, Thomas, 65
Carniani-Malvezzi, Countess Teresa, 8, 18
Carsaniga, Giovanni, 219
Casale, Ottavio M., 61, 64, 65, 85, 87–88, 190
Caserta, Ernesto G., 130, 134
Cassi, Gertrude (Lazzari), 7, 10, 142

Castelvetro, Lodovico, 103, 126
Casti, Giambattista, 130
Castiglione, Baldassare, 81, 126–27
Cecchetti, Giovanni, 72, 74
Cesari, Antonio, 127
Chateaubriand, René de, 41, 107, 114, 195, 196, 197
Christianity, 41–42, 190–91
Cicero, Marcus Tullius, 11, 18, 57, 89, 90, 198
Cirillo, Domenico, 57
classicism, 103–4, 105, 155, 212–13
Coleridge, Samuel Taylor, 34, 102, 108, 109–10, 112, 115, 196, 198, 213
Colletta, Pietro, 20, 22, 23, 24
Colli, General Michele, 134
Columbus, Christopher, 91, 156
compassion, 63–64, 67, 95, 100, 199
Condillac, Etienne, 66
Consalvi, Ercole Cardinal, 14, 15
Consoli, D., 177
Constant, Benjamin, 65
Copernicus, Nicolaus, 39, 43, 95–96, 212
Croce, Benedetto, 32–33, 75, 104, 163, 175, 193

D'Adamo, Gian Carlo, 35, 135, 177, 190–91, 206
Dante. *See* Alighieri
death, 13, 41, 43, 46–58, 59, 60, 66, 68, 74, 89, 97, 100, 161, 165, 166, 168, 170, 171, 175, 176, 178–79, 181, 192, 198–99
De Feo, Italo, 31, 69, 75, 141, 189, 206
Delalande, Pierre Antoine, 83
Delille, abbé Jacques, 107
de Lisle, Charles Lecomte, 196, 199
de Maistre, Joseph-Marie, 192
Democritus, 52, 53
De Robertis, Giuseppe, 35, 90, 154, 163, 166, 168
De Sanctis, Francesco, 32, 46, 63, 70, 138, 139, 140, 145, 157
Descartes, René, 33, 39, 46, 52, 53, 109
De Sinner, Luigi, 23, 28
Diamantini, Alessandra, 208
Di Carlo, Franco, 219
Diderot, Denis, 97
Didimi, Carlo, 14
Diogenes, 81, 90
Donadoni, Ernesto, 133
Donatus, 90
Dotti, Ugo, 208

Duro, A., 205

Edwards, Paul, 206
Eliot, Thomas Stearns, 116, 138, 190
Emerson, Ralph Waldo, 197
Empedocles, 52
empiricism, 45
Empson, William, 115
enthusiasm/emotion, *115–18,* 121, 138, 141, 158, 178
Epictetus, 10
Epicurus, 53, 89, 90
Este, Eleonora d', 211
Eunapius, 97
Euripides, 198
evil, 64, 75
existentialism, 33, 40, 87, 90, 194

fame, 88–89, 155, 156
Fattorini, Teresa ("Silvia"), 7–8, 159
Ferdinand, King of Naples, 134
Ferretti, G., 205
Ferrigni, Giuseppe, 28, 30
Figurelli, F., 144
Firenzuola, Agnolo, 81
Flaubert, Gustave, 117
Flora, Francesco, 72, 74, 166, 167, 204
Fontenelle, Bernard de, 82
Foscolo, Ugo, 3, 10, 12, 39, 65, 113, 144, 145, 189, 212
Foucault, Michel, 189
Francis I, Emperor of Austria, 134
Frattini, Alberto, 33, 58
freedom/liberty, 51, 61, 102, 126, 128, 178, 189, 200
Freppa, Giovanni, 25
Freud, Sigmund, 51, 55, 56, 189
Friedrich, Caspar David, 41
friendship, 51
Fubini, Mario, 72, 86, 141, 149, 191, 210

Galilei, Galileo, 22
Galimberti, Cesare, 73, 189, 208
Gassendi, Pierre, 52, 53
Gautier, Théophile, 102, 196
Gentile, Giovanni, 70, 71
Gentilianus ("Aemilius"), 91
Gessner, Solomon, 165
Getti, Pasquale, 209–10
Getto, Giovanni, 101, 164, 210
Giannessi, Ferdinando, 210, 213
Gioberti, Vincenzo, 21, 32, 133, 134, 135

Giordani, Pietro, 6, 7, 10, 12, 13, 20, 31,
    127, 133, 144, 152, 196
Giusti, Giuseppe, 133
Gladstone, William, 193
God, 13, 66, 87, 101, 155, 188, 193, 197
Goethe, Johann Wolfgang von, 3, 10, 35,
    50, 65, 83, 102, 106, 155, 195, 197,
    200, 201
Gogol, Nikolai, 194
Graf, Arturo, 137, 191
Grassi, Giuseppe, 203
Gravina, Gian Vincenzo, 124
Gustarelli, Andrea, 99, 165, 177

habit, 44, 58, 60
happiness/unhappiness, 12, 17, 28, 46–47,
    48, 53, 56, 57, 66, 71, 73, 74, 83, 86,
    90, 93, 94–95, 98–99, 100, 104, 155,
    156, 157, 158, 159, 165, 166, 168, 175,
    176, 191, 194, 199, 201
Hartmann, Eduard von, 40, 45, 195
Heath-Stubbs, John, 5, 34–35, 193
Hegel, Friedrich, 46, 134, 195
Heidegger, Martin, 55
Heine, Heinrich, 201
Helvétius, Claude, 51
Herder, Johann Gottfried, 33
Hesiod, 79
Hobbes, Thomas, 52, 53, 60
Holbach, Baron d', 33, 52, 53, 63
Hölderlin, Friedrich, 106, 198
Homer, 3, 6, 90, 108, 113, 125, 130, 131,
    132
Horace, 3, 33, 80, 90, 103, 123, 198
Hufeland, Christoph Wilhelm, 86
Hugo, Victor, 109, 126, 137, 196, 197,
    214
Hume, David, 68, 109, 112
Hutcheson, Francis, 44

idealism, 45, 194, 195
Ideologues, the, 39
illusion, 11, 12, 13, 17, 25, 45, 47, 50,
    51, 55, 56, 58, 64, 67, 71, 75, 87, 88,
    93, 95, 105, 106, 111, 115, 137, 138,
    149, 156, 158, 161, 163, 165, 176, 177,
    181, 190, 194, 195, 196, 198, 199, 200,
    202
imagery, 29, 102, 121, 137, 138–39, 159,
    164, 166, 189
imagination, 51, 102, 107, 109–12, 113,
    123, 125, 148, 155, 156, 158, 167, 176,
    178

inequality, 60, 62
infinity, 47, 48, 52, 55, 125, 149, 168,
    191, 201
irony/satire, 71, 77–78, 80, 98, 99, 100,
    131–36, 166, 180
Irving, Washington, 197
Isocrates, 3
Isomachus, 54
Ivanov, Aleksandr, 41

Jacopssen, A., 17
James, William, 210
John the Evangelist, 181
Jonard, Norbert, 66
Jones, Ernest, 56
Joyce, James, 135
Julian, Emperor Havius Claudius, 90

Kant, Immanuel, 38, 44–45, 46, 65, 109,
    194
Keats, John, 67, 68, 102, 117, 119, 195,
    198
Kierkegaard, Sören, 33, 194
Kingsborough, Viscount Earl of Kingston,
    205
knowledge, 99, 106, 109, 121, 155
Kroeber, Karl, 173

Lacan, Jacques, 55
Laertius, 90
Lamartine, Alphonse de, 41, 137, 143, 197,
    200
Lambert, Mme de, 49
Lamennais, Félicité de, 13, 132
language/style, 58–59, 69, 71, 75, 76–77,
    93, 102, 108, 109, 111, 112, 115, 118,
    121, 140–42, 148, 149–51, 153, 163,
    167, 173, 191, 215–16; Italian, 125–29
Laplace, Marquis de, 197
La Rochefoucauld, François de, 34, 51
Leibniz, Gottfried W., 33
Lenau, Nicolaus, 196, 197
Leo XII, Pope, 15
Leopardi, Giacomo

    FAMILY: Antici, Countess Adelaide
        (mother), 2, 4, 10, 21, 25, 29, 30;
        Antici, Carlo (uncle), 14, 15, 16, 29;
        Carlo (brother), 1, 6, 8, 15, 21; Luigi
        (brother), 1, 20; Mamiani, Terenzio
        (cousin), 182, 218; Mazzagalli, Paolina
        (cousin), 21; Melchiorri, Marquess
        Ferdinanda (aunt), 13; Monaldo, Count

(father), 1–2, 4, 7, 10, 15, 21, 25, 29, 30; Paolina (sister), 1, 14, 15; Pier Francesco (brother), 1

WORKS:
"Amore e morte," 25, 55, 99, *175,* 179
"Angelo Mai, Ad," 11, 73, 80, 91, 143, *156–57*
"Appressamento della morte, L'," 5, 56, 136, 142
"Arimane, Ad," 26, 27, 179, 218
"Aspasia," 8, 24, 27, 48, 50, *177–78*
Aspasia Cycle, 175–78
"Bruto minore," 14, 63, 98, 156, *157–58*
Canti, 23, 27, 34, 56, 71, 75, 76, 78, 92, 130, *136–91*
"Cantico del gallo silvestre," 56, 84, *92–93*
"Canto notturno di un pastore errante dell'Asia," 22, 49, 66, 138, 139, 159, *167–75,* 191
Carte napoletane, 206
"Comparazione delle sentenze di Bruto minore e di Teofrasto vicini a morte," 73
"Consalvo," 8, 25, 138, *175,* 199
"Conte Carlo Pepoli, Al," 18, *155–56*
"Copernico—Dialogo, Il," *95–96,* 197
"Crestomazia" (of Italian literature), 21
"Dallo stesso" (Simonides), 143
"Detti memorabili di Filippo Ottonieri," *90–91*
"Dialogo della Moda e della Morte," 56, 59, *80–81*
"Dialogo della Natura e di un'Anima," *83,* 179
"Dialogo della Natura e di un Islandese," 39, 84, *87–88,* 179
"Dialogo della Terra e della Luna," 77, *83–84*
"Dialogo di Cristoforo Colombo e di Pietro Gutierrez," 75, *91*
"Dialogo di Ercole e di Atlante," 77, *79–80*
"Dialogo di Federico Ruysch e delle sue mummie," 56, 75, *89–90,* 136
"Dialogo di Malambruno e di Farfarello," 57, 75, *82–83*
"Dialogo di Plotino e di Porfirio," 20, 63, 75, *97–98*

"Dialogo di Timandro e di Eleandro," 70, 71, 72, *94–95*
"Dialogo di Torquato Tasso e del suo Genio familiare," 66, 75, *86–87,* 98, 155
"Dialogo di Tristano e di un amico," 26, 40, 57, 62, 72, *99–100,* 179, 180
"Dialogo di un cavallo e un bue," 210
"Dialogo di un fisico e di un metafisico," 57, *85–86*
"Dialogo di un Folletto e di uno Gnomo," *82*
"Dialogo di un venditore d'almanacchi e di un passeggere," 25, 75, *98–99*
"Dialogo tra due bestie p.e un cavallo e un toro," 210
"Dialogo tra Galantuomo e Mondo," 70
"Elogio degli uccelli," 76, *91–92*
"Enciclopedia delle cognizioni utili e delle cose che non si sanno," 22
Epistolario, 1–31, 102
Final Canti, 179–91
"Frammento apocrifo di Stratone da Lampsaco," 75, *93–94*
"Frammento XXXVII: Odi, Melisso, io vo' contarti un sogno," 146, 197
"Frammento XXXVIII: Io qui vagando al limitare intorno," 142
"Frammento XXXIX: Spento il diurno raggio in occidente," 142
"Ginestra, La," 28, 29, 36, 41, 62, 63, 67, 87, 98, 104, 138, 179, *181–91,* 200
Great Idylls, 159–75
"Greco di Semionide, Dal" ("la speranza"), 143
"Infinito, L'," 11, 67, 69, 110, 139, *146–49,* 191, 195
"Imitazione," 143
"Inno ai patriarchi, L'," 14, *155*
"Inno a Nettuno," 3
"Italia, All'," 6, 143, *144–45,* 156
"Luna, Alla," 12, 138, *146*
"Memorie del primo amore," 3, 142
"Murco, Senatore romano, filosofo greco," 210
"Nozze della sorella Paolina, Nelle," 14, *154*
Operette morali, 11, 17, 18, 20, 21, 23, 25, 27, 28, 32, 34, 53, 56, 57, 70–*101,* 102, 104, 120, 130, 179
"Osservazioni," 3

"Palinodia al marchese Gino Capponi,"
27, 99, *179–80*
Paralipomeni della Batracomiomachia, I, 27–
28, *130–36*
"Parini, ovvero della gloria, Il," 75, *88–*
89, 102
"Passero solitario, Il," 22, 138, 139, *164*
Patriotic Canzoni, 143–45
Pensieri, 32, 34, *35,* 39, 58, 61, 64, 90,
130, 189, 218
"Pensiero dominante, Il," 8, 24, 50, 139,
141, *176,* 177, 179
Philosophical Canzoni, 154–59
"Pompeo in Egitto," 3
"Primavera, o delle favole antiche, Alla,"
14, *154–55*
"Primo amore, Il," 3, 7, 142
"Proposta di premi fatta dall'Accademia
dei Sillografi," 77, *81*
"Quiete dopo la tempesta, La," 22, 91,
166, 167
"Ricordanze, Le," 3, 22, 120, 139, *164–*
66, 179
"Risorgimento, Il," 20, *159,* 176, 179
"Sabato del villaggio, Il," 22, 98, 139,
166–67
Saggio sopra gli errori popolari degli antichi, 3
"Scherzo," 143
"Scommessa di Prometeo, La," 77, *84–85*
"Senofonte e Niccolò Machiavello," 70
Sepulchral Canzoni, 178–79
"Sera del dì di festa, La," 12, 120, *149–*
54
"Se stesso, A," 7, 8, 26, 41, 50, 55,
176–77, 178, 195, 218
"Silvia, A," 8, 20, 120, 138, 146, *159–*
64, 191
Small Idylls, 145–54
"Sogno, Il," 14, *146*
"Sopra il monumento di Dante," 6, 143,
144
"Sopra il ritratto d'una bella donna," 27,
138, 141, *178*
"Sopra un bassorilievo antico sepolcrale,"
27, *178–79,* 199
"Storia del genere umano, La," 51, 70,
75, *78–79,* 84
"Sua donna, Alla," 8, 17, *155,* 176
Telesilla, 3
"Tramonto della luna, Il," 30, 138, 141,
179, *180–81*
"Ultimo canto di Saffo, L'," 63, 138,
158–59, 179

"Vincitore nel pallone, A un," 14, 73,
154, 200
"Vita solitaria, La," 12, *146*
Zibaldone di pensieri, 9, 13, 25, *32–69,*
34–35, 71, 72, 74, 75, 76, 77, 83,
86, 90, 98, 102, 103, 119, 198, 200

Lermontov, Mikhail, 198, 199
Leucippus, 52
Levi, Giulio, 168, 216
life, 41, 69, 71, 86–87, 97, 103, 175,
181, 218
Linnaeus, 60
Lloyd-Jones, Hugh, 213
Locke, John, 33, 58, 59, 66, 120, 122
Longfellow, Henry Wadsworth, 197
Lorenzino de' Medici, 90
Louis-Philippe, King of France, 134
love, 25, 26, 40, 43, *46–58,* 60, 61, 71,
74, 90, 100, 158, 159, 161, 175–78,
191, 194, 197, 199
Lucian, 17, 71, 80, 84, 85, 90, 212
Lucignani, Teresa, 203
Lucretius, 33, 42, 52, 53, 200
Luporini, Cesare, 32, 104, 191
Luther, Martin, 33
lyric, *118–20*

Machiavelli, Niccolò, Lo, 33, 81, 127,
130, 180
Mai, Angelo, 6, 156
Malagoli, Luigi, 213
man, 29, 55, 70, 90, 96, 130, 156, 166,
170, 172, 188–89
Mannella, Dr., 30
Manzoni, Alessandro, 20, 23, 24, 41, 62,
76, 122, 126, 127, 128, 144, 182,
190, 193, 216
Marx, Karl, 52
Massano, Riccardo, 213
materialism, 40, 45, 47, 52, 53, 55, 73,
75, 94, 106
Maupertuis, Pierre M., 54
Mazzali, Ettore, 213, 214
Mazzamuto, Pietro, 213
Mazzanti, Luca, 204
Mazzini, Giuseppe, 134, 193
Mazzocca, Maristella, 74, 93, 137, 218
melancholy, 48, 50, 102, *112–15,* 119,
125, 136, 141, 152, 154, 159, 164,
167, 191
Melchiorri, Giuseppe, 204
Melissus, Gaius, 90

Melville, Herman, 87–88
memory/remembrance, 102, 109, *120–22*, 125, 146, 148
Merivale, H. C., 219
Mestica, Giovanni, 207
metaphysics, 45, 53
Metastasio, Pietro, 81
Metternich, Klemens von, 134
Michelangelo. *See* Buonarroti
Milton, John, 83, 199
mimesis/imitation, 102, *122–25*, 138
Minturno, Antonio, 103
misanthropy, 42, 191
moderns, 63, 155
Momigliano, Attilio, 149, 156, 163, 210
Montaigne, Michel de, 56, 200
Montani, Giuseppe, 211
Montesquieu, Baron de, 10, 39, 45, 48
Monti, Vincenzo, 6, 25, 142
Moravia, Alberto, 65
Moroncini, F., 130, 141, 205
Moroni, A. M., 204
Moschus, 3
Mountcashell, Lady, 205
Mountcashell, Lauretta, 205
Mozart, Wolfgang Amadeus, 77, 196
Murat, Joachim, 134
Musset, Alfred de, 50, 197, 201

Napoleon(e) B(u)onaparte, 2, 134
nature, 13, 14, 26, 28, 29, 33, *36–43*, 46, 47, 52–53, 56, 57, 60, 61, 62, 65, 71, 74, 75, 83, 87–88, 97, 103, 104, 105, 124, 135, 137, 151, 155, 158, 163, 168, 176, 179, 183, 185, 186, 188, 189, 192, 194, 195–96, 197, 198, 200, 201
necessity, 39
Nerval, Gérard de, 120, 199, 214
Newton, Isaac, 197
Niccolini, Giambattista, 20, 23
Niebuhr, Baron G. B., 15, 18
Nietzsche, Friedrich, 56, 189, 193, 202
Nifosì, Carmelo, 44–45
Nims, John Frederick, 150
Novalis, 114, 197, 198, 199, 201

originality/invention, 109, *112–15*, 124, 128
Origo, Iris, 5, 34–35, 76, 197
Ortes, Giammaria, 54
Ovid, 79

Papadopoli, Antonio, 204
Parini, Giuseppe, 80, 88–89, 113, 146
Pascal, Blaise, 33, 39, 40, 65, 66, 67, 190, 194, 196, 197, 199
Pascoli, Giovanni, 107
Paul III, Pope, 212
Peer, Larry, 122
Pellico, Silvio, 41
Pepe, Guglielmo, 134
Pepoli, Carlo, 156
Perella, Nicholas J., 103, 121, 146, 170, 171, 190, 212, 213
Pericles, 175
Perticari, Giulio, 203
pessimism, 33, 50, 54, 55, *58–67*, 64, 67, 73, 74, 84, 86, 90, 94, 98, 100, 104, 106, 125, 144, 156, 166, 180, 189, 191, 193, 195, 200, 202
Peter (the Great), 212
Petrarca, Francesco (Petrarch), 10, 17, 18, 20, 45, 46, 118, 144, 146, 156, 160, 164, 199
Petronio, Giuseppe, 163, 167
Phaedrus, 130
philology, 16, 156
philosophy, *32–69*, 38–39
Piatti, Guglielmo, 23, 27, 70
Pindar, 14
Pirandello, Luigi, 194
Pius VII, Pope, 15
Plato, 10, 15, 17, 33, 39, 43, 50, 61, 68, 79, 90, 94, 97, 109, 122, 155, 176, 177, 194, 214
pleasure/desire, 12, 43, *46–58*, 67, 71, 74, 82, 87, 89, 90, 100, 165, 175, 200, 201
Plotinus, 3, 28, 92, 97–98
Plutarch, 90
Poe, Edgar Allan, 102, 119, 122, 136, 197
poetics, *102–29*
Poggioli, Renato, 148, 149
Pompey, 82
Porena, Manfredi, 207
Porphyry, 3, 97–98, 100
Pound, Ezra, 141
Prete, Antonio, 34, 35, 51–52, 59–60, 121, 213
progress, 17, 41, 62, 65, 81, 100, 135, 180, 182, 189, 191
Puccinotti, Francesco, 3
Pushkin, Aleksandr, 50, 67, 200

Ranieri, Antonio, 24, 25, 26, 28, 29, 30, 31, 35, 70, 181
Ranieri, Paolina, 29, 30, 31, 143
reality, 17, 45, 73, 87, 100, 105, 137, 155, 156, 176, 190, 200, 202
reason/rationalism, 12, 13, *36–43*, 45, 50, 56, 61, 65, 66, 73, 103, 106, 110, 115, 155, 157, 194, 198, 202
Reinhold, F. G., 15
relativism, 44, 47, 64
religion, 13, 42, 53, 101, 190
Reynolds, Barbara, 216
Richter, Jean-Paul, 197
Rigoni, Mario Andrea, 214
Rimbaud, Arthur, 125
Robertson, William, 212
romanticism, 9–10, 44, 103–4, 105–8, 114, 117, 122, 127, 136, 137, 155, 175, 212–13
Ronsard, Pierre de, 103
Rosini, Giovanni, 205
Rousseau, Jean-Jacques, 9, 10, 13, 29, 37, 39, 42, 46, 60, 61, 85, 86, 87, 90, 114, 132, 134, 196
Roverella, Giannantonio, 203
Ruffilli, Paolo, 73
Runge, Philipp Otto, 41
Russell, Bertrand, 120
Russo, Luigi, 78, 156–57, 167, 171
Ruysch, Friedrich, 89, 100

Sainte-Beuve, Charles A. de, 140, 193
Saint-Pierre, Bernardin de, 107
Sansone, Mario, 9, 77
Santayana, George, 136, 193
Sapegno, Natalino, 106, 165
Sappho, 11, 14, 45, 199
Sartre, Jean-Paul, 33
Savarese, Gennaro, 133
Scaligero, Giulio Cesare, 103
Scarpa, Gino, 206
Schelling, Friedrich, 137, 200
Schiller, Friedrich von, 36, 106, 114, 195
Schlegel, Friedrich, 33, 102
Schleiermacher, Friedrich, 197
Schopenhauer, Arthur, 32, 62, 63, 67, 68, 193, 195, 199
Schulz, H. Wilhelm, 181
self-esteem, 47, 51, 54–55, 83, 90
self-preservation, 47, 54–55, 97
Sénancour, Etienne de, 65
Seneca, 33, 198
sentiment/sensibility, 107, 119, 137

Shaftesbury, Earl of, 68
Shakespeare, William, 35, 60, 109, 217
Shelley, Mary Wollstonecraft, 205
Shelley, Percy Bysshe, 50, 106, 137, 196, 200, 201
Sidney, Philip, 103
Silvia (Neapolitan maiden), 29
Silvia. *See* Fattorini, Teresa
Simonides of Samos, 143, 144
sincerity, 102, *115–18*, 125
Singh, Ghan, 102, 108, 112, 114, 115, 119, 123, 125, 141
skepticism, 45, 46
society, 60, 61, 189
Socrates, 54, 72, 86, 90, 98
solitude, 157, 164, 165, 168, 178, 181, 201
Solomon, 198
Sophocles, 33, 57, 198
Spencer, Herbert, 195
Spinoza, Baruch, 64
Staël, Mme de, 10, 39, 62, 76
Stampa (ed.), 70
Starita, Saverio, 27, 28, 70
Stella, Antonio Fortunato, 6, 10, 18, 21, 22
Stendhal, 11, 20
Stevens, Wallace, 67
stoicism, 33, 40, 41, 64
Stolnitz, Jerome, 44
Strato of Lampsacus, 46, 93–94
suicide, 17, 20, 62–63, 97–98, 157, 158
Swift, Jonathan, 17
Swinburne, Charles, 196

Taine, Hippolyte, 109
Targioni-Tozzetti, Fanny, 8, 24, 175, 176
Tasso, Torquato, 16, 67, 86, 90, 92, 156, 167, 213
tedium, 60, 65, 66, 67, 68, 71, 74, 75, 78, 85, 87, 91, 97, 156, 164, 167, 177
Theophrastus, 3, 45
Thompson, James, 193
Tilgher, Adriano, 51, 54, 209
Timpanaro, Sebastiano, 104, 191
Tommaseo, Niccolò, 20, 193
Tommasini, Antonietta, 203
Tommasini, Giacomo, 204
Trissino, Leonardo, 203
truth, 68, 78–79, 87, 90, 95, 114, 124, 139, 140, 156, 198
Tundo, Luigi, 56

Uhland, Johann Ludwig, 201
Unamuno, Miguel de, 32, 65, 193
Ungaretti, Giuseppe, 201

vagueness/indefiniteness, 52, 110, 111,
    125, 139, 141, 150, 163, 167, 189,
    196
Varchi, Benedetto, 127
Verri, Pietro, 54
Vico, Giovanni Battista, 33, 114, 214
Vieusseux, Giampietro, 18, 20, 23, 177,
    218
Vigny, Alfred de, 39, 41, 106, 196, 197,
    198
Vinciguerra, Mario, 43
Virgil, 3, 6, 35, 50, 81, 82, 90, 113,
    118, 119, 133, 139, 167, 181
Voltaire, 10, 85
Von Platen, August, 26

Vossler, Karl, 4, 61, 163, 190, 210

Wackenroder, Wilhelm, 117
Wellek, René, 119, 121, 212
Wergeland, Henrik, 10, 196, 198, 200
Whitfield, J. H., 41, 42, 70, 194
Whitman, Walt, 197, 201
wonder, *115–18*
Wordsworth, William, 36, 67, 102, 106,
    108, 109, 118, 190, 196, 197, 198

Xenophanes, 82
Xenophon, 54, 90, 212

Young, Edward, 153
youth/childhood, 93, 107, 121, 152, 159,
    161, 163, 165, 181, 194, 195

Zannoni, Giambattista, 74
Zottoli, Angelandrea, 157, 210